Lights & Shadows:
Discoveries Away From Home

LIGHTS & SHADOWS: DISCOVERIES AWAY FROM HOME

PERSPECTIVES ON AMERICAN, GERMAN AND CHINESE CULTURES

GERTRAUDE ROTH LI

Published by Gertraude Roth Li

Cover Design: Michelle Li Bothe

Print ISBN 978-1-9855-5785-7

Typesetting services by BOOKOW.COM

To Jane, with gratitude

PREFACE

As a little girl, perhaps around seven or so, I remember often lying in the grass near my home in a small village in Germany looking at the sky and dreaming of going to see the big wide world. When I saw a plane crossing above I'd imagine being in it traveling to far-away places. At the time—this was post-war Germany—I had no reason to believe I would ever get any further than the next town down the road. My family was poor. We had no running water, no electricity, no car and certainly no thoughts of traveling anywhere. By high school my dreams became more specific, wanting to go to Tibet and Mongolia, probably because these were two places farthest away around the globe from where I lived. Then, still in high school, it occurred to me to visit the local book store and ask for a textbook on Asian languages, unaware there might be more than one language. The store clerk had nothing to offer but referred me to a large store in the city of Hamburg, one specializing in foreign language books. When I eventually made it to that store and found a two-volume textbook for Chinese on their shelf—there were no other Asian language books that might have confused me—my mind was made up: I was going to study Chinese after graduation. The fact that until then I had never met a single person from Asia nor had ever heard a word of spoken Chinese was not a deterrent.

All that was long ago. But the desire to learn about the world, study different languages and live in unfamiliar places remained with me throughout my life. It has led me to travel around the world three times, learn six languages, dabble in several more, live in Taiwan, Japan and Switzerland before finally settling down for good in the United States. During the years I was involved in international exchange programs at the University of Hawaii it gave me enormous pleasure to encourage young Americans to take the leap and leave home to broaden their mental and geographical horizons. I also enjoyed reading widely on cross-cultural topics though over time I found the books generally to be either too theoretical or too shallow for my taste. Gradually the idea emerged in my mind to do my own book, one that would be practical but also have depth. This is how *Lights & Shadows: Discoveries Away From Home* came about. Though it represents the culmination of my own life's journey, the quotes in this book come from others, the nearly one hundred individuals whom I personally interviewed over the course of about a decade and who shared with me their views of and insights into living abroad.

By juxtaposing Chinese, German and American experiences, *Lights & Shadows* illustrates how the people in these cultures think and act differently. It also gives us insights into how others view our culture and interpret our actions. At times what they have to say may please us. Other times we may be shocked, perhaps to the degree we feel compelled to discuss some of their statements with our friends. Whether we agree or disagree with the particular stands taken, we are likely to learn and grow by seeing our own beliefs and values in a new light.

If you live or plan to live in a country not associated with German, Chinese or American cultures, the reflections in this book will nonetheless open up new perspectives on how to communicate and relate in the wider world. Whether you are a participant in inbound or outbound exchange programs, someone involved in diplomatic endeavors, a business person on the international stage, a member of a military family stationed overseas, a global nomad of another kind, or simply a world traveler who enjoys meaningful encounters with the people along the road, I hope you will find *Lights & Shadows* to be a useful and stimulating companion. I thoroughly enjoyed my own journeys, both the mental and the physical ones. I hope you will enjoy yours.

GRL

Highlands Ranch, Colorado

February 2018

CONTENTS

INTRODUCTION

Only he who is capable of a genuine encounter with the other is capable of an authentic encounter with himself and the converse is equally true.

—Pierre Hadot, French philosopher

Experiencing other cultures

PEOPLE who immerse themselves in another culture have an opportunity to see themselves and their own country in a new light. Like friends who enrich each other by exchanging thoughts and feelings, living in a different culture heightens our awareness of who we are, both individually and culturally. Cultural norms or standards, which shape our notions of what is good and morally appropriate, are passed on to us as children but often are not clear to us until we live in an environment in which they do not apply.

This book examines elements of American, German, and Chinese cultural values. In these pages, Americans—in this context I use this term to refer to the people of the United States—who live or have lived in German or Chinese societies; Germans who live or have lived in the US, Taiwan or China; and Chinese who live or have lived in the US or in Germany, share their insights into this process of self-discovery. Whether they admire certain traits of the foreign culture or complain about something they do not like, both reactions imply that in their view things are different "at home." If, for example, they are struck by Chinese politeness, they are indicating that where they come from the people are not as polite. If a Chinese describes Germans as "animal loving," it indicates he thinks the Chinese are less so. This applies to both positive and negative impressions. An American telling her friend she thinks Germans are "unfriendly" means that in her experience the people in the world she is most familiar with are friendlier. In the vast majority of cases, it is a matter of more or less, rarely one of the presence or total absence of a particular trait.

Interpreting our cultural experiences in the light of what we are, or are not, is both kinder and more accurate. It turns harsh judgments and criticisms of the other into self-reflection and self-knowledge. Rather than taking our impressions as valid judgments of a foreign culture, this approach allows us to realize that many of our irritations, upsets, and strong reactions when living in another country are telltale signs of what is important to us. They represent valuable signposts that can help us clarify our own values and priorities. Culture is difficult to see from both the outside and the inside; as outsiders we do not know enough, while as insiders we may be simply unaware.

Why compare American, German, and Chinese? The answer to this question is simple: German, American, and Chinese ways and cultures have been an intrinsic part of my personal, educational, and professional life. I grew up in Germany, have been married to a Taiwanese for over forty years, and lived in the US for most of my adult life, a time interrupted only by several year-long stays in Taiwan, Switzerland, and Japan. I earned a Ph.D. at Harvard in Chinese History and Far Eastern Languages and worked professionally in refugee resettlement and university international programs. Knowing German, American, and Chinese cultures well and being able to communicate in the respective languages was important for the many conversations I had with individuals who shared their views for this book. However, beyond my personal familiarity, I believe the three cultures also happen to make for a good combination because they include two, American and German, that are both thought of as "Western" and therefore expected to be quite similar, and Chinese, which is based on very different philosophical foundations. In real life the expectation of a high similarity may actually present an additional roadblock to cultural adjustment in that people find themselves unprepared for the differences they encounter.

Cultural diversity and change

One way to understand the concept of culture is to think of it as a forest made up of many kinds of trees. Standing inside the woods you only see the different individual trees, but from afar you can see the totality of the forest. Or we can compare culture to a fern with many leaves. From a distance they all appear to look alike, but when you look up close, each leaf is different.

Although there will always be individuals who do not subscribe or adhere to certain common values in their society, there are dominant cultural patterns. Therefore, when looking at a particular characteristic it is important to ask whether or not it is significantly present in the culture. If so, there is no need to get sidetracked by tangential arguments such as "but Aunt Mary is not that way." Nor does the presence of various subcultures negate the existence of cultural commonalities in the mainstream society.

As living traditions, cultures are moving targets, meaning that attitudes and values change over time and place. In many countries historical experiences have led to cultural differences between geographic regions. In the US people often point to differences between East and West and North and South. Though on a smaller geographical scale, similar distinctions apply to Germany. In many ways the people of Bavaria are quite different from those in the northern part of the country and the Soviet-era political division into East and West Germany has left a mark which continues to be felt.

Dealing with Chinese culture raises the question of which country best represents this culture today. Currently the Chinese culture extends over three, possibly four, political entities: the People's Republic of China (PRC) or Mainland China; Taiwan, known as the Republic of China (ROC); Hong Kong; and Singapore. Each of these have undergone their own particular changes. Because my personal ties are closer to Taiwan, many of my Chinese respondents were Taiwanese. Initially this might seem a shortcoming. However, given the history and size of mainland China, Taiwan is actually a better representative of modern Chinese culture than the PRC. In part that is so because it is smaller and more homogeneous than the mainland, but also because the communist government in Mainland China spent years trying to destroy traditional Chinese culture to fit the communist doctrine. The Cultural Revolution in the 1960s and 1970s wiped out not only historical artifacts but also cultural norms.

Since the opening of the country to modernization in the 1980s, Chinese culture in Mainland China has undergone further dramatic changes. The lifestyle of middle class Chinese living in China's eastern provinces, especially in the major cities like Beijing and Shanghai, has changed in ways that have distanced it from traditional cultural values. Another factor is China's one child policy which, even though now abandoned, fundamentally changed the Chinese family structure, especially in the cities. This policy did away with the extended family, which for centuries embodied and passed on Chinese values. Thus, in terms of values and traditions, modern developments in the PRC have created a very uneven cultural landscape. Taiwan too, lost some of its "Chineseness" when it was occupied by the Japanese during the first half of the twentieth century. Still, the effects of that occupation were less harsh on Chinese traditions than the events during the second half of the twentieth century in the PRC.

In recent decades there has been an enormous expansion of international travel, commerce, and migration that, along with the technical revolution brought about by computers and the internet, has greatly accelerated the pace of change. Still, it is doubtful these changes will result in a homogenized culture throughout the world any time soon. In fact, as more people from different parts of the world interact with each other, there will be an ever greater need for cultural awareness; for acknowledging rather than ignoring or discounting our distinctive cultural aspects.

Perceptions of culture

Americans, Germans, and Chinese differ in their perceptions of "culture." According to various studies, Americans overestimate their individual diversity, differences, and uniqueness and underestimate their commonalities. In contrast, Chinese tend to underestimate their individuality and overestimate their commonalities; German perception seems to lie in between those two poles.

Over the course of working on this book, many Americans, usually individuals without international living experience, questioned my efforts because they felt there was no such thing as an "American culture," preferring to view all people as individuals who are basically the same under the skin and who, like them, desire to be free of boundaries, restraints and traditions. "We Americans don't have the foggiest notion of where our culture is," one person told me, "I don't think we have a character that is definable." Another person expressed the same idea saying, "We don't believe in culture. We are a people who came from all over the world, a people who wanted to be free. So don't burden us with concepts of culture. Whatever that thing called culture was, we left that baggage behind when we emigrated in order to get a fresh start."

The American imperception of distinct cultures eases the initial acceptance of immigrants and foreigners and makes for an openness to personal intermingling. However, discounting the significance of culture also contributes to the view that there is no need to learn about other people, study their languages, and understand or adjust to their ways.

"Americans have to understand the foreignness of foreigners," wrote Stanley Hoffmann, a retired Harvard Professor of political science, "instead of believing that they are simply misguided or not well-guided Americans. . . . The assumption that people everywhere are all alike is something you have to get out of your system. In old age, I am more and more convinced that people are intensely different from country to country, and not everyone is motivated by the same things." [1]

Assuming our own values and cultural norms to be "normal," we tend to judge those that differ as "unusual." If another culture does not exhibit a particular trait we cherish, we probably think the culture is "lacking" something. Whereas, if we had a universe of cultures in our heads for comparison, our own culture may very well be the oddball; the one that is "unusual" or "lacking" something. By using three cultures, I hope to somewhat reduce this bias.

Information gathering

Notwithstanding the well-meaning advice from friends in the academic world that I needed to narrow my topic from the start, I decided to undertake my information gathering without a set agenda. Instead of using a questionnaire I wanted to let my conversation partners decide which topics were most important in their overall experience, hoping that certain themes would emerge naturally. It was not an efficient approach because it was bound to generate a vast amount of data that eventually would not be part of the book. At the time, a comment by author E. L. Doctorow, made during an interview with Bill Moyers, helped me along. "There may be great chaos in the mind," Doctorow said, "but out of the chaos of that mind somehow will come an orderly vision. If the writer knows what he feels before he writes and knows indubitably what's right and what's wrong and who's good and who's bad, he's going to write worthless prose." [2] Ah, there, I was on my way!

With very few exceptions, and then only at my interviewees' request, I conducted the interviews in their native language. With culture and language channeling us into certain modes of thinking and with it into certain topics, it was important to me that my conversation partners were on their cultural turf, not mine.

Most of the conversations were extensive and the majority lasted from four to six hours. While I often started out by asking what impressed or irritated them the most in the foreign culture, we spent most of our time together examining what their judgments and reactions said about their own priorities and values. For example, if a particular Chinese told me that she found Americans to be naively open and trusting, we might explore her own perception of a less hospitable world. To remind the reader that statements made about "the other" are best understood as self-descriptions of the speaker, those types of entries are marked with an arrow (⇒).

Though this book is primarily based on the personal accounts of the individuals I interviewed, occasionally I refer to written accounts. This has the benefit of being able to draw on perceptions from an earlier time, which provides some longitudinal perspective. For example, a 1914 account by the Chinese ambassador to the United States, Wu Tingfang, *America Through the Spectacles of an Oriental Diplomat*, or the various books by Lin Yutang from the 1930s serve this purpose. For an earlier American perception of Germany, Price Collier's 1913 book *Germany and the Germans from an American Point of View*, offers a glimpse of pre-World War II Germany. Collier's book has the additional benefit that his comments on Germany do not interpret German life in the light of Nazi history, as do so many books and movies written or produced since.

Process of writing the book

As author I have tried to be unbiased and fair. That does not mean that the views in the various quotes cited in this book are necessarily objective or even factually correct. As quotes they represent one individual's view or reaction to a particular impression or a series of experiences at a particular point in time.

Time frame

The idea of writing a book on cultural values first occurred to me around the year 2001. After poring over various studies on the topic, I decided to base my own work on verbal input from individuals with relevant living experience. When I first tested the idea during a three-month stay in Germany in 2003, I found the conversations to be so stimulating that I have been pursuing opportunities for similar discussions ever since, whether that be at home in Hawaii or overseas. A year split between Germany and Taiwan in 2005 and 2006 and extended visits to Germany in 2010 and 2012 allowed for intensive periods of interviews, not only with Germans and Chinese, but also with Americans who lived in those countries. To my delight I found that in almost all cases my conversation partners enjoyed the discussions as much as I did.

Conversation partners

When looking for Americans, Germans, and Chinese to interview I had two basic criteria. First, the individuals should have lived in one of the two other countries, ideally for not less than a year and not more than three or four years. Second, they should be well enough versed in the local language to participate in the daily life of their host society. The reason for the limited number of years is that when we live in another country for a long time, we tend to become so familiar with its way of life that we are no longer conscious of the differences. The majority of my conversation partners did fit the criteria, although there were also some who, in spite of lacking language skills or having shorter or longer living experiences, had excellent insights to share.

Most people I spoke with were in their late twenties or thirties. Although I would have liked more diversity in terms of age and class, many were living or had lived abroad as students when I met them. A small number were older than fifty. I did not ask about economic status but the reality is that sojourners in another country tend to belong to the educated middle or upper middle class in their home countries. Except for a few first-generation American-born Chinese (ABC) and one Hispanic individual, my American conversation partners were Caucasians. While that represents a limitation, it had the benefit that they compared their host culture to white mainstream America, whose norms and values at this moment in history still prevail in the public sphere. It is also what German and Chinese newcomers to America predominantly experience.

Throughout the book, speakers are identified by name (altered to preserve anonymity), followed by their country of origin, and the foreign country or area they were familiar with. Thus "US/Ger" stands for Americans who lived in Germany, while "Ger/US" refers to Germans who lived in the US. "Tw" stands for Taiwan and "PRC" for the People's Republic of China (Mainland China). Because Chinese names do not reveal gender, I have added *m* (male) or *f* (female) for clarity. The occasional quote by an American-born Chinese is noted as "ABC."

Anticipated concerns versus reality

Prior to starting the project I anticipated that it would be easy to engage Americans in conversations but I was concerned that as an outsider and stranger it might be difficult to find Germans or Chinese willing to sit down with me, or if they did, that they would not fully open up. As it turned out, Germans, who generally shy away from casual chats with strangers, were extremely responsive to my requests for a conversation and enormously generous about spending time with me. As I found out, when there is a meaningful purpose to a proposed interaction, Germans are very forthcoming. In fact, in some cases a purposeful conversation may be the starting point of a lasting friendship.

It was also a happy surprise that my being a stranger did not deter the Chinese from being willing to meet with me. In some cases being an outsider may actually have been helpful because it eliminated possible concerns that what they told me would somehow get back to their families and friends, which might lead to being chided for having shared personal details and family secrets with a stranger. Nor did the customary politeness and tendency to say what the other person wants to hear seem to interfere with their openness and honesty regarding the topics we discussed. At the end of our sometimes marathon-like conversations, nearly every one of my Chinese interviewees thanked me—in my estimation sincerely—for the opportunity to share thoughts and feelings on their experiences overseas.

Having expected it to be relatively easy to find Americans with the appropriate experience and willingness to engage in a conversation I was surprised to encounter several obstacles. Although it was not difficult to find Americans who were living or had lived overseas, many lacked sufficient language skills to allow them to truly see their host society from the inside. The second obstacle was time. Americans were generally open to the idea of getting together when initially approached, but it was very difficult to pin them down to a specific time and place. They were always "busy" or had other priorities that took precedence over a leisurely conversation. Also, rather than pondering questions that have little practical application, Americans overall tend to prefer more useful topics, such as problems that can be solved or measured quantitatively. "We Americans are more into doing things," Paul R. (US/Asia) told me. "We are not into deeper thinking or open ended discussions. I myself am not particularly fond of reflecting on things either." Nonetheless, quite a few Americans did enjoy our conversations and gave generously of their time, although as a group they presented me with a greater challenge and my conversations with them tended to be shorter and have less depth compared to the ones I had with Chinese and Germans.

For the vast majority of my interviewees, our conversations seemed to feel liberating. Often the years overseas had been a life-transforming experience and they were eager to talk about it, especially since after returning home the interest of family and friends in hearing about the details was limited.

> *"Sometimes I feel that nobody understands me when it comes to my experience in Germany. I think you cannot understand it if you haven't experienced it yourself." (Chung C.Y., f, Tw/Ger/US)*

> *"After I returned to Germany, only very few people wanted to hear more than the superficial stuff from my ten months in Hawaii. So I was really happy when one time, sitting with three of my friends, all three of them fired questions at me all evening long. It felt exhilarating, but then I realized that all three of them had lived overseas themselves!" (Olga K., Ger/US)*

Not only the Chinese, but also the Germans, and sometimes the Americans, would thank me for the stimulation to rethink and reevaluate their experiences. "I very much enjoyed our evening together and I received a lot of food for thought from you," Ilse F. (Ger/US) told me. "The encounter will motivate me to continue to pursue my dream to meet the world." Of course, I was the one who owed them thanks for so generously giving me time and sharing their thoughts. It was a wonderful experience for me. With gratefulness I dedicate the book to each one of them, wishing all of them full and satisfying lives while they continue to broaden their understanding of themselves and the world.

Structure of the book

The reader will notice that the internal organization of the first three chapters differs, reflecting the priorities each culture attaches to different parts of the human experience. Thus my Chinese conversation partners dwelled at length on family relationships, especially the parent-child relationship, often describing the gulf they perceived to exist between Chinese and Western values in this regard. In comparison, Americans and Germans said relatively little about this topic. Instead, an individual's actions assumed a much higher priority in American thinking, while a person's thoughts and feelings stood out more in my conversations with Germans.

Why read the book?

In writing *Lights & Shadows: Discoveries Away From Home* I would hope to stimulate more awareness of the cultural lens through which we view ourselves and the world. Though international tourism has greatly expanded and allows travelers to visit unfamiliar places, taste different foods, or observe interesting local customs, rarely does short-term travel allow people to gain a deeper cultural understanding. Truly immersing oneself in another country takes time and effort and often, at least initially, entails a good amount of loneliness. Yet, I know of no one who in hindsight had regrets over having embarked on such an adventure. It is my hope that those who have not had such opportunity will enjoy the indirect experience they can gain through the views and insights of those who contributed to this book. Those who have lived overseas know that the experience helped them grow and change, often to a degree that makes it difficult to resume their former lives upon returning home. At that point they may look for a new and different set of friends. Perhaps this book can be one such friend.

* * *

Notes

[1] "Harvard Magazine" (Jul/Aug 2007), harvardmagazine.com/2007/07/le-professeur.html.

[2] Bill Moyers, *A World of Ideas* (New York: Doubleday, 1989), 90.

I. THE AMERICAN DOING SELF

It is my heritage to stand erect, proud, and unafraid: to think and act for myself, enjoy the benefit of my creations and to face the world boldly and say, this I have done. All this is what it means to be an American."

—John Adams, second president of the United States

An identity

MANY of my American conversation partners concurred that Americans continue to define themselves to a large degree by what they do and have accomplished. The reality of this shared American value became clear as they discovered that neither the Germans nor the Chinese identified themselves in this way.

I am what I do

Americans commonly introduce themselves by talking about what they do, which determines much of their self-worth and who they are. It also determines what others think of them. Quite possibly, due to Europe's most enterprising immigrants settling in the United States, achievement oriented action took on an increasingly dominant role, overshadowing other human abilities such as thinking or relating when judging oneself and granting status and social recognition to others.

"When I took a university class in Hong Kong and the professor had us introduce ourselves, I was struck by the way the other students did so. They would start out with 'I am the daughter of so and so' and everything they said was in the context of their larger relationships. My own introduction was about me, my name, my hobbies, my achievements. That's the norm for us, but, gee, what I said was very different from what the others said." (Rose C., ABC/Hong Kong)

"I judge people by what they do; not by what they are or know, or how they relate to others." (Richard M., US/Ger)

"We don't judge people by who they are or by what they know. We judge and are judged by what we do." (Mark R., US/Ger)

"After I was unemployed for a period and then found a job, I recognized that work in our culture is not self-actualization. Instead work fulfills a huge protective function. It protects us from the question of who we are and what we want. When the job defines you, you don't need to think about who you are. But when you don't have a job, you immediately start to doubt yourself." (Pete Z., US)

"I am obsessed with my job to the point that it has become my life. I am personally driven and need to prove to myself that I can shape an idea, make it happen and achieve a desired result. It's very American—it's our entrepreneurial spirit." (Paul R., US/Asia)

"When people say somebody is a nice guy, that means that's all he is. Basically he is a loser." (Jonathan L., US/Eur/PRC)

Americans living in Germany took note of a different attitude toward work.

⇨ *"I see a big difference between Americans and Germans in our attitudes toward the job. In America we rather work more to get that car, that big TV, a new computer, whatever. Here in Germany there is more to life than work. People work hard but they also put time away for other things, and this time is very important to them. During vacations and over the weekends they spend time with family and friends. And when I am with my friends here in Germany we don't talk about work. It's just not a central concern. Now, after having lived and worked in Germany for five years I think I am more suitable to life here than in the US, where life is primarily about work and where passion and enthusiasm is mostly about having a big dream about making big money. Here life is broader than that." (Peter W., ABC/Ger)*

⇨ *"When I was in Europe I sensed a different priority. People there seemed to be doing what they were doing out of pride in doing the job well, not because of any reward or money. For them it seemed to be more a reflection of their self, more like 'I am the quality of my work.'" (Jane M., US/Europe)*

⇨ *"I think Germans strive much more for quality than we do. Whatever the task, most people seem to take real pride in doing a job well." (John D., US/Ger)*

Americans often say, if you keep busy, you'll live longer. Being busy makes people feel good and capable. Susan, one of my retired friends regularly greets me and others by telling us what she just did or what she is about to do. She'll say, "I have to do all this stuff. My calendar is a mess and I am leaving for a trip next week." Indeed for the doing self it seems hard to slow down. It is no coincidence that America invented fast food, for time is far too important to be wasted on preparing food and eating it leisurely at home. Every so often we read in the paper of someone who makes a great deal of money, perhaps millions of dollars a year, and who says something like, "I am now making so much money. I could sit on the beach and do nothing for the rest of my life. But that would be boring. I would rather work one hundred hours a week. It's my life!"

"When I lived in California it was go go for me, especially at the time I wanted to get over a bad relationship. Being super busy helped me forget; but I also really wanted to do all those things. In the evening I'd be thrilled to tell myself, 'Oh I finished all this today.' I did not think of enjoying each task and I was exhausted." (Angelina H., US/Europe)

"A couple of days ago my husband discovered Planet Earth on the web and played with it all night. Afterwards he groaned, 'Oh I just wasted a whole evening!' 'Why, it must have been enjoyable,' I told him. 'Yes, but I did not get anything accomplished!' Enjoyment does not seem to count. Americans always need to have accomplished something." (Jenny S., US/Europe)

"Even my eighty-year-old mother feels that she has to be busy. In Asia I don't see people living by set times or their calendars." (Larry R., US/Ger/Asia)

⇨ *"I was amazed to see that people in Germany had so much time for each other. We are always in a rush and never take the time." (Jim S., US/Ger)*

"We don't know where we are going but we are on our way." This American saying points to the importance of doing something fast, even if it is not well thought out. A former boss of mine was an enthusiastic and creative university administrator. "I sometimes feel as if I am flying an airplane without a bottom," he once admitted to me, when his ideas were flying and he was talking about his visions as if they were already reality. And when one house of cards collapsed, as it usually did, he did not dwell on the collapse but immediately built a new one. Working for him felt as if we were permanently on the verge of some astounding accomplishment, yet somehow none ever came to fruition.

"We Americans want to get things done fast and we can bully our way into things. If you just shout loud enough something is going to happen." (Elizabeth M., US/Europe)

"My mother used to tell me, "Do something! Even if it is wrong. It's better to try and fail, than fail to try." (Tim C., US/Europe)

"While working for a large company I learned several things. The ability to come up with results quickly is more important than thinking ahead. As long as you can come up with something for your boss right away, never mind if the next guy has to clean up the mess. I was told 'We don't care how carefully you look at those documents. Just get them done, pump them out!' The principle is, don't lose money and time. Dump and run, pass the buck. On the surface it appears that a lot is being done." (Dorothy W., US/Ger)

"If you are trying to do something, put forward the image. Fake it until you make it. What we learned in massage therapy school in New York was this: the best therapist will be the one who has the most success. Your product may be average, but in your marketing you must excel. What good is it if no one knows about you? So we got training in making two minute elevator speeches, to learn how to market ourselves and get our message across quickly." (Jenna H., US/Ger)

Given the emphasis on speed, Americans prefer to start projects quickly and then make necessary adjustments as the implementation gets under way. People who are fond of this style have little patience for the German habit of considering all possible ramifications before starting a task. Nor do they appreciate the German emphasis on formal education and degrees over practical experience.

⇨ *"When we want to undertake a project or design a program we just start and improve as we go along. In Germany they want to design quality programs, and for that purpose they emphasize knowledge and training. But it means that if the project is very demanding it may never get off the ground. In the US we say let's get started and then make adjustments as we need to." (Rick F. US /Ger/Asia)*

⇨ *"Germans are perfectionists. They always think it could be better, which means it's never good enough. We Americans see room for improvement and get going. Germans complain about imperfections." (Phil B., US/Ger)*

⇨ *"In Germany people are held back from maturing by not entering the workforce sooner. I could not wait to get out of junior high school to leave home and start working. In Germany education is more important than experience, but I think not working retards you from blossoming, from becoming your independent self. Besides, in the US ninety percent of the people don't work in the field they studied. In America we always need to reinvent ourselves, to re-educate ourselves to keep up with the market." (Richard M., US/Ger)*

Americans living in Chinese society recognized that the Chinese generally work longer hours than Americans, but did not seem to share the American sense of individual responsibility and fairness. Defined by their individual accomplishments, Americans expect to be given credit for their personal achievements, but in return they also generally accept the responsibility for their work and actions, something they found lacking in Chinese society.

⇨ *"We Americans internalize values. The Chinese will not feel bad if nobody finds out that they have done something bad. They only get upset when the boss finds out. Even if nobody tells us what to do, we take responsibility and we may feel guilty when we do something we should not do. The Chinese don't feel guilty. If a politician is caught taking or giving bribes and then apologizes, people forgive him and all is well." (Nellie W., US/Tw/PRC)*

⇨ *"When Taiwanese are instructed to do something they will spend a lot of time on the task. Most of us in the US will not work as much, but we are more committed to the job and take more responsibility." (Matthew T., ABC/Tw)*

⇨ *"For Asians it always seems easier to blame someone else for your mistakes than to look inward and take stock of your own weaknesses and strengths." (Harry M. US/Asia)*

⇨ *"When I worked in a large organization in Taiwan, I noticed that as soon as the boss was not present, the workers stopped working and started playing computer games or chatted with the person sitting next to them. The change from working to slacking off was abrupt, almost comical. When I pointed it out to my coworkers they laughed and said, 'Why, that's human nature!'" (Erica L., US/Tw)*

⇨ *"I spent several years working for Voice of America supervising about fifty Chinese employees. During that time I gained some insights into their attitudes towards work. There was a lot of factional infighting among them. Though usually these conflicts were over personal dislikes, it affected their productivity. Also, they had no sense of a common task or contributing to a greater cause. If someone tries to be good, or do something extra, the others will pull him down. They may sabotage others even when doing so does not bring them any personal advantage. I also became aware that they tried to hide their mistakes and did their own business on work time." (Jonathan L., US/Ger /PRC).*

⇨ *"The Chinese business people engage in more cutthroat practices than any other people I know. Maybe it has something to do with the fact that the Chinese have plenty of rules on how to keep conflict under wraps, but no rules or laws for fair play. Competitive sports teaches rules for fair play, but China has no native sports tradition. Their tradition prescribes harmony, not competition." (Douglas T., US/Tw)*

I am what I have

In the decades following World War II money and material possessions have slowly but increasingly become a measure of American self-worth. No longer is making money a mere side product, a symbol of success. In Somerset Maugham's 1944 novel *The Razor's Edge* the author has one of his main characters say, "You Europeans don't understand anything about us Americans. Because we amass great fortunes, you think that we are only interested in money. It has no value for us. From the moment we have it, we spend it. For us, money is nothing; it is simply a symbol of success. We are the greatest idealists in the world." [1] Times have changed. Doing and keeping busy are still important, but wealth and possessions are increasingly replacing doing as identity markers.

> "We now increasingly judge people not by what they do but by what they have. Nowadays things help create our identity." (Mark R., US/Ger)

> "As I see it, the most important thing in the American purpose driven life is having stuff. For us being unemployed is terrible, but when I talk to my brother and sister, they say provided you have some savings it's not so bad. But being without a house or without a car is bad. At least in the Midwest buying things, such as a house or a car, is more about who you are than anything else. It's not the family and it's not what you think. People study in order to get the degree in order to buy stuff. Look at all those self-storage places. They tell us, I am the sum total of all this stuff." (Phil B., US/Ger/PRC)

> "At my university new buildings used to be named after famous professors or intellectual leaders. No longer. Now the university waits for somebody to give a lot of money and then extends recognition by using the donor's name for the building." (Judy K., US/Europe/Asia)

> "The option of doing what you like and feeling satisfaction even with making little money is still available, but doing so means missing out on recognition from others. For example, as a university English professor I know that English majors tend to be idealists. They enjoy their studies, but in most cases they do not receive the support from their families. Nowadays most young people, Asian immigrants even more so, go for money, though later in life some may opt for early retirement in order to do what they want." (Bess E., US/PRC)

As the measuring stick for determining worthwhile goals changes from "I am what I do" to "I am what I have," Americans attribute an ever greater importance to how they compare to others and how others see them.

"We spend a lot of time thinking how we appear to other people, especially on social occasions. It's like being up on a stage with people looking at me, ready to judge me." (Mary L., US/Ger)

"Though everybody is afraid of being a loser, what is driving things and what is really important is not being a winner but rather the penalty of being a loser. Our focus is not on the work per se, but rather on how we stack up against others." (Larry R., US/Ger)

Beliefs

The American faith in doing builds on beliefs in the capability of the individual and in his God-given rights and freedom. With an underpinning faith of "in God we trust," self-reliance, freedom and optimism are at the heart of the American doing self. Though rooted in Calvinist tradition, according to which God helps those who help themselves, Americans tend to assume these values to be universal, shared by people around the world. However, being based on beliefs, other cultures do not necessarily accept the basic premises behind these concepts or may interpret them differently.

Self-reliance and freedom

The belief in self-reliance assumes that the individual is capable and independent of others. For Americans self-reliance is a good feeling and enhances motivation. Asking others for help means a lack of ability and is best avoided while the thought of being dependent instills fear.

"The belief that you can do anything if you just put your mind to it and apply yourself is a basic American value. It means that in this land of opportunity anybody can be rich. That is the American dream, an idealism, not reality. It's behind many ideas and initiatives, such as Special Olympics and 'No child left behind.'" (Jenny S., US/Eur)

"We Americans can't say no if we are asked to do something; it's because it means I cannot do it, I am not capable of doing it." (Angelina H., US/Eur)

"When I accept help I have just lowered my ability to do it myself. It's not a matter of being unable to do it myself, it's a matter of wanting to do it myself. It's similar to covering the good eye when the other eye is not working well. It's a way of forcing your eyes to make the adjustment. Same thing when you don't push yourself hard enough and quit doing things, you become less and your mind and body lose their abilities. It means that I am not as strong as I should or could be. The thought of being dependent—whether it means being poor, ill, or not mobile—that is what scares people." (Jane M., US/Eur)

"In America our whole educational system is geared to making the young independent. I have plenty of friends who at the age of eighteen are on their own and without a family to fall back on. There are some ethnic groups, like some Scottish Irish I know, that do have extended families, but in the average American family the children are pushed out into the world with the promise that it's a fair world out there with opportunities to make it." (Mark R., US/Ger)

For the I-am-what-I do self, doing it my way is the hallmark of the free individual. It assumes that I am in control of my life, not unduly restricted by family or excessive governmental rules. "What America gives you," Richard Rodriguez wrote in Bill Moyers' book *Ideas*, "is an 'I,' the individual. The possibility that your father's ghost will not pursue you. That you can escape the civil wars of your ancestral village, that you can escape your ancestors, that you can escape all that ties you to the past. That you can begin anew. . . . We mustn't forget the freedom and the extraordinary joy that comes with that." [2] That idea also rang true for my American respondents.

"My sense of individual freedom is that you can do what you want to do when you want to do it. When I grew up, the only limitation was money." (Bess E., US/PRC)

"The thing I came to appreciate most about America is our sense that everyone is free to go their own way, and is expected and encouraged to take full advantage of this freedom. In Asia, I feel that this dynamic is missing. There is negative instead of positive pressure. In America it seems that each individual pushes to expand his space, while in Asia there is pressure not *from* the individual but *upon* the individual. Individuality is discouraged, which means

the fullness of human nature is not given room to flourish. In my view it re-
flects a narrow view of humanity." (Jason N., US/PRC/Asia)

"In my mind the Reformation, which established a personal relationship be-
tween man and God by sweeping aside all intermediaries, such as govern-
ments or laws, gave people a sense of personal liberty and responsibility.
Though this sense never came to fruition in Europe, it transported itself over
here, and became the underpinning for everything. It's the basis for our faith
in personal liberty and for wanting opportunities and freedom, rather than
security. It makes it impossible to say you can't do this or that." (Alan K., US/
Tw/Ger)

The American belief in self-reliance and freedom contrasts with the Chinese
ideal of mutual interdependence and respect for authority.

⇨ *"I could see that many in my Chinese husband's family were stunned and*
shocked that we wanted to make our children self-reliant, so that they can go
off and live their own lives. Some asked us, 'But who is going to take care of
you when you are old?' I think that some Americans might envy the Chinese
family situation as they grow older, but I come from a tradition that is very
different. At the age of eighty-five, my mother preferred to die rather than
become dependent on my sister. She lived alone for twenty years in order
to maintain that independence. Looking at myself as I approach old age, I
understand my mother's stubbornness." (Nellie W., US/Tw/PRC)

⇨ *"When I lived in China, an expat colleague of mine in Shandong was sent to*
the hospital when she had pneumonia. After she felt well she was ready to go
home. So even though the doctor told her that she had to stay longer, she just
put on her clothes, walked out of the hospital and came back to work in our
school. In that one action of getting up and walking out on her own, she was
more American than I could say. Her Chinese students were appalled because
it was something they could not even think of doing. Another time when I
was in the Shanghai library talking to a couple of staff members somehow
the concept of self-reliance came up just as David, our then thirteen-year-old
son, emerged from the stacks. I called him over and asked him, 'The people
here are interested in knowing when you started to make your own decisions
about when and what you would do for school.' He thought for a moment and

said, 'Kindergarten?' You can't just become self-reliant. It's a process. Years later, after David had just graduated from college, he told us that he'd like to come home for Thanksgiving but that he couldn't afford it. For our kids, the last thing they want to do is ask us for help. Grown children feel shame to ask their parents for help. My Chinese acquaintances are shocked when I tell them that we are proud not to help our college son find a job. We want self-reliant children." (Bess E., US/PRC)

⇨ "In Asia people commonly give people presents, not only as a sign of respect, but frequently also with the intent of creating an indebtedness. Many Americans have a difficult time accepting things. We want to be free and independent, not indebted." (Julie L., US/Tw/PRC)

Several of my American interviewees questioned the American beliefs in self-reliance and freedom.

"Believing in self-reliance means 'I can do it.' That attitude is instilled into us, making us self-confident and optimistic. But it neglects the fact that the world is not fair. In the real world, it's who you know not what you know or what you can do." (Jane M., US/Eur)

"Germans know better that people have talents in specific areas. In America we assume you can learn anything. It's an optimism which allows us to believe in ourselves, but it also has social consequences for our educational system and society at large." (Mark R., US/Ger)

"The word 'freedom' makes me cringe. We forget about the fact that our freedom to do requires that we have the ability to do what we want. In America everybody is for himself. If the other person can't make it, tough luck." (Peter W., ABC/Ger)

Self-confidence and optimism

Americans are expected to be self-confident and optimistic. Confidence and optimism complement each other, both spurring the individual into action in the pursuit of goals. By keeping negative thoughts at bay, self-confidence and optimism create a fearlessness that encourages risk-taking. Dr. Jason Selk, a mental toughness coach for individuals, businesses, and professional athletes and their coaches, put it this way, "Ask any successful person to divulge their secret to winning, to meeting and exceeding goals, and to feeling fulfilled and accomplished, and they'll usually say that optimism is key." [3] Even when inner feelings do not correspond, it is important for Americans to project an optimistic and self-confident image.

> "Because the core of my self depends on what I do, if I am not doing or producing something, I lose self-confidence. For example, as a writer if I am not sitting down and writing something, or if as a masseuse—which is what I do—I don't do massages, I am going to lose the ability as well as confidence. I had a crisis and took a drop in confidence when after moving to Germany I did not have clients for a while." (Jenna H., US/Ger)

> "I teach legal writing in China to Chinese law associates. So in my classes I talk to them about self-confidence, because it's what our clients expect. People want someone who is an expert and projects that image. It's like going to the doctor. We want someone who is confident, not someone who hems and haws and says he has never seen anything like your problem. It's the same in the service industry. You need to portray knowledge. Much of it is the skill of presenting yourself. Sometimes a person may excel at presenting himself, oozing confidence but in reality lack know-how and substance. That's the bad side of the acting part." (Lance F., US/PRC)

> "I'd say fifty percent of American demonstrated confidence is show, fifty percent is real. It's part of our education and our family upbringing. We are taught to present ourselves well." (Arnie E., US/PRC)

> "When I lived in New York and later in Baltimore, I lived in pretty rough neighborhoods. So I learned to walk tall, stare people down and be ready with a whole set of reactions. If someone talks to you aggressively you need to talk back, make fun of them, perhaps say something like, 'You can be looking like that? In those pants!!!' If you talk like that they'll let you go. If you ignored them, they take it as a sign of fear and will come after you." (Jenna H., US/Ger)

> "In order to do things Americans have to be eternally positive, like the early pioneers. In those days only strong doers and strong optimists would have had the disposition to emigrate." (Mark R., US/Ger)

Americans living overseas observed a lack of confidence among the Chinese, while those in Germany were particularly struck by what they saw as a pervasive pessimism.

⇨ *"I think that people who are confident generally do not worry about failing. It seems to me that Asians cannot handle rejection or even impersonal criticism or information. For example, they'd rather not apply for a certain job than risk rejection." (Harry M., US/Asia)*

⇨ *"My girl friends in Taiwan may be confident in their own way, but they are very much insecure about their abilities. For example, take their language skills. It's okay for me to make mistakes when I speak Chinese, even though I am embarrassed. But for them it's not okay to make mistakes. They want to practice their English, but then they really don't want to." (Julie L., US/Tw/PRC)*

⇨ *"The Chinese tell me that they don't have self-confidence. They put a premium on showing respect toward others, especially toward elders and people with authority, but this respect does not seem to include respect for themselves which may be behind their lack of self-confidence." (Nick H., US/Tw)*

⇨ *"I have lived in Japan for many years and learned that in everyday encounters the Japanese are busy acting shy, reticent, and hesitant because these attributes are considered attractive. In Japan one should never act as if one had confidence. I find the whole process of communicating with people very time-consuming, tedious and laborious. But this layer of superficiality that coats the Japanese has made me think about myself as an American. Our American hallmark is to be confident, friendly and outgoing. Now I wonder, is our own confidence also just a cultural layer?" (Helen V., US/Jap)*

⇨ *"Germans are terrible pessimists. They are always waiting for the next shoe to drop." (Jason H., US/Ger)*

American authors of articles on topics such as global warming, increasing crime, or some other negative development that threatens people's sense of well-being tend to end their piece of writing on an optimistic note, even when the facts they have just presented do not seem to warrant it. "I have no reason to be optimistic," one wrote, "yet I am optimistic, because I need to retain my optimism in order to go on, to have faith that the future will come out okay."

Feeling and thinking

The American doing self is not an inward looking self. Acting out enthusiasm and passion is more appealing than quiet self-reflection. "Nothing great has ever been created without passion," wrote Ralph Waldo Emerson, a well-known nineteenth century American essayist and poet.

Feeling

Several generations ago Americans were still taught to keep their feelings to themselves. At that time showing your emotions would have been considered impolite and undisciplined. However, times have changed and beginning with the postwar baby boomers expressing feelings has become the norm: Show your enthusiasm. Get the adrenaline flowing. Matt Cohen, an American film and television actor, once said, "I'd rather be around a passionate nerd than a non-passionate cool person. Because if you lack passion, your soul is diminishing by the second. You have to be passionate about something. Call it obsessed or whatever you want, but be obsessed about something. Obsessed people care." [4]

Appealing to feelings is also an effective sales tool. The American entertainment and advertising industries, in particular, are built on the principle of excitement. Whether the topic is sports, news, or the latest laundry detergent, more often than not television presents its subject matter by dramatizing the content through heavy sensationalist voices.

> *"American emotions freely flow when we waive our flags during sports events or scream at football matches. Being passionate about religion is okay. If you want to proselytize, people have the right to be passionate about it—though I also have the right to reject it. It is also expected and valued that you are passionate about your children and grandchildren and it is acceptable to gush over their accomplishments. In academic life intellectual passions are expressed through lively interactions at meetings and university forums. We've been trained since high school to deliver presentations with enthusiasm, and so we usually outperform our European and Asian colleagues in this respect." (Jenny S., US/Europe)*

"Stores in America are better than German stores at appealing to my feelings and therefore they make me want and buy more. They light up my imagination and help me create my identity." (Katja P., US/Ger)

Americans' own propensity for appeal to and display of emotions is clearly reflected in their observations of Chinese and German societies. Americans describe the Chinese as stoic and Germans as cold and lacking in empathy. Confirming the cultural discrepancies, Germans commonly describe American emotionalism as excessive and insincere, while the Chinese interpret it as a sign of immaturity.

⇨ *"On my first visit to China I was amazed how much 'in control' people in public seemed to be. Their facial expressions were so stoic, even when getting shoved or almost run over on their bicycles in the street. Gradually I understood that for the Chinese showing, or worse, losing, your temper is terrible, and I was afraid that one day I might lose mine—again—as I had once out of sheer frustration over living in China. So I had my Chinese students debate the issue in English class. They decided that it was okay to lose your temper when something really preposterous occurred, but only then and only very rarely. So I came to realize that I just could not be as emotional as I had been at home and I knew that I had at most three opportunities to lose my temper, at the right time and for the right cause, as long as I was in control of myself the rest of the time." (Bess E., US/PRC)*

⇨ *"The Germans are the coldest people I know. The way they deal with each other is cold. Their affect is low. They have a huge ability to shut down emotions and passion for the sake of objectivity. Without regard for empathy they narrowly focus on the facts, always trying to be objective, not be passionate. Nobody will accuse the Germans of being subjective. In school they are well trained to be objective, and they are proud of it, showing a kind of superiority to the point of rudeness or arrogance." (Mark R., US/Ger)*

⇨ *"When I have a problem my German friends tend to help me analyze my actions or feelings, even though sometimes maybe I just want a hug." (Joanne E., US/Ger)*

⇨ *"Germans have one week a year, during carnival (Fasching), to let loose of their emotions!" (Mary L., US/Ger)*

Not all of my American respondents shared the American flair for passion.

> "Many Americans dream big and are passionate about what they do, but usually it is about business and making money, making contacts and deals. I envy the people who have a passion. I don't have a passion and so don't have the opportunity to live it out. I don't get emotional. When I am really excited I won't scream and shout, and I don't like it when people go overboard with emotions or when I feel it's fake. My favorite kind of excitement, joy and happiness is quiet satisfaction. But in America when we speak, we go for shock therapy and tend to exaggerate, sensationalize things. We say we 'love' something, or 'hate' something. In Germany lieben ('to love') means you really, really mean it." (Dorothy W., US/Ger)

Thinking

To Americans the value of thinking lies primarily in its practical application. Thus the American educational system emphasizes experiential learning and problem solving, and encourages practical creativity and on-the-spot thinking. With thinking viewed as the starting point for action, there is little room for naysayers and pessimism. Positive thinking is expected and flexibility, not theories, principles, or rules, dominates American thinking. In his article for Phi Beta Kappa, the oldest honor society for the liberal arts and sciences, Leroy S. Rouner summed up his view, "Americans are a people who both built a better mousetrap and dreamed a grander dream. At best our practicality has enabled our visions . . . but we are not always at our best. . . . The one indigenous American philosophy is that use determines meaning and that ideas are instruments for achieving goals. Americans are suspicious of intellectuals whose ideas do not have some practical application but you can't predict what will be useful." [5]

This kind of thinking contrasts quite sharply with the kind of thinking Americans encountered in Germany. Some Americans who recently lived in Germany might agree with what Price Collier wrote over a century ago in his book *Germany and the Germans from an American Point of View*: "[The German] loves things of the mind, not because he thinks of them as of divine creation, but because they are the playthings of his own manufacture. . . . [He] imagines he has done something when he has had an idea. . . . The German flair of translating facts back into philosophy and then dancing through a discussion of theories is not understood, much less appreciated by the rest of the world. We can never get on if we are to introduce the discussion of every new battleship by arguments as to the seaworthiness of the ark. . . . You cannot think out life ahead of the living of it. Life is to live, not to think after all. It's wrong to mistake thinking for living." [6]

Nathan Heller, a Harvard student studying in Paris described, with a bit of tongue in cheek, the difference between American and French thinking in a similar way. Though he happened to be in France, I believe his perception holds true for German thinking as well. "Academic papers and lectures in the United States," he wrote, "are based on the idea of the thesis. The thesis advances an original idea and shows how this idea can be used to explain the obvious and unobvious aspects of a particular topic. The French, on the other hand, do not seem to trust anything that comes to a conclusion. They favor something called the *problématique* ('the problem of the problem'), which identifies the problems at stake and elaborates them until no explanation is in sight. Whereas the thesis is an answer, the *problématique* is a question. A thesis brings some sort of order to apparent chaos, while a *problématique* suggests why a given problem is much, much more complicated than it looks and, actually, probably impossible to solve at all." [7]

⇒ *"Germans analyze things to death. They plan and plan and plan and are obsessed with understanding the bigger picture before they can decide any-thing. It's true, we Americans rush to implement and we don't see peaks and valleys. But the Germans feel burdened, whereas we Americans seem freer." (Mary L., US/Ger)*

⇒ *"I agree with what I read recently. The Germans don't just go by bike. They need to have an ideology to support it. They always need a reason for doing something." (Tim C., US/Ger)*

However, the majority of my American interviewees appreciated the broader thinking they encountered in Germany and Europe and were quite critical of what they saw as a nonintellectual climate in American mainstream society.

"I think we Americans are on the whole rather superficial in our thinking. People are open to beliefs, where the answers are given to them, and they stop there instead of engaging in deeper reflections of their own." (Paul R., US/Asia)

"I think we Americans have very little interest in thinking, whether it's thinking about ethics, principles or thinking in general. To me that's missing an important human dimension. It makes us less human. We Americans are creative in matters that lead to an end result, to something that can be measured in money, but to my mind there is a lot more to life than making money." (Jane M., US/Europe)

"American society is not an intellectual society. Here money talks. Just look at the $800,000 salaries for athletic coaches in the universities!" (Brian G., US/Europe)

"Americans of Anglo descent have little ability for introspection. Central Europeans, meaning Germans, Austrians, Czech and Central European Jews, tend to ask themselves, 'Why do I feel the way I do?,' 'Why do I think this way?' In the US it's the Jews and Germans who are the archetype of this thing." (Mark R., US/Ger)

"As an undergraduate who majors in philosophy I feel alienated from other students. For them I am up in the clouds somewhere." (Gerry S., US/Ger)

"Americans do not think broadly. They think locally. They don't know what's going on within the next state and don't necessarily want to know." (Peter W., ABC/Ger)

"American students are fine with problem solving, but not good at thinking per se. In order to have something to think about, you need a knowledge base, but in the US knowledge per se is devalued." (Jane M., US/Europe)

⇨ "As an American I am much less informed than the Germans I have been meeting here in Berlin. Many Americans have little interest in the rest of the world. We don't read newspapers, and even if we read them, there is less world news in them. It strikes me that the news here in Germany is all about the US. In fact I am shocked that there is so much. There is a general dismay among Germans about American ignorance of the world. But the information is just not provided to us." (Jenna H., US/Ger)

⇨ *"Maybe there is no greater divergence between the US and Germany than in our attitudes toward thinking. Germany is a deep culture, and its people are thoughtful, deep people. We Americans don't value long thinking conversations and we tend to think of the Manhattan intelligentsia as snobs. And snobbery is a big negative." (Alan K., US/Tw/Ger)*

⇨ *"Europeans are much more intellectual than Americans. Not smarter or more intelligent, but they have more intellectual interests. With my German student friends we often got into some heated arguments. I learned more in the streets with them than in the classroom. In America we are more into sports and physical activity, doing things. People are much less interested in intellectual conversations, though more so than people in Asia." (Rick F., US/Ger/Asia)*

⇨ *"To the Europeans thinking is an intellectual exchange. With Germans of a decent education you can have a cultured, intellectual discussion and have it be enjoyable. Americans do not view ideas as valuable. To them a conversation like that is just hogwash and they would not find pleasure in it." (Larry R., US/Ger/Asia)*

⇨ *"I think Americans are very shortsighted. Europeans pay more attention to the bigger picture. Their thinking is more thought-provoking, more open-minded. We don't think broadly enough, and we don't take on the big story. By excluding the negative, our positive thinking is delusional." (Angelina H., US/Europe)*

⇨ *"One of the things I really like about Germany is that people are not expected to think the same as everyone else." (Anne F., US/Ger)*

Americans in Chinese society also encountered a different mode of thinking, one that zeroed in on people and relationships rather than the task at hand. Less concerned about principles and established rules via á vis Germans, compared to the Chinese, Americans found themselves to be more concerned about such issues.

⇨ *"What I have learned over the years is that we Americans think in linear ways while the Chinese in Taiwan think in circular ways. There are two different thinking patterns that go with our respective cultures. When we Americans want to solve a problem, we think about how to get from point A to B in a straight line. For example, in America if a rule says the apartment manager is not available between twelve and two o'clock, then even if you have a situation where you need to contact the manager during this time the manager is unlikely to make an exception. In a way this manager is oblivious to other factors. The Chinese tend to take the path with the least resistance to obtain a goal. By circular thinking this means getting from A to B can also have a factor of C or D. We still arrive at B but we got there via C. In my view, the Taiwanese have a greater tendency to 'go with the flow' while we Americans can get all fidgety or uncomfortable if something is not done by a preestablished pattern or procedure. With this in mind, I find the Taiwanese to be more pragmatic than Americans. An American friend of mine here in Taiwan told me that he experienced similar situations." (Nathan N., US/Tw/PRC)*

⇨ *"People in Taiwan have become much more aware of world affairs, and are now more willing to state political views than before. However, much of talking politics is still about who, not about what. There is a lot of finger pointing, attention to whom to blame instead of thinking what needs to be done to solve the problem." (Julie L., US/Tw)*

⇨ *"I don't care for the usual gossip or chit chat conversations amongst the Chinese and other Asians. However, my (Chinese) mother-in-law who lived in the US for many years, is very different from the rest of her large extended family in that she engages in a lot of self-reflection. I enjoy my conversations with her, but the rest of her family thinks I am just very patient to put up with her." (Harry M., US/Asia)*

Relating

Informality and tangentiality represent the core differences between American, Chinese, and German dominant modes of relating to others. Informality refers to a friendly communication style, which minimally differentiates between friend and stranger, superior and inferior, junior and senior. Tangentiality, literally meaning "merely touching, slightly connected," implies relationships that do not curb one's independence and freedom through obligations or long-term bonds. Together informality and tangentiality provide ways of relating to others with ease and freedom through casual relationships, suitable for individuals who value independence and mobility in order to pursue opportunities wherever they might present themselves. Besides offering easy ways to connect with others without a compelling reason or commitment, informality and tangentiality require little investment of time, so important to a busy doing self.

Communicating

American informality is a one-size-fits-all approach that uses light and friendly conversation to communicate with everyone. Although there are regional differences within the United States, showing interest in the other is part of politeness and does not necessarily aim at establishing a relationship. Small talk expresses friendliness, while silence conveys a lack of cordiality and feels awkward.

> "We are all on a first name basis. In the United States my students called me Elizabeth even when I was sixty years old and they were twenty. We go for extreme informality. In most other cultures there are several levels of form you go through before becoming friendly. But here in America we basically have only one level, which applies to strangers as well as friends." (Elizabeth M., US /Europe)

> "Making conversation with people we don't know is the polite thing to do. You don't want to make them feel bad." (Angelina H., US/Europe)

> "As Americans we are trained to be friendly, and it is unfriendly to have nothing to say, no matter how little we know that person. To refuse to talk is to be arrogant, snooty." (Pamela Y., US/Europe)

> "Though I am usually shy with strangers, I talk to people in the elevator and in bathrooms, because I feel the need to fill up that uncomfortable silence." (Kay M., US/Europe)

> "My wife talks to everybody. When she does not know someone, she asks a lot of questions. 'Tell me about your children' she might ask, even though she

doesn't even know if the person has children. 'Are they married?' For her it is not about a conversation with content. It's an interaction, a process. I myself would not initiate a conversation with people I don't know and I would not ask anything personal. I take after my father, who had European—including some German—roots and who preferred to be quiet, to not say much. For him sitting together in silence could be a wonderful silence, a demonstration of some depth in the relationship. But I remember my mother telling him every so often that he was not holding up his part in the relationship. I know this was a point of contention in our home." (Larry S., US/Asia)

"For us, if someone speaks to you in the street—in a friendly manner, not aggressively—that's a new acquaintance. And in the South and Midwest, people might stop and ask whether you need a ride. That is old fashioned American openheartedness, a kindness toward strangers." (Jenna H., US/Ger)

American communication aims to make the other feel comfortable. Along with easy smiles and an appeal to emotions, Americans generally prefer topics that are light or entertaining, avoiding those that risk offending, such as discussions involving philosophy, religion, moral or political beliefs. With conversation being more a process of interaction than about content, courtesy, and friendliness take precedence over truth and honesty.

"Generally our conversations are not centered on a topic. Instead we want to make people feel comfortable. So we tend to say not what we feel or think, just what we consider to be polite." (Angelina H., US/Eur)

"I grew up in the South and still went to charm school where I learned not to talk about religion and politics at parties. I also learned that when you go to someone's house you say something complimentary even if the place looks rotten." (Sarah V., US/Asia)

"We are taught to find a nice way to say things. Before you make a negative comment, find something good to say. And if you can't find something good to say, don't say anything. It's part of our upbringing. Instead of going with the truth and risking to hurt feelings I play it safe and use a lot of dishonest white lies." (Kathy R., US/Europe)

"In theory, expressing our opinions is part of free speech. Still, there are many circumstances where being too honest violates American expectations of interpersonal relations. I think we expect honesty to come out in actions rather than words. I judge people more by what they do than what they say. Actions speak louder than words." (Jenna H., US/Ger)

"I grew up in Manhattan, where people are very outspoken and direct, if not rude. I knew even then that New York was not representative of the rest of the country. In the Midwest, if I said something negative, they might say something positive as a response, because you just can't have disharmony or voice a negative thought. Not so in New York!" (Mark R., US/Ger)

When not engaging in small talk or other light conversations, Americans like to talk about themselves, especially about what they do. The topic is safe in that it does not offend, can fill an uncomfortable silence and is enjoyable for the speaker because what one does lies at the heart of the doing self.

"When you are raised to be independent, you are out there by yourself. You are to excel as an individual, be the star of basketball, a movie star, get your picture in the paper, wave to the camera. . . . It's all about you. So we talk about all the stuff we did. Since you are it, there is nothing else to talk about." (Phil B., US/Ger/PRC)

"Americans talk about themselves. Some of them, including my own children, talk about themselves incessantly. I talk about myself especially when I feel uncomfortable, because I can be sure it does not offend. Once in a public bathroom I saw a woman toward whom for whatever reason I felt an antipathy. Still, I was telling her about my life, things she did not care hearing about and I did not want her to know. But for me it meant putting the best face on it, because you don't offend. You can't ask others what they do, because the person might be a janitor or not have a job at all." (Kay M., US/Europe)

"Other than talking about work, we Americans usually don't discuss topics, unless you count shopping and talking about spending money a topic. It's a kind of anti-intellectual attitude and climate. That's why my friends are mostly foreigners." (Cara B., US/Eur)

Given the importance to make people feel comfortable and included along with a tendency to fill each day with activities, Americans have relatively little interest in and time for longer, deeper conversations or serious discussions.

"We Americans are so busy. Most of us have a long list of things we want to do. Doing things is so valued that we never have time to sit and talk. It's no wonder that we have no decent coffee shops in America." (Jenny S., US/Eur)

"Americans talk about what they do. They are not into intellectual discussions. When I was in the army, where you are surrounded by the average person, I could find very few people I wanted to sit down with and talk. You can't talk with them about deeper or philosophical things. Nor can I have those kinds of conversations with my relatives." (Jonathan L., US/Ger/PRC)

"I remember that not long ago a small group of us, all fellow students, happened to talk about the weather and how it was changing. When we got to the topic of global warming, one person said that it was just hype, a lie by the media. When another person agreed with him, the rest of us all pounced on them with arguments about ice melts and such. One of the two could take it and came up with counterarguments, but the other stopped participating and seemed offended. When we noticed that he felt uncomfortable, we changed the topic to not make him feel bad. But I thought to myself, what's the point of a discussion, if it isn't to discuss different views?" (Angelina H., US/Eur)

"In America conversations do not have much value, a fact I am especially aware of when eating out with friends. For example, last week, when I went out to dinner with some friends the music in the restaurant was so loud that we had to shout to hear each other. A restaurant should be a place where people can meet and where it is not so loud that you can't have a conversation. Also, American waiters usually keep coming to the table to ask if everything is okay, each time interrupting the ongoing conversation. The assumption must be that conversations are just chatter which can be interrupted any time. In Europe restaurants are generally quiet and the waiters don't disturb the diners in the same way." (Kay M., US/Eur)

"When I lived in New York as a student many of my friends were foreign students. When I went out with them for a drink we would talk about all sorts of interesting topics. When American students got together they probably would buy

a case of beer and sit in a house on a Saturday morning and watch sports. The American male has nothing to say. At most they talk shop, or they kick a ball or do something. If people don't sit down and have discussions there is no intimacy." (Mark R., US/Ger)

Accustomed to a friendly and light informality toward all, the majority of Americans react negatively to the German clear distinction between friend and stranger. Particularly vexing to Americans is the lack of social smiles, which makes Germans appear distant and uncaring.

⇒ *"I think most Americans find Germans to be too serious. Germans need a reason to smile. To them, someone smiling too much is considered weird or crazy." (Alan K., US/Tw/Ger)*

⇒ *"People look at you in Germany without smiling. Worse, they stare and don't look away which in the US would be considered aggressive. It took me a while to realize that they mean no harm." (Susan F., US/Ger)*

⇒ *"Germans are more serious than we are. When I first went to Germany I'd smile at people. Until a salesperson in a department store asked me, 'Why are you laughing at me?' Germans are serious about what they say, and they take themselves more seriously. Life for them isn't such a cheerful business." (Arnold B., US/Ger)*

⇒ *"In the subways in Germany people look very stern. So here I came and smiled at people until I realized that smiling in public places was not the cultural norm. We smile at people we don't know or do know. It's a social smile. We are not trying to communicate happiness, we are simply following the norm. To Germans truthfulness is more important, so for them a smile is an honest smile, coming from a happy person. They have no social obligation to smile. It took me a long time of living in Germany until that insight sank in. Before that I just kept smiling and people probably thought I was strange. Now I realize that my cultural norm is different. Just as I wouldn't smile in certain parts of town in America, where the men would think you are a hooker if you smiled. People from countries that are used to be more reticent are nerved by our ever present smiles." (Mary L., US/Ger)*

⇨ "Many years ago I was passing through Paris with time to kill. Since I had heard that the French were unfriendly, I decided to try an experiment to find out whether that was true. For two hours I went through the airport with the express intention to get people to smile at me. I did not succeed. I didn't get a single smile. Not one!" (Kay M., US/Eur) [Though this experiment took place in France, the result would probably have been similar in other parts of Central and Northern Europe, including in Germany.]

To many Americans, German directness and focus on the topic rather than the feelings of the listener comes across as impolite and insensitive. A reporter once asked Sir Simon Rattle, the British music conductor of the Berlin Philharmonic, how language affected his relationship with the orchestra. "Language plays a huge role," Rattle said. "German sounds clear and is well articulated but it is not allusive. My language teacher came to some of my rehearsals and told me afterwards that I did not know how to talk to Germans. You can't say 'Perhaps you could. . .' or 'Don't you think that . . .?' They have none of our layers of politeness." [8]

⇨ "Germans have strong opinions and they state them bluntly. One German academic colleague told me that he thought American talk was terribly wishy washy. As an example he pointed out that when Americans want to make a critical comment on an academic presentation they use expressions like 'It might be a good idea. . .,' or 'Have you ever thought of such and such. . .' even when there is no doubt that it's hogwash. For us Americans it is important to be tactful and for criticism to be constructive." (Jack H., US/Ger)

⇨ "I don't like the verbal part of the Germans. Their words are like sharp knives. They'll tell me, 'What you are doing is all wrong. I know the right way and I don't like the way you are doing it.' It is very aggressive, a kind of bullying. We use courtesy to grease the wheels when there is a conflict." (Richard M., US/Ger)

⇨ "I discovered that when a German makes a statement such as 'You are doing this all wrong' what they actually mean to say is 'I think you are doing this all wrong.' Expressing opinions like that is considered a good thing—it means you are thinking! Sometimes their insistence that they are right is related to accuracy. For example, if I say 'Look at that gorgeous blue sky,' someone is bound to point out to me that the sky isn't entirely blue, that there is a tiny little cloud over there somewhere." (Mark R., US/Ger)

⇨ "Germans have no taste for small talk. They want to talk about 'real' topics, such as discussing the environment, global warming, or recycling. It makes you feel as if you have just walked into an academic seminar." (Eric M., US/ Ger)

Some Americans, whether by nature or heritage, feel comfortable with the German seriousness and directness. Several talked about their own discomfort with small talk and about missing deeper conversations in American life.

"I can't handle small talk very well and I am not good at it. I had to learn it, but it still does not come naturally to me. Perhaps that's because I was an only child, as well as an only grandchild and I grew up in a formal family with British heritage." (Elizabeth M., US/Eur)

⇨ "I like the German directness because it is honest. Instead of trying to make everything sound wonderful, they state matters how they are. Living in Germany I have learned to be more direct. I find it works well and does not create hard feelings." (Louis Y., US/Ger)

⇨ "I like that with Germans I can be more honest in what I say. People are not as easily offended. They assume that people can handle the truth." (Rick F., US/ Ger)

⇨ "Germans are very critical, but they are honest which means you know where you stand. Also, in my experience, their criticism is usually based on pretty solid factual knowledge. And what's more, the criticism I have heard has never been directed at me personally." (Eric M., US/Ger)

⇨ "One of the things I like about Germany is that I can talk about big political, economic and social issues without the conversation ending in personal animosities. There is a wider variety of views than what I experience in the US." (Peter N., US/Ger)

⇨ "I miss deeper conversations in America. In my home we rarely had conversations around the dinner table, and if so, they tended to be explosive conversations. Generally Americans do not linger after the meal as people do in Germany." (Jane M., US/Ger)

⇨ *"I thought it was funny when at a recent American party two German men stood there with their glasses of wine in hand having a serious conversation in the midst of a noisy crowd. For all I know they might have been discussing death and dying. Yet, they seemed to be having a good time." (Eric D., US/Eur)*

⇨ *"You can talk about god and life in Germany. That's normal, but here in the US, if you start a topic like that, people will say, 'Gee, I've got to run now.' They don't want to go where there might be a controversy, where there is probing the depth of the soul. Of course, it depends on the neighborhood. In my own family we had no serious discussions, but I spent a lot of time in the home of a Jewish friend, where I was exposed to all sorts of interesting topics. Then I'd go home and raise a topic I had heard at my friend's place during dinner. But my dad did not feel comfortable talking about these things. 'That's nice,' he would say. 'Please, pass the salt.'" (Dorothy W., US/Ger)*

If Americans in Germany encountered an unfamiliar and, to some, unpleasant, directness and honesty, those living in Chinese societies experienced the opposite. The polite and indirect Chinese way of communication seemed excessively concerned with pleasing and not offending others. More mindful of the relationship than the message, honesty appeared to have little value. At the same time, Americans observed that the Chinese could be rude when no authority or personal relationship was involved, such as in the public sphere or within their own families where relationships are assumed to be unbreakable. Overall Americans considered Chinese communication to be complicated and stressful and given the Chinese taboo against even slight criticism, ill-suited to getting things done.

⇨ *"We Americans tend to compliment more honestly than the Chinese I know. We elevate the other without lowering ourselves, meaning you pick up something positive about the other and stretch it a bit." (Dorothy W., US/Ger)*

⇨ *"As the wife of a Chinese politician I was introduced to many people. Usually the person who introduced me would then continue to talk to the others about me, saying all sorts of good things about me, but treating me as if I was a child. I felt it was very demeaning to be talked about while I was standing there next to them and could have spoken for myself. Yet to them it was part of politeness." (Linda L., US/Tw)*

⇨ *"As Mormon missionaries we knock on many Chinese doors seeking an opportunity to talk with people about our faith. I have been here in Taiwan for two years now, and I can count on the fingers of one hand the times the door was slammed in my face. The Chinese have a cultural requirement to be polite, and that includes telling a lie. People need some way to tell us they are not interested, and there are more or less polite ways to do that. It's a matter of directness and indirectness. I remember one case when a little girl answered the door and after we asked whether we could speak to an adult, she ran back into the house to tell her mom, or whoever was there. She came back telling us 'Nobody is home.' I could see on her face that mom had told her to tell me she was not home, but the little girl was having a rough time with that lie and I felt sorry for her." (Jim M., US/Tw)*

⇨ *"When it comes to the question and answer period after an academic talk, my Asian audiences clap politely but never question anything. For them there is no such thing as impersonal criticism. Western presenters at academic or professional meetings expect some real questions from the audience, perhaps challenges, being asked to defend their data. Asians don't challenge people in public, because it means embarrassing them and represents an open conflict. Both are very serious matters to them." (Harry M., US/Asia)*

⇨ *"In the West we expect people to be explicit. Since I won't know unless you tell me, we count on people to express themselves clearly. In China you are supposed to rely on your power of observation. What does this person really want? What makes him happy? The Chinese are good observers and they do spend a lot of time together, but do they really know? I don't think so." (Rose C., ABC/Hong Kong)*

⇨ *"For the Chinese it is important to always be polite, to be indirect, evasive and not tell people what they really think. We Americans want to get something done, achieve a goal, solve a problem, but it takes a lot of effort to know what the Chinese really mean. Because you cannot take things at face value, there is a lot of guessing going on. There is a bit of that everywhere, but the Chinese culture is based on reciprocity, which means much of the time something is done with an ulterior motive in mind. People do something so that it will benefit them later. There is more manipulation and opportunism in Chinese society than we are used to seeing at home." (Margo V., US/Asia)*

While Americans are familiar with white lies being part of politeness, the Chinese lack of truthfulness appeared to be of a different nature. Instead of being a positive trait, honesty seemed to be viewed as foolishness and naïveté, especially when dealing with the public.

⇨ *"Honesty is not a value for the Chinese. They sometimes laugh at Americans, finding them naïve. A Chinese may tell his friend, 'I told that American this and he believed it! That is so funny!' For them communicating with others is a game. But it means you can't take things at face value which makes it hard to figure out what is meant. It makes life complicated and stressful." (Nellie W., US/Tw/PRC)*

⇨ *"When I lived in Taiwan I realized that we Americans are a very transparent people. What you see is what you get." (Alan K., US/Tw/Ger)*

⇨ *"My (Chinese) wife has told me on more than one occasion that I am too honest. At first I was a bit perplexed by her saying this because I always thought being honest was a good personality trait. In American culture we are taught to be honest. When I grew up my mother occasionally praised me by saying that I never lied. So naturally I thought that in all cases to lie is wrong. English uses the term 'white lie' which is a lie but it is for a good reason. If your girlfriend bought a new dress and you think it is ugly, rather than telling her the truth which would hurt her feelings it would be better to come up with a white lie to make her feel good. I think most Americans would not have a problem with this kind of a white lie. Both Taiwan and American cultures have their white lies though they seem to be applied differently depending on the topic and the relationship to the person. But when my wife says I am too honest she means that in certain situations it is better to lie or omit certain details so that the outcome of the situation will benefit oneself or achieve a desired outcome. In her opinion, offering too much information for the sake of honesty is a negative trait because it puts yourself at a disadvantage. Therefore it is better to only state part of the truth or even lie if that is to your advantage, or at least does not make things worse for yourself." (John G., US/Tw)*

⇨ *"As missionary I have had to find my way to a lot of addresses. But when I ask people for the way, instead of saying they don't know, they tell me to go this or that way. Half the time they did not have a clue, but just could not admit* it. I interpret it this way. For them it's important to appear smart, to not look stupid." (Jim M., US/Tw)

⇨ "Visitors to China realize that if you ask three different people for directions you average three different answers. They can't say that they don't know." (Jonathan L., US/Ger/PRC)

Though Americans and other Westerners living in Chinese society most often experience Chinese politeness, those who as members of Chinese families or other established groups gained insights into the Chinese familiar mode of speaking found the latter to clash with certain basic American norms of communicating.

⇨ "If you want something from someone who is not family, you don't ask directly but feel him out first. But when you are related you have rights and obligations. There is no need to be humble." (Nellie W., US/Tw/PRC)

⇨ "Within my husband's Taiwanese family there is a constant stream of unsolicited judgments shelled out. For example, my sister-in-law tells me that I have a terrible taste, that the dress I am wearing looks terrible, or that my haircut is bad, and on and on. I respect that tastes are different but I find her way of saying it offensive. In America we voice a lot more judgments about politics or social issues or about how to improve things in a given organization, but we are more tactful when we speak to people we know. Within my Chinese family here I feel smothered by all the criticism on a daily basis. And I know, so do many Chinese when they come back home after having lived in the US for a long time." (Linda Y., US/Tw).

⇨ "I have interacted with Chinese since 1983 and over the years have observed that in some aspects the Chinese are more honest than Americans and that they have a different kind of humor. The younger generation of Chinese tease each other more than Americans do and they do so in a different way. One such example that I experienced occurred when I attended a Chinese church for about three years. In one of our group meetings some people joked about a girl's overweight, making comments about her 'carrot legs.' Whether the teasing focuses on a personal flaw, such as being fat or singing out of key, the person with the flaw never seems to be offended by the teasing. The Chinese *do not consider this kind of talk to be a mean joke, but it struck me because in American culture I do not think Americans would so freely comment in a joking way about someone being overweight and the person subject to such teasing most likely would be offended." (John G., US/Tw)*

Besides such unfamiliar ways of teasing each other among the younger generation, Americans also noted that Chinese conversations generally revolved around different topics. Instead of people talking about what they do, food, family and gossip were the dominant subjects.

⇨ *"Here in Taiwan conversations revolve primarily around the topic of family, which of course includes talking about aunts, uncles, distant cousins and relatives by marriage. It's very different from what I am used to in America. When I go back home and visit with my former high school friends we hardly ever talk about our parents or our family life at home. We like to zero in on the person before us, not the family." (Chris M., US/Tw)*

⇨ *"At the many Chinese family gatherings I have attended over the years people talk predominantly about food. It's the number one topic of conversation. People talk about what they are eating, what they ate in the past and what they are going to eat or want to eat in the future. There is also quite a bit of gossip about mutual friends, about people not present at the gathering though they would never say anything negative in front of the person. For me this is more vicious than open criticism, because it gets the rumor mill flying and you can't defend yourself." (Douglas T., US/Tw)*

⇨ *"In my (Chinese) wife's extended family intellectual discussions are just not part of anyone's agenda. I know that if I started one I would put them ill at ease. Long conversations with an individual are felt as uncomfortable or boring, perhaps even suspect, especially if they are with a member of the opposite sex. For most people talk is about how much money somebody is making or has just wasted, and how much this or that costs. Or else it is gossip about somebody, maybe a relative or a politician." (Stephen T., US/Tw/PRC)*

The Chinese way of interacting with others in situations where no authority and no personal relationships or interests are at stake is particularly jarring to Americans whose one-size-fits-all way of communicating prescribes a friendly courtesy toward all. Under those circumstances none of the habitual Chinese politeness seems to apply.

⇨ *"During my first trip to China in the 1990's I looked for a certain cemetery, hoping to find a specific tombstone inscription that I had read about in my research. But the Chinese official in charge of foreigners told me that no such cemetery existed and so there could be no such inscription. Telling a pesky foreigner that what he is looking for does not exist was a simple way to minimize his involvement, work and trouble. On other occasions I have found Chinese may just say 'Ask somebody else,' when you ask for some information. It is another way of saying, 'Don't give me trouble.' And yes, I did eventually find that cemetery I had been looking for!" (Jonathan L., US/PRC/Ger)*

⇨ *"In my opinion the Chinese in China (PRC) have almost no concern whatsoever for people they don't know. Their first impulse seems to be to cheat and to squeeze as much personal profit out of a given encounter as possible, and it didn't appear to me that they devoted much time afterwards to reflect on their actions. Time and again I and other foreigners in China were gleefully and brazenly lied to, duped, misled, and ripped off. I found that even when I gave what I thought were unmistakable signals of impatience, unwillingness, or even a flat-out refusal, the Chinese either did not interpret my signals as I intended them to be interpreted or did not want to understand them. I can't remember meeting any Chinese in China who were as self-reflective and other-oriented as I know the Koreans or the Japanese to be." (Jason N., US/ PRC/Asia)*

Relationships

In line with the light and friendly communication style, American relationships tend to be casual relationships, easily entered into and free of lasting commitment, well-suited for a mobile society of self-reliant individuals who cherish independence and freedom of action. While those familiar with Chinese relationships of reciprocity and obligations were likely to see American noncommittal casualness in a positive light, others, especially those who had lived in Europe took a more critical view.

"We have a frontier mentality. We wave and wink, but don't stop." (Mark R., US/ Ger)

"In the old days, we had the saying, 'Move west young man.' It's still a bit like that. If you have a problem in your relationships you can run away from the problem. That's different in cultures where people tend to stay in one place." (Judy K. US/Europe/Asia)

"We want to be on our own, to be left alone. It's hard to get off that urge to be self-reliant. For us relationships are transitory. So we don't open up as much." (Bess E., US/PRC)

"When we answer a 'How are you?' with something like 'Fine' or 'Never better' it's partially self-protection, partially not burdening the other." (Peter W., ABC /Ger)

"I never talk about my personal issues with people, not even with my best friend. I don't want to take up people's time with that." (Sarah V., US/Asia)

"I will tell others only about the good things in my life. For example, when meeting with my old high school classmates, I tell them everything is fine. The other stuff I will eat up." (Kevin T., US/Tw)

"In our culture not only are products disposable. Our enormous mobility has contributed to making our relationships disposable too. We think it gives us freedom." (Dorothy W., US/Ger)

Though American casual and tangential relationships generally do not create closeness and lasting bonds, Americans excel at demonstrating interest and concern for others through spontaneous actions, such as offering assistance to an individual or a community with a specific temporary need. They readily come to the aid of a stranded motorist, an injured tourist or a disaster stricken community, and a heartbreaking story on TV of a worthy person in distress usually elicits somebody's immediate help. Under such circumstances American warmth, though temporary, is sincere and their generosity shines.

"When there is a crisis everybody comes and helps, but then you go back into your shell, back to being independent and feeling insecure." (Elizabeth M., US /PRC/Europe)

"When things are rough, we help each other, but when things are reasonably good we go back to our 'rugged individualism.'" (Jane M., US/Europe)

"We are supposed to have all those good qualities for communicating with others but then we also have this thing called privacy. At what point is your interest in the other intrusive to the other person? Some people at church take a mental attendance of who is there and who is not there. So if people do not show up they may check up on them to see whether they are sick and need help. I don't take that mental attendance and I am unaware of anyone who might need help. In my mind such awareness can be intrusive or it can be helpful." (Beatrice A., US/Asia)

Americans who lived in Germany talked a great deal about the difficulty of getting to know people there; about the lack of interest among Germans in meeting others. Though some Americans, often those of more recent European heritage, came to like the German way of relating, many did not. "In the end," one of my American conversation partners told me, "you'll love it or hate it in Germany."

⇨ *"I don't like the way Germans treat each other, nor the way they treat me. When I am trying to be social, they have an opportunity to meet an American, to find out about me. But they are not taking advantage of it. They are missing an ingredient of the educated person, a lack of curiosity about the other person. This is what I think goes on in the German head: 'When I meet a new person, I don't want to get to know you. I don't know whether I can fit you into my life.' So here I am, this American, jumping into your life, who doesn't do the usual things that form requires, who feels that there are no prerequisites to knowing you. I see myself as an open book and tell you anything you want to know about me. But you make me feel like an infection, something that is being rejected. This kind of thing takes place in the United States occasionally with a given individual, but here in Berlin there is a whole population of this type!" (Richard M., US/Ger)*

⇨ *"Once I joined a walking tour in Berlin. Since there were only six of us, all German except me, I found it strange that the tour guide did not have us introduce ourselves before starting out. Even more surprising to me was that during the two hours we spent together walking side by side nobody made a single personal remark or asked anyone any personal questions, which meant that after two hours we still didn't know as much as each other's names. I can't imagine this happening in the US. Another time, when I was invited by a German friend to have dinner at his house, we spent an entire evening sitting around the table talking about various topics. There were three other guests who had been introduced to me earlier. But even though I tried to participate in the conversations, none of the three ever directed a single comment or question at me during the entire evening. It seemed as if to them I was not even there. It felt very odd." (Erica L., US/Ger)*

⇨ *"I learned that in Germany showing interest in a person is perceived as an intrusion, or worse faking interest. On a recent visit back to the US I was in the supermarket looking for rice, when a lady came up to me and asked what I was looking for. She told me where to find it and also told me that I could get it much better and cheaper in an Asian store and how to get there. People were so nice. I miss those kinds of friendly encounters in Germany." (Cara B., US/Ger)*

⇨ *"In the streets in Germany the expression on the faces of the people says 'Don't come near me!' And yet, even though there is this distance, when you ask for something, people are very responsive to the request." (Dorothy W., US/Ger)*

Friendship

In line with the casual American way of relating to strangers and acquaintances, American friendships are likely to be light and inclusive. Friends are easily made and willingly shared. Often social success is measured in numbers of friends, as is evident from the common practice of high school yearbooks, which include lists of "the most popular," "the most successful," etc. Having a large number of Facebook friends and earning their "Likes" seem to have a similar meaning.

For Americans, friends tend to be playmates and companions for fun activities and entertainment when there is time. Some friendships revolve around common interests such as work, children, political activity, or charities, which often means that friends know each other only in certain aspects, not as whole persons. Most friendships are loose enough to allow others to join in. Those who do have a more personal relationship periodically get together "to catch up," filling in some gaps in what they know about each other.

"Friends are for doing things together. I have a lot of friends for different things. For example, one set of friends in church, another as a soccer mom. In the US we don't sit around and talk at length. Usually it's just filling in the gaps, but we don't really know each other." (Jenny S., US/Europe)

"I have one friend who is really very different from me and there are lots of topics we disagree on. But when we do things together it works well. We just dwell on what we have in common and ignore certain other aspects." (Jane M., US/ Europe)

"When I am out with my friends, whether it's for coffee or sightseeing, if people approach us, we start talking to them and sometimes invite them to come along. All of my friends are very social, very inclusive." (Angelina H., US/Europe)

"I am a member of a lot of groups. Except perhaps for the church group, the others are totally impersonal, loose organizations. I join because I like to do the things that they do." (Beatrice A., US/Asia)

"My best friend is Susie whom I see quite often, because we are both active in many clubs, but we never talk about personal things. I do not need to have a personal closeness." (Sarah V., US/Asia)

In America friends are expected to be your cheerleaders, be supportive and give approval, but not judge or criticize or make demands on your time. Friends extend help when convenient, but mutual help is not a major feature in American friendship, nor are friendships for airing your troubles. The idea is to be self-reliant, not to bother or impose on your friends. Support for more serious emotional needs may come through other sources, such as professionals and churches.

⇨ *"For us self-reliance means that we should not put a burden on others, but as I now see it affects the quality of our relationships. Here in the US, if you ask for help it means you can't do it alone, and so people don't ask. Living abroad made me change. I found that over there I could not do everything myself, and that I would need to call on my friends, for example, to help me clean out the current place and help me move my things. Under those circumstances they would all come and we'd have a great time getting the job done really fast. One of my friends there liked to give dinner parties and often she would ask some of us to come early to help prepare the food. So when I got back to California, I sent an email to my friends inviting them to dinner, maybe at six o'clock, adding that it would be great if some of them could come earlier to help me prepare things. People reacted, 'Oh, you are inviting us and want us to work?' Of course, it was said as a joke and they did come but it's not the natural way to do things." (Angelina H., US/Eur)*

"My closest friend is a woman whom I came to know when my children were young. We were very close. Now we live in different parts of the country and we don't communicate much, but I know if everything fails, she would be there for me. If I asked her to come she would say yes and would be here tomorrow. But—I would never ask her. It would mean owing her." (Jane M., US/Europe)

Given the American preference for lightness and inclusivity, Americans reacted strongly to the German way of making friends, or rather to the German reluctance to make new friends. Instead of being inclusive and welcoming, Germans appeared to be extraordinarily exclusive, abiding by some unknown codes.

⇨ *"Americans and Germans have different criteria and a different time frame for when they start calling an acquaintance a friend. For Germans 'friend' implies a commitment, whereas 'acquaintance' does not. During my first year I did not get invited at all, and when I got to a point of wanting to do something together—after knowing them from my English class—it was too soon for them." (Cara B., US/Ger)*

⇨ *"While studying in Europe I did make one good friend among my class mates, but the others were not very friendly. They were nice enough in class but if after class I bumped into them at a café, they would say hello, but would never ask me to sit with them. They didn't seem to seek more friendship." (Angelina H., US/Eur)*

⇨ *"When meeting German speakers who I will see frequently, I like to find out how fast we can transition from the formal 'you' (Sie) to the informal 'you' (Du). I will be polite and not force it, which means that more often than not I do not succeed." (Paula B., US/Ger)*

⇨ *"What I find disturbing about German friendship is that they have silly rules about it; like you can't be friends within a month, and you can't talk about certain things. I had a German friend who practiced law in Texas. We used to have dinner together quite often, but once when I started chatting about his law practice he said talking about business over dinner was vulgar. For Americans there is no such taboo, even if you did so at your mother's funeral. Gee, give me a list of things we can talk about. Here in Germany I don't know the rules, so if I break them I don't know that I am breaking them."* (Richard M., US/Ger)

⇨ *"When living in Germany, I found it hard to read the unwritten rules of friendship. I would not know that I had done something wrong, like not visited often enough. For example, once I stayed with an American friend which meant they did not see me for a week. Afterwards they treated me as if I had done something wrong. I feel I don't have to announce my presence or absence in advance and I was nerved by their inability to understand Americans."* (Mark R., US/Ger)

Despite the difficulty and slowness of developing friendships in Germany, most of my American conversation partners liked the closeness and commitment they experienced once they did make friends. More than in America, German friends seemed to open up to each other and nurture their relationships over long periods of time. The extensive comments of these Americans provide a good description of what the dominant form of American friendship is not.

⇨ *"We Americans are open, which is nice. But basically we are saying, if we can get together that will be fine, but it is not a priority for me. I am busy. Germans are thoughtful, deep people, which comes out through long conversations. I have had a lot of German friends in my life and found that they wanted their relationships to be deeper."* (Alan K., US/Tw/Ger)

⇨ *"Friendship in Germany implies commitment. Being acquainted with somebody does not. This difference in my mind explains why Germans don't make friends the American way. Since friendship means to commit your time, energy, and attention, valuable resources that you don't want to waste on somebody you don't really know or care for, friendship for Germans starts at a later point in time than for Americans."* (Jenna H., US/Ger)

⇨ "In the US I often go shopping with friends and we talk about things we bought or want to buy. Here my German girl friends don't like to hang out at the shopping mall. They seem less materialistic, buying things only when they need something, not impulsively. They also are not into girly things, like doing their nails together. My German friends don't look to others to be entertained. Instead they rather sit in a café and talk. Here in Germany I have both American and German friends, but I am probably a better fit for German friendship." (Cara B., US/Ger)

⇨ "Germans have time for each other and they have time for long conversations. You see it in the many coffee shops, side walk cafes or beer gardens. Often these places offer a beautiful ambience which is conducive to people spending hours enjoying each other's company. In America, we have Starbucks instead, where most people just run in to get their cup or they sit there alone with their computers." (Harry M., US/Ger)

⇨ "In Germany, when people do something for another, they do it out of the fullness of their hearts. There is a cordiality when they shake hands with a friend, and when they send someone off by train by waving goodbye with a handkerchief. In America we smile, but it is not a heartfelt connection. In America we try not to get in someone's way, because we don't want to take up someone's time." (Mark R., US/Ger)

⇨ "I found that people in Europe tend to have lifelong friends. It may be their neighbors or coworkers, or others who have lived in the same place for a long time. In America we have much more mobility which means that our friendships depend on where we happen to live at any given time." (Jenny S., US/Europe)

⇨ "I like it that German friends take the time to visit each other. I see my German friends here much more than I used to see my friends in the US. In fact, there we might not see each other for months. We were too busy with our careers, with boyfriends and what not. Friendship ranks below work and family. I like the fact that in Germany true friends are true friends. It just takes such a darn long time to make friends, and they are high maintenance. There are a lot of expectations: help you move; buy presents for a birthday; go and talk. In the US, there is much more distance between friends. We don't know that much

about each other's lives. Time is money and I can only donate so much free time. Some of my friends in America have trouble asking me for help when they feel depressed. It's like 'Call only when you are in a happy state of mind.'"
(Jenna H., US/Ger)

Sooner or later most Americans living in Germany become aware of the German stereotype of American superficiality, which refers to both the American light style of communicating as well as their preference for quick and casual rather than deeper and lasting relationships. Some of my respondents deemed this characterization unfair, while others were self-critical, lamenting the lack of depth in American relationships.

⇒ *"In Germany Americans are known to be superficially friendly. But that mode is just our way of courtesy. To label it is superficial is unfair." (Jim S., US/Ger)*

⇒ *"As an American, I am expected to answer the question of 'How are you?' with a casual 'Fine' or 'Great' or, if I want to be particularly positive that day, maybe even with 'Terrific!' After living in Germany for a while I noticed that people do not do that here. I found out that to their ears it's superficial and sounds phony, because it is not how you really feel. Germans want an honest answer." (Peter W., ABC/Ger)*

⇒ *"The German stereotype of Americans is that we are superficial. I tell them that they are right. When I walk into a store and people greet me with a friendly 'Can I help you?' smiling at me, maybe thanking me for coming—even if all that is fake, what's the harm? What is the downside to that? If I had a great day and feel great, I am happy. If somebody then looks at me like a grouch, with a face that seems to ask me, 'What do you want from me?' their negative feedback ruins the day for me." (Richard M., US/Ger)*

⇒ *"Germans think Americans are superficial. But as an American I might say, 'Maybe being superficial is not so bad. Maybe I don't want to be that hedgehog, always be deep down there.'" (Edward M., US/Ger)*

"We don't know how to relate to others on a deeper level. When we talk with our friends, we mostly talk about what we do, about our sailing, surfing, our jobs." (Jonathan L., US/Ger/PRC)

> *"When I recently mentioned to a friend that I wished I had more friends, she said, 'But we are friends!' 'Yes,' I said, 'but we never see each other.' That is so because she is always busy." (Beatrice A., US/Asia)*

Compared to what they were used to at home, some of my American respondents who lived in Taiwan or China found Chinese friends to be closer and more willing to help each other. Others, however, were wary of what they saw as a Chinese tendency to manipulate and take advantage of friendly relationships.

⇨ *"I have now lived in Taiwan for over twenty years. I think Chinese friends are closer to each other and they share a lot more about each other's families than we ever did when I was young. My Taiwanese friends are also more thoughtful, and more readily ask favors of each other." (Kevin T., US/Tw)*

⇨ *"I like my friends in Asia. I like it that friends there are really friends, people who value having a good time together. In the US my really good friends were people I went to high school or to college with. Not only are they all scattered, they are also always too busy to pay much attention to friends." (Larry R., US/Ger/Asia)*

⇨ *"When we lived in China I found that it was easy to become too friendly with some people, who then will ask for favors for the rest of their lives. For us it was easier to not become so dependent on them since we were there as a family, but other foreigners who were single had a harder time and were more vulnerable." (Bess E., US/PRC)*

⇨ *"I hate to play detective and figure out the motivation of my Chinese friends. In America we focus on the person; the Chinese estimate your status, your money, how useful you might be to them which makes friendship a means to an end. I feel closer to my American friends. In Chinese society I never know who my real friend is." (Jonathan L., US/Ger/PRC)*

⇨ *"When I am with my Taiwanese friends there is a lot of flattery, not just towards me but also amongst the Chinese themselves. Much of it is about establishing or consolidating a relationship." (Julie L., US/Tw)*

Family relationships

Despite an enormous variety in family cohesion and individual parental styles, the traditional ideal in mainstream America envisions close emotional bonds between marriage partners as well as between parents and their children, along with room and encouragement for independence and freedom. Unlike Chinese families, which provide their members with a life-long security mantle in return for mutual obligations, the American goal is to provide a nurturing and loving environment for the children to grow and mature into independent selves, able to make it in the world on their own. However, reality often differs as is evident from the views of my American conversation partners.

> *"I grew up not really knowing closely any of my cousins and only very infrequently had occasion to meet any of my aunts and uncles. The family was spread all over the U.S. Beyond my brother and my parents, family was not something that I ever thought of as a support system. We were kept informed of what everyone was doing largely through annual Christmas cards and lengthy letters from one aunt who was the self-appointed scribe for the family." (Harry M., US/Asia)*

> *"We will only be there for family at the end of life. For the last six months of life it is often a family member who will take care of you." (Jane M., US/Europe)*

> *"For some of us the church is the center of our lives. In such case the church fulfills a function similar to the family. It's okay to not like one's family because you don't choose your family, but as church members people can have that same sense of belonging. For my brother it definitely has been the church. It not only provides him with moral guidance for right and wrong, but it is also there for him for more practical needs. People find their realtor, their contractor and other specialists they need in life there. Wherever you turn there is always somebody there." (Jenny S., US/Eur)*

> *"I see a breakdown of family communication, a poverty of spirit in my generation. Our father-son relationship is particularly poor when compared to other cultures, such as Chinese or Arab cultures. Our boys and young men are father hungry. Due to the lack of it, they don't know which direction to turn*

when facing opportunities and challenges. As a result we are like adult children, parading around." (Dorothy W., US/Ger)

"Perhaps for us it's either independence or emotional closeness, one way or the other. Either the parent-child bond is so close that as a child you don't want to leave or else you are not close and can't wait to get away and conquer the world. If it were an either or, I know which side I am on for my own children. I'd rather have them go out and see the world." (Helen V., US/Asia)

Overall Americans living in Chinese societies had little taste for the prescribed roles applying to members of Chinese families or for the tight Chinese family bonds based on blood relationships and mutual dependency. Given the value of independence and personal emotional bonds between spouses and between parents and young children, what they encountered in Chinese society was different and difficult to accept. What might feel like security and acceptance to the Chinese, looked to Americans like a lack of personal bonds or in some cases like immaturity.

⇨ "The Chinese relationships are roles, not personal bonds. We like our relationships to be personal, to include emotional closeness." (Diana L., US/Asia)

⇨ "My (Chinese) wife is often irritated with my brother because of the way we relate to each other. 'He is your younger brother,' she tells me. 'He should not talk to you this way!' For the Chinese a relationship is all about playing the proper role. Confucian rules and regulations determine how you should behave in the hierarchy of relationships. It's a straightjacket." (Doug T., US/Tw)

⇨ "I like many of the Chinese values. I just don't like the reality! 'Family harmony' turns out to be mostly conflictual, and 'mutual concern' turns into heavy duty control." (Nellie W., US/Tw/PRC)

⇨ "Within the Asian family, an individual plays different roles and has different statuses at the same time. Having to play all these roles correctly creates a lot of stress." (June M., US/Asia)

⇨ "My Chinese friends have commented to me that the parent-adult child relationship in America seems closer than in the Chinese social structure. In America an adult child may talk to a parent about something for hours and do so in *a manner similar to how you talk to a friend. From what I have observed Chinese parent-child relationships are more distant, preserving respect." (John G., US/Tw)*

⇨ *"We expect marriage to be a close and twosome relationship, free from interference by parents and other relatives. That seems rarely to be the case in Chinese marriages. There is a lot of give and take between parents and adult children, but in my view much of it is parental interference." (Kevin T., US/Tw)*

⇨ *"My spouse or significant other is a lot more important to me than a relative. In China I miss closer emotional bonds between spouses and between parents and children." (Nathan M., US/PRC)*

⇨ *"When we went back to live in Taiwan, my (Chinese) husband reverted to being a mama's boy, becoming very selfish. I started to feel like an adjunct and eventually got divorced." (Linda Y., US/Tw)*

⇨ *"For Asian parents making money and passing it on to the children is what they live for. When they talk about sacrifice, which they do often, it's usually about giving or leaving money to their children. As soon as the child, especially the son, gets married, he receives a sum of money to buy a house or an apartment. As an American I am not earning my money to give my children an inheritance. My (Chinese) mother-in-law is appalled and tells my wife, 'What, you don't want to buy a house for each of your boys? I didn't realize how Americanized you have become!' We paid a lot to put our two kids through an expensive private high school and we helped with college. Now they want to be independent. As for us, we are getting ready to retire, and the money is ours now." (Harry M., US/Asia)*

⇨ *"For the Chinese being independent from the family means not being filial. It is not good. Also, traveling alone is seen as courageous, not because there might be some dangers out there, but because you are doing something by yourself. There is nothing in their upbringing to prepare them for independence. Leaving the family is usually done in the name of family duty. Getting an education or seeking a better job, both with the aim to make money to support the larger family." (Andrew M., US/Asia)*

⇨ *"Here in Taipei (Taiwan) I room with a fifty-eight year old woman who lives with her mom. She still sleeps in the same bed with her mom, feels like a care-free teenager and acts like a sixteen-year old. Chinese parents only teach their children to study and to make money. I know quite a few Chinese adult children who live at home and have no independent thoughts or desires of their own. I see it as emotional infantilism, though it also seems to make them emotionally very stable." (Ellen H., US/Tw)*

The insights of Mary V., an American woman who grew up on the Pacific island of Palau and then married into a Palauan family, provide a friendly, and at the same time critical, perspective of what American family relationships are not. By the time I met Mary, she was divorced and living in the United States. Even though her story depicts family closeness in Palau, her experience and her reactions are similar to what an American might experience as a member of a Chinese family. This is how Mary described Palauan family relationships to me:

"In the American family world I know, we have a lot of isolation. The Palauan family offers you a sure and stable foundation of watertight personal insurance. It's a group in which you feel totally secure and taken care of. There is always someone who is checking up on you, who will stop your unhealthy behavior and make you feel useful by giving you a role. A lot of times even the lazy ones, or those without talents, will be drawn into the fold. Someone will insist on involving you, saying something like, 'Come on we need your help.' Even if you are only part Palauan, or someone like me, an American married into their family, they just envelop you.

When you are married to a Palauan, you are owned by the extended family. It feels good, but you give up liberties and personal expression. My husband's family expected me to cook certain things for them; for example, regularly bake bread. My in-laws also would take my son for days at a time, which I had to accept. We were not at odds with each other, but I learned to be quiet, to be subservient. People who grow up in that kind of family environment welcome the stability, but to me it felt like a straightjacket. Once my husband's family asked me to bake five hundred doughnuts for a funeral. Ordinarily my own family would have been my work force but since my parents had already left the islands by that time, I went to the Peace Corps to find people to help me. When the family asked me to bake those doughnuts for them, I saw it as an intrusion into my life. I was busy doing my own work of illustrating books and I didn't want somebody else telling me how to use my next three days. Still, I found it easier to comply than not to. Fitting in brings many advantages. People come to your house, bring you food and presents, help you, and are nice to your baby. Not fitting in would have meant becoming a non-entity in their eyes. No love, no attention, nothing. Tied into the social web, you lack personal freedom, but all the aunts and uncles will take care of you when you need it. In America we have one set of parents. In Palau you have many aunts and uncles who act like your real mothers and fathers. And when you tell them that you are off to college, they all give you money and remind you to come back and help them."

The feel of life

Vitality

The combination of faith in self-reliance, freedom and optimism generates a vitality that is expressed with energy, exuberance and passion, along with risk-taking. "Fail fast, fail often" is a Silicon Valley mantra. This sense of vitality is reinforced on many occasions. Motivational speeches by those who have scored successes are a staple of business seminars and graduation ceremonies. The message is, "We've made it, so can you! It's within yourself. Go at it with ambition, optimism and audacity." Chinese and Germans alike tend to admire this sense of vitality in America.

"Our fearlessness is the best part of our culture. I once had two jobs in the US, not enough money for decent food, and lived in public housing. BUT, did that discourage me? No, not at all. I worked very hard to better myself. Was I worried about the future? No, I didn't have time for that because at the time I lived in the present and everything else was secondary." (Jenna H., US/Ger)

"For me life is what I do: experiences, not purpose. Every action counts as an experience, whether it's going out to a restaurant or buying something. It leads

59

to a rush, which keeps me going, always in need of another experience." (Tim
C., US/Europe)

"I want to take calculated risks; to dream and build, to fail and succeed. We work
toward something, and if one initiative does not pan out, we find something
else." (Andrew M., US/Asia)

"The belief that you can do anything if you just put your mind to it is a basic American value. Immigrants had been oppressed and came with nothing, but this
is a land of opportunity where anybody can be rich and move upward. Just
look toward the future, set a goal and apply yourself. It's idealistic, it's a dream,
but it's an idealism geared toward implementation. Like special Olympics, it
means working towards your goal and feeling accomplished with what you
achieve given the confines you work under." (Jenny S., US/Europe)

"I think Americans see infinite possibilities, long highways. It's a dreaming idea
thing which does the initiating, but lends itself less to bringing things to
fruition, to completion. The energy lies in the initial step of ideas, the brainstorming, which does not allow us to look at negatives. We tend to cultivate
a child-like energy for possibilities, meaning we enjoy being full of ideas. It's
a sort of freedom, a spontaneity, in the sense of, 'I love this today, so let's go
with it.' As a culture we are not much into steadiness. It's vitalizing, but it
wears you out." (Dorothy W., US/Ger)

Americans did not encounter their sense of vitality in Germany. "German
dreams are modest. To live in peace, build a house and have a garden with
a tree," wrote Frederick Kempe in his book *Father/Land: A Personal Search for
the New Germany*. "You don't ask Germans what their dreams are. Those who
had great dreams emigrated." [9]

⇨ "During my years of working in Europe, some of them in the United Kingdom,
some in Germany, I felt very American. The difference was my ambition to be
what I wanted to be. Over there people are much more reined in by the class
they are in and they don't think of breaking out of the circumstances in which
they find themselves. Here in the US, we also have class differences and maybe
they are no different from those in Europe. But individually we are taught that
we can break out and be anything we want to be. So we have this desire to

move up the ladder which goes into our ambition and gives us energy." (Elly D., US/Europe)

⇨ *"I have a do-it-yourself attitude, which means I spend a lot of time doing advertising and marketing my massage services, while my German counterparts spend much of their time applying for small government grants or subsidies. So much time wasted in order to get that little bit of money, but it seems they just can't let go of these small grants. It's their safety net. I don't have that fear, so I take more risks. That is my culture and comes from my upbringing. That is American for me." (Jenna H., US/Ger)*

Nor do Americans find their kind of vitality in Chinese society. Chinese work long hours, but rarely with the kind of passion and enthusiasm that characterizes American life. While in Taiwan I once asked a second year graduate student in biology at Taiwan University, how she liked her studies. "It's okay, I don't hate it (*hai hao bu taoyan*)," she said. The answer troubled me. For someone starting to prepare herself for a lifelong career I had expected a more positive answer. "We are all like that," my Chinese respondents later assured me, one after another, when I asked them about the student's response. "We don't like studying and we are not enthusiastic about work. Usually our parents decide what we study and besides, it's clear to us that work is about making money, not about liking what you do."

⇨ *"There is no question that many Chinese work very hard, often harder than Westerners would be willing to do. But they rarely work with enthusiasm and interest. In fact, I noted that to them the show of enthusiasm tends to be a trigger for suspicion and caution. If someone's eyes sparkle with interest, they assume that the person must have a hidden agenda or be expecting to gain some personal benefit from the matter." (Erica L., US/Ger/Tw)*

⇨ *"I think our self-reliance gives us the energy to take more risks, though at the same time we know that when we take the risk we don't have a social safety net, if we fail. The Chinese have family support in the case of failure. They won't be starving or go begging. On the other hand, to take a risk and fail also has a bigger cost for them because it affects more people." (Jim M., US/Tw)*

In pursuit of happiness

All explorers are seeking something they have lost. It is seldom that they find it, and more seldom still that the attainment brings them greater happiness than the quest.

—Arthur C. Clarke (British explorer and writer).

American vitality is mainly driven by the pursuit of happiness, which is written into the American constitution as a basic right for all. Indeed, Americans talk a great deal about wanting to be happy, often assuming that being happy is, or should be, the normal state of affairs. If happiness is lacking, something needs to be done or "pursued" to revert to this natural state. "We don't laugh because we are happy," William James wrote, "We are happy because we laugh." [10] "When life gives you lemons, make lemonade" is a saying used to encourage optimism and a can-do attitude. If you feel down, respond with action because doing something will make you feel better. This motto has been an integral part of the American spirit. More than Chinese or Germans, Americans respond to personal tragedy or difficulties with action. If made blind, help other blind people. If your child has gone missing, set up a foundation for missing children. Those may be exceptional cases, but some sort of action to overcome negative feelings is common. If the activity provides meaning or purpose, chances are that it will generate a deeper and more lasting sense of satisfaction and contentment.

"When I was still living in California, I overbooked myself. At the time I wanted to get over a bad relationship and doing stuff helped me forget. Rushing around served as a kind of therapy and avoided thinking." (Angelina H., US/Europe)

"The only thing that you regret are things that you did not do." (Rob L., US/Europe)

"For me happiness is being successful in what I do. Success makes me happy and content. But it's not enough to say I love the work I do. In order to recognize and celebrate it I have to quantify it. For me, a massage therapist, it might read, 'Yesterday I worked a party of four women, and I was paid fairly for my work.' Every New Year I make a list of things that have brought me pleasure. In order to enjoy my accomplishments and be happy and grateful I have to write them down." (Jenna H., US/Ger)

Since Americans define themselves increasingly by what they have, making money and accumulating wealth is no longer merely a symbol of success. It has become an important goal in the pursuit of happiness.

> *"There is nothing like being gainfully employed to lift the human spirit." (Rob L., US/Europe)*

> *"For most of us Americans happiness is not deep. Usually it's money. For me money gives me a sense of psychological freedom." (Larry S., US/Asia)*

In spite of the important role that the pursuit of happiness plays in American life, the goal of feeling happy remains largely elusive. Easy smiles, light hearted cheer, and optimism in American daily interactions often do not reflect a true feeling of happiness. The assumption that the people around us are self-confident, joyous, and successful begs the question: why is it that everybody around me is happy, but I am not?

> *"One of my friends, a very nice sweet woman whom I like a lot, writes the most obnoxious, bragging Christmas letters! I'm sure she doesn't mean them to sound the way they do, but her letters basically recount the fun and fabulous life she and her family lead, full of joy and satisfaction with nary a problem! They make me want to jump off a cliff because my life is not like that at all!" (Pamela Y., US/Europe)*

> *"Life just isn't what we Americans make it out to be. We look at the world through 'rose-colored glasses,' focusing on what we like and ignoring what we don't like." (Richard Y., US/Eur)*

> *"I grew up being told to pursue my goals and live my life with passion, but now a decade or two later I have come to realize that I was actually a peg in somebody else's goal. It leaves me with the feeling that 'I have been had.'" (Jane P., US/Asia)*

Not only does the pursuit of happiness fail to generate happiness, the American action-driven life frequently leads to exhaustion and restlessness. Donald Campbell, past president of the American Psychological Association, called the direct pursuit of happiness a recipe for an unhappy life. In an interview with Bill Moyers, Willard Gaylin, clinical professor of psychiatry at Columbia College of Physicians and Surgeons, said that, "American society is a classless society in which everyone is restlessly struggling to change his social status. The success drive is killing us because no matter where you are on the rung of success, there is always a rung above you. So you are a failure no matter where you stand." [11]

> *"We have high expectations, with a hierarchy of wants and needs. Since new ones always come up, it's a restless pursuit, with little time for true enjoyment. We also confuse achievement or recognition with happiness. If I have reached my goal, what do I do next? It ends in restlessness or depression." (Jim M., US/ Tw)*

Antidepressants are the most widely prescribed medicines in America. "The two most common reasons why students come to see me," a psychological counselor on a California university campus told me, "are anxiety and depression."

Even though the pursuit of happiness generates a vitality rarely seen elsewhere, a subset of Americans prefers a slower lifestyle and quiet satisfaction. Several of my interviewees encountered it overseas.

> *"When I taught high school we teachers sometimes talked about our students as being like motor boats or sailboats. But the analogy applies to older adults as well. Some people live their lives like a motorboat, pursuing a goal by heading in a specified direction. Others are more like sailboats. They want to enjoy the sail, live a calmer way of life, aiming for quiet contentment rather than speeding toward a destination. But in America motorboats outnumber the sailboats. More people aim for action, fun, and emotional highs, modeled by the American entertainment industry, than for quiet reflection and simple contentment." (Jane M., US/Eur)*

> ⇨ *"I like the way the Chinese and other Asians live, one day at a time. They are less organized than we are, less time conscious. They don't prioritize things, making lists of things to do the way we do. The Chinese might be more productive if they followed a better time management, but many are content and take pleasure in eating well." (Ellen H. US/Tw)*

> ⇨ *"I admire the Chinese simple folks for their attitude to living life. Even when they have little, they often radiate a sense of contentedness." (Julie L., US/Tw)*

⇒ *"When I spent the summer in Asia, I realized that the people there had so much less. Yet they seemed perfectly happy and content! We don't accept life. We want to be in control." (Andrew M., Asia)*

⇒ *"Often we Americans think that Germans are less content because they look serious and do not smile, or we assume that they can only be happy with beer. But we confuse happiness with gaiety. For gaiety Germans resort to alcohol and special occasions, like carnival. But their happiness has a depth which gaiety does not have." (Rob L., US/Europe)*

⇒ *"Life in Germany is slower, with less energy exerted, and less frenzied doing. Instead people enjoy and appreciate occasions of Gemuetlichkeit, for which we don't even have a word. The German word refers to a feeling of well-being that comes from being in a comfortable and pleasant place and not feeling rushed." (Rick F., US/Ger/Asia)*

Insecurities and fears

In spite of their display of confidence, Americans are not free of insecurities.

"We are confident about making decisions, but we have many social insecurities. We are always trying to project an image, needing to present ourselves in a certain way. The Chinese know who they are." (Rose C. ABC/Hong Kong)

"There is a lot of underlying insecurity among Americans." (Lance F., US/PRC)

"In my view, when people go overboard on telling you all their achievement it's really a sign of feeling inadequate." (Mark R. US/Ger)

"As a child I only felt good about myself when I got praised, so I became an over-achiever. I kept doing something to get praise and at the same time doubted my abilities to achieve my goals. I was so afraid what other people thought of me that I always tried to do nice things, so that they would like me." (Pamela Y., US)

"In America we have more choices than we can handle and often we are not sure the choices we are making are the right ones. We are on our own and only have ourselves to blame. For example, we thirty-some year olds are very

cautious about getting married and settling down. My generation of young women has so many options that it is very hard to make a decision. We may agonize or question whether we made the right choice or avoid a commitment altogether because there may always be something better around the corner. It's stressful." (Karen H., US/Eur)

"American society strikes me as a very fearful society. It's especially evident from the way people overprotect their children. In Germany parents raise their children differently." (Mary L., US/Ger)

Isolation and loneliness

People who need people are the luckiest people in the world. . . .

(Song from the 1964 Broadway musical *Funny Girl*)

The American values of self-reliance, freedom, and mobility along with a preference for tangential relationships foster the vitality of American life. However, they also contribute to a sense of isolation and loneliness due to a lack of human connectedness, both in the Chinese sense of unquestionable mutual support as well as in the German sense of opening up the inner self to others.

"In America you tell others about all the great things you did but then you go back to feeling insecure and lonely, with only superficial relationships." (Phil B. US/Ger/PRC)

"There is no camaraderie among my neighbors. I wish we could have a cup of tea together now and then, but people are cool. It's not fear that keeps us away. It's just that people are busy. They are friendly when you see them, but the doors are always kept closed." (Beatrice A., US/Asia)

Both Germans and Chinese talked about being baffled when Americans shared personal, even intimate information with them during casual encounters, such as when sitting next to each other as strangers on the plane. To them this kind of sharing personal information is inappropriate and belongs to well-established close relationships. To Americans this kind of circumstance presents a safe environment to release troubling and negative thoughts, sharing them with people they will likely never see again. It offers a temporary connectedness with others. Nowadays social media provide many additional avenues through which to create the illusion of closeness and connectedness, even while retaining anonymity.

In his book *Healing and the Mind*, Bill Moyers discussed the issue of people feeling emptiness and loneliness with Dean Ornish. "What is different now," Ornish said, "is that cultural isolation is pervasive in our culture. We used to have extended families, and at the church or synagogue or workplace or in the neighborhood we felt a sense of safety and community. We often don't have that now. There aren't many places where people can feel safe enough to just be who they are without having to create a mask or a façade, and to experience the intimacy and the community that we are all looking for." [12] At the Commonweal Retreat Center for cancer patients in California, Moyers recalled witnessing new arrivals who first reluctantly, then joyously, made connections with each other with an intimacy occurring quite rapidly between these strangers. "Brought together by disease and then forming communities around illness, people were finding each other through pain." [13] One of the Commonweal patients expressed her feelings in a poem [14].

Mother knows best:

Don't talk about your troubles.
No one loves a sad face.
Oh, Mom, the truth is
Cheer isolates,
Humor defends,
Competence intimidates,
Control separates,
And sadness,
Sadness opens up each to the other.

* * *

Notes

[1] W. Somerset Maugham, *The Razor's Edge* (New York: Doubleday, 1944), 306.

[2] Bill Moyers, *A World of Ideas II* (New York: Doubleday, 1990), 85.

[3] www.mindbodygreen.com/0-7949/7-ways-to-become-a-more-optimistic-person.html

[4] www.quotetab.com/quotes/by-matt-cohen\#TBbPUsoev88UmTaH.97

[5] Leroy S. Rouner, "Resolved: That Phi Beta Kappa is gloriously useless," *Key Reporter*, (October 2000) www.uncg.edu/faculty.groups/pbk/gloriously_useless_rouner.html

[6] Price Collier. *Germany and the Germans from an American Point of View* (Charles Scribners' Sons, 1914), 167.

[7] harvardmagazine.com/2005/07/an-american-in-paris-html

[8] Andrew Clark, "Lunch with the FT: Sir Simon Rattle," *Financial Times* (September 6, 2008).
www.ft.com/cms/s/0/fb4b5fe8-5c52-11de-aea3-00144feabdc0.html

[9] Frederick Kempe, *Father/Land: A Personal Search for the New Germany* (Indiana University Press, 2002), 164.

[10] www.goodreads.com/quotes/10656-we-don-t-laugh-because-we-re-happy-we-re-happy-because-we

[11] Moyers, *A World of Ideas II*, 122.

[12] Bill Moyers, *Healing and the Mind* (New York: Doubleday, 1993),106.

[13] Ibid., 101.

[14] Ibid., 319.

II. The German Inner Self

An identity

I am what I think and feel

THE German self is primarily an inner self whose identity is strongly tied to thoughts and emotions. It is an I-am-what-I think-and-feel self more than an I-am-what-I-do self. Though formed by innate characteristics and the social environment, the process of becoming an independent and authentic self includes the freedom to adapt or reject what is given from the outside. This understanding of the independent self is part of the legacy of Europe's Enlightenment, an intellectual movement of the late seventeenth and eighteenth centuries that emphasized reason and individualism.

"In my mind I come into this world as an 'I,' as an individual who will shape her own life. If I didn't have a chance to live my life authentically, as that 'I' that I came into the world with, it would be terrible. I certainly don't want to and don't need to run with the crowd." (Christina G., Ger/US)

"What matters most to me is the person I am within. Even though everything influences us, I'd like to be like a rock, not being blown about by life's events. I aim for a kind of steady core, an inner stability. We change with new insights, gradually over time but we should not be blowing with the wind or be opportunistic. That steady inner self is my dignity." (Erhard A., Ger/Asia)

"For us it is important that we are authentic. You can't hide things before yourself, or, if you are Christian, before God. God sees everything." (Steven B., Ger/Tw)

Maturity means that an individual has formed a steady core based on stable values that provide guidance and give direction over time and place. It includes the expectation that the individual feels free to express himself and stand up against social pressure. Though gradual change is natural and desirable, an authentic self should be steady, not one that negates thoughts and values in order to seek a personal advantage or please others. It means having integrity. This kind of understanding of the mature self differs from what my German conversation partners observed among the Chinese.

⇒ *"For us, the concepts of good and bad are like an anchor holding a ship on its course. For the Chinese good and bad is a moving target." (Karl M., Ger/Tw)*

⇒ *"I have not seen self-reflection among the Chinese. My children are half Chinese, but if they looked within, probably all they'd see would be what they did wrong." (Ursula L., Ger/Tw)*

⇒ *"To me having integrity means personal honesty and consistency. It means that your act matches your words. It means admiring someone for standing up for his beliefs. At the other end of the scale is opportunism, something I see a lot in Chinese society." (Juergen S., Ger/US/Tw)*

⇒ *"In the Chinese Confucian society individuals play roles—but with playing roles, where am I?" (Karl M., Ger/Tw)*

⇒ *"In the West we ask a lot from the individual. Often we are more or less on our own. We don't have many generally binding rituals, and some of us come from broken homes. Therefore it is important to have a good relationship to the self, in order to cope in life. Perhaps it's because the Chinese are much more bound into their families that they don't need to care as much about the self. In fact, one Chinese friend of mine once told me that the whole idea of having a relationship to one's self was a very strange thing to him." (Anne B., Ger/PRC)*

Thinking and feeling

The inner self is expected to develop gradually through a liberal education, one that strengthens intellectual reasoning by providing a broad knowledge base and enhances emotional maturing through the arts (*Kultur*), such as literature, music, art and craftsmanship. To that end the German government offers free education, subsidizes theatres and orchestras, and maintains an enormous number of museums and historical buildings. To many Germans foreign language skills, travel, and study or living abroad are also important for the intellectual and emotional development of the inner self.

Thinking

The high value attached to the ability to think clearly and broadly is reflected in the recognition of intellectual achievement. Over time, various non-German writers have commented on the difference between Germany and other countries in this respect. For example, Julian Marias, a well-known Spanish philosopher writing about the United States in the 1950s and 60s, wrote that while there were outstanding academics in America, they were known only within their own limited circles. American society at large did not know about them or pay attention to them. [1] Peter F. (Ger/US), a professor amongst my conversation partners, agreed, "In Germany, education and knowledge are more valued than in the US," he said. "One way it shows is in the status of university professors. Compared to Germany, where professors are highly respected, the status of professors in the United States is lower."

Not only does good reasoning ability rank higher on the scale of desirable attributes in Germany than in American society at large, but the German prevalent thinking pattern is also different. German thinking tends to be holistic, aiming at understanding the larger picture and wider implications, regardless of whether this knowledge is necessary for practical application. The American author Hampden-Turner, in his *Seven Cultures*, described the German thinking pattern in this way: "For Germans, the whole is prior to the part. . . . Identifying patterns and regularities gives broader meaning to the individual parts: A necklace is more than its pearls, the train is more than a series of compartments and the forest is more than the sum of its trees." [2]

A German film director once described the difference between German and American movie making saying that American movies sought out the different and unique, whereas German movies sought out commonalities. Germans like to find broader meaning, which is reflected in a widespread interest in philosophy, a subject that includes the search for unifying ideas behind life.

A holistic perception also goes into the many practical professional training programs Germany offers to young people who do not intend to pursue academic careers. Whether training to become a carpenter, gardener, or hairdresser, the programs generally encompass two- or three-year apprenticeships alongside schooling that adds a strong theoretical component.

This is how my German conversation partners described themselves in terms of holistic thinking:

> "I want to understand the world, find some overarching truths. And that implies some generalization. In my mind, you can't have interesting conversations without looking for the bigger picture." (Else B., Ger/US)

> "In Germany we value knowledge, because knowledge lies at the heart of making good judgments." (Kirsten B., Ger/US)

> "For us, having a small horizon, not knowing anything about the geographic world beyond your home town means being uneducated. However, Germany is becoming more like the US in terms of lack of geographic knowledge. In German high schools (Gymnasien) children continue to be taught well in this area, but many of the children who graduate nowadays from the less demanding schools (Hauptschulen) do not have much geographic knowledge." (Susanne B., Ger/Tw)

> "As parents we consciously modeled a broad variety of interests for our children. So they came to ask a lot of questions on things they encountered. For example, when they saw new plants, they would ask and learn about them. New questions came up all the time. Now that our children are grown, they are open and thirsty for knowledge. If I look at the kids in the US, they are interested in and good at computers or sports, but they do little else. Nor were the parents we met a model for instilling a broad curiosity." (Hannelore G., Ger/ US)

Neither the Americans nor the Chinese tend to appreciate the German desire for a larger understanding and their bent for abstract thinking and generalizing. In the Chinese world such persons would be considered self-centered or selfishly independent, while the majority of Americans might label them impractical idealists, or worse, elitists. However, seen from a German perspective, Americans' love for practical application, their low regard for a broad general knowledge base, and their inclination to judge people by popularity rather than intellectual ability tends to arouse an equally unsympathetic reaction. Though my respondents found value in American style "on the spot" thinking, suitable for brainstorming and spontaneous creativity, they had much to say about what they perceived to be a lack of knowledge and narrow thinking among Americans. Clearly, this was a topic close to their hearts reflecting the important role that thinking plays for the German self.

⇨ *"Americans are ignorant, meaning their scope of knowledge is narrow. They don't know their geography, they don't know languages, and they don't know about foreign countries and the world." (Susanne C., Ger/US)*

⇨ *"Americans have a lot of good practical ideas but they lack factual knowledge. They don't think less, but they know less and therefore can make fewer connections." (Else B., Ger/US)*

⇨ *"I've found Americans to generally have little interest in thoughts and ideas, unless it's about something that can be implemented." (Manuela M., Ger/US)*

⇨ *"I learned that in America it's not so much the academic content in school that's important for children to learn, rather they should prepare themselves for life by finding 'their' sport. Of course, physical activity is important, but we need information along with a general reference system that lets us categorize our knowledge in the brain for recall. Yes, there are Americans who also think this way, but I am afraid they are a much smaller minority than in Europe." (Helga B., Ger/US)*

⇨ *"I find the American form of quick thinking liberating, but only in a sense. Americans tend to feel free to burst out with their thoughts or their ideas. To speak their minds without much hesitation can make for a pleasant spontaneity, for a good brain storming session and it expresses a self-confidence that is highly valued in American communication. But this spontaneity relies on quick thinking, not on forethought. When it becomes the main mode, the art of a deeper form of thinking and conversation can get lost." (Inge L., Ger/ US)*

⇒ *"Being educated in the sense of knowing things has a higher value in Germany. There are ignorant people here and there. But in Germany we tend to think that if you don't know something that you ought to know, it is a bad thing. Here in the US people are not embarrassed when they don't know. Instead they think it's funny. I remember a TV program in which students who majored in history were asked simple questions. When asked in what year Columbus landed in the US, one student answered, "In the seventeenth century, and his ship was called the 'Mayflower.' When these students found out they were wrong, they laughed and thought it was so funny. In Germany not knowing things you should know is viewed negatively and people feel some pressure to find out and learn more." (Rainer M., Ger/US)*

⇒ *"In America you always need to quantify, but quantified information is so much hogwash. If you can't generalize, it means you can't see the bigger picture. For example, when I study a foreign language, I see grammar as a form of generalization that helps me become aware of the language's patterns and regularities. Knowing the grammar is a shortcut to better speaking." (Juergen S., Ger/US)*

⇒ *"Americans tell me that the Germans love for principles makes us rigid in our thinking. But I find Americans to have just as many rigid principles and truths as Germans. In politics and religion they hold almost sect-like opinions." (Oliver K., Ger/PRC/US)*

⇒ *"There is way too much political correctness in the US. You can't make any statement about a group or culture. So they check little kids and feeble grandmothers in the airport from head to toe simply to avoid being seen as biased. Any kind of categorization is suspect, even when it makes sense." (Barbara S., Ger/US/Tw)*

Chinese thinking is predominantly focused on a specific situation, quite different from the German preference to consider the larger context. During my years living in Taiwan I was often struck by what I came to call the "water lily concept," a strong Chinese tendency to focus on a specific item without taking its surrounding environment into account. Occasionally I found it admirable, but more often I did not. It first occurred to me during an outing with a group of Chinese friends. We had taken a trip into the mountains, where we came across one of those bright red pavilions with a little pond next to it. The natural surrounding was stunning, and a water lily bloomed in the middle of the pond. But the water was dirty and littered with garbage. Whereas I could not take my eyes off the filthy water and the litter all around, my Chinese companions seemed to only see the beauty of the flower. I envied their ability to concentrate their vision on the beauty of one item, but I also could not help but note their being oblivious to the surrounding ugliness. Later I saw examples of this "water lily" concept in many other places: a hodgepodge of things put together into a single space, a room, a street, a town, without any effort to create some unity or order to encompass the entirety. To me the majority of Chinese homes and gardens—this does not apply to well kept and professionally manicured classical Chinese gardens that are open to the public—had a scattered look, dividing the available space into many tiny spaces and overloading each with a multitude of different things. In towns and cities there are no or few city wide planning laws that would prevent an owner of a small odd shaped lot from building an odd shaped building on it. As a result, an ugly, dilapidated building might sit right next to an ultramodern or beautiful one. Though some of my Chinese friends saw the explanation for the water lily concept in the fact that Chinese live in crowded conditions and have little space, over the years I have come to believe that the water lily concept has more to do with a different way of thinking than with not having enough space. Steven B. (Ger/Tw), a professor at a university in Taiwan, shared this view.

> "The Chinese see things more in isolation, less in the larger context. I notice it among my students at this university. They may study for a specific course or exam, but when they take another course after that they don't see that these two courses are related to each other, or to their lives, or to society. So everything is separated, valid only for short-term specific goals. For me, as their professor, it is important that what they learn is meaningful, that they develop an educated personality. But the reality is that for them what they learn is

just mental junk food. Nor do my Taiwanese students have a student identity. They play being a student, but they are not students. Parents and schools will teach effort and obedience, two traits that are admired and well taught. But students don't learn to think for themselves, to become confident and stand up for themselves. In my view the Chinese kindergarten is a school, the Chinese school is a prison, and the university is a kindergarten for adults."

Feeling

Germans feel deeply but their feelings are primarily inner directed. Love and friendship play an important role in people's personal lives but there are many types of intense feelings unrelated to human relationships. Feelings may be nurtured by learning and expanding one's horizons, but most often German feelings are stirred by beauty, whether it is beauty in music, the arts or beauty encountered in nature.

> *"I think we Germans feel more intensely than Americans. Rather than aiming for 'highs,' Germans aim for depth. Whether it's the head or heart speaking, I don't know." (Ingo R., Ger/US/PRC)*

> *"Sometimes I think that only traveling and seeing new places can produce big excitement and big emotions in me. But that would be sad, wouldn't it?! Yet, travel is something that combines several emotionally intense interests for me: seeing, learning, smelling, listening." (Olga K., Ger/US)*

> *"I think the inner person needs to be nurtured by beauty which means it's also something that can be hurt or damaged by surrounding ugliness." (Karin W., Ger/Tw)*

> *"We Germans reserve feelings and emotions for the inner self. It's something to dwell on when alone or in nature, when reading poetry or listening to music." (Jonas K., Ger/US)*

Feelings nurtured by beauty in the arts and in nature

According to an Italian filmmaker who worked in Germany, Germans are timid about showing feelings, instead expressing them through art, poetry, and music. Simon Rattle, the British conductor the Berlin Philharmonic Orchestra, made a similar comment. "Germans are among the most emotional people on the planet. Maybe it has to do with the fact that as a nation they are always drawn back to nature and the forest. . . . That's one of the reasons the Berlin Philharmonic plays as it does—volcanic emotions from deep within. There are lots of nationalities in the orchestra now, but they are there because they are attracted to that type of temperament." [3]

"For most of us, film, theatre, literature and music are very important. It's part of life for the middle class, not just for the elite. It includes people you would not expect to have that sort of interest. And it's not for show. We talk a lot about the plays we have seen, the literature we have read, the music we have heard. It's one way to learn about human life and about ourselves." (Lisa K., Ger/US)

Nature and a beautiful environment play an enormously important part in German life for young and old, evident in their spending much time adorning their homes with flowers and plants, tending to beautiful yards, taking walks in parks and woods, and sitting in sidewalk cafes. A few years ago when I visited Berlin during very cold weather with subzero temperatures I never stopped being amazed at seeing people eating or drinking at sidewalk tables, sometimes keeping the cold at bay with blankets supplied by the establishment.

Children are taught to enjoy nature from an early age. Quite a few German nursery schools have a weekly "forest day." On that day, rain or shine, the children are expected to come properly dressed to walk and spend the major part of the day outside.

"Nature is something that touches deep feelings within me. Being surrounded by nature gives me a feeling of awe. It makes me feel small and insignificant, but it also makes me feel free!" (Heather L., Ger/US)

"We Germans direct and train our feelings by talking with plants in flower boxes, with animals, and with nature. It seems painful to have to fell a tree." (Friederike G., Ger/Tw)

"I often feel a very deep happiness when I am out in nature. Last year when I walked the Way of St. James (an ancient pilgrim route in northwestern Spain), there were several times when I felt such an intense joy and gratefulness for the beauty of nature surrounding me that tears were streaming

> down my face. Actually I may experience a similar happiness when I have
> the time and leisure to work in my garden, or when I see the first snowdrops
> and tulips sticking out of the snow. For me this intense feeling of happiness is
> closely connected to being in nature. I like to travel and see new cities. I enjoy
> beautiful exhibitions and museums, or a nice concert. But these things don't
> trigger the same intensity of happiness. Only being in nature does that. It has
> occurred to me that we human beings need nature, but that nature does not
> need the human being." (Betty S., Ger/US)

⇒ "Compared to people in Germany, I think Americans don't feel as strong a con-
> nection to nature. More Americans than Germans go on wilderness trips, but
> often that is more for adventure and challenge than out of love for nature."
> (Olga K., Ger/US)

Mark R., an American, married to a German and living in Germany, saw the
difference between German and American attitudes toward nature in a similar
way.

> "Germans like to be in nature and it is my impression that for them being in na-
> ture is much more part of who they are than it is for Americans. For us Amer-
> icans nature either means something inborn, as in nature vs. nurture, or it
> means complete nature, as in wilderness. Americans may be rafting down
> a wild river, or go hunting in upstate New York, but they don't go for walks
> in order to be in nature the way many Germans do. More than Germans, we
> Americans move between air-conditioned homes, cars, offices and shops. We
> are not so much exploiting nature, as wasting it. Thinking that there is always
> enough, our sense of abundance leads to waste and pollution. There is little
> consciousness about its preciousness."

Though an increasing number of individual Chinese now take the time to enjoy nature and share a concern about the environment, my German respondents
were dismayed at what they saw as a strong disregard among the Chinese toward the natural world as well as the lack of beauty in the Chinese man-made
surroundings. Both in Taiwan and in China convenience and making or saving
money seemed to prevail over caring for the environment.

⇒ *"I spent a couple of years teaching at a university in China. Everything around me was so dirty and ugly, that I remember placing two pieces of a nice fabric on a little box in my apartment, so that I could have something pretty to look at. I had a need for something beautiful in an ugly world."* (Friederike G., Ger/PRC)

⇒ *"When I lived for a year in Tainan (city in central Taiwan) I felt like being buried alive for lack of beauty."* (Elena M., Ger/Tw)

⇒ *"A few months ago we were invited to a large party at the house of one of our Chinese friends in California. As we were the first to arrive, the lady of the house, an American born Chinese, proudly showed us their garden: beautiful flower beds near the house, some vegetables and fruit trees further back. When I complimented her about the flowers, she was truly happy, even grateful for my comments. 'Our Chinese visitors usually disregard the flowers, maybe even step on them, in order to get to the veggies and fruit trees,' she told us. 'They have no appreciation for flowers.'"* (Barbara S., Ger/US/Tw)

⇒ *"It's incredible what animals have to suffer in Chinese society. People still commonly believe that an animal in the home is the source for all sorts of diseases. When living in Taipei (Taiwan) I recall many occasions where my Chinese companions would react to my talking to an animal in the streets by telling me 'Dirty, dirty, don't touch it' and pulling me away. Recently it has become somewhat fashionable among certain Chinese urbanites to have pets. Some treat them like family members but for many others, the commitment to an animal is thin. When the novelty of having a pet wears off or when it becomes inconvenient to have a pet, the animal is simply abandoned, put out in the street or park. The way I see it, in spite of all those wonderful nature poems in Chinese classical literature, the Chinese have little respect for nature and animals."* (Petra L., Ger/Tw)

⇒ *"The interest of the Chinese lies in human relationships and in the realities of the world. The Chinese may well exhibit fewer escapist notions than we Germans do, but is it very human? Where are the feelings? The romantic?"* (Ingo R., Ger/US/PRC)

Silence, solitude and Gemuetlichkeit

Many of my German conversation partners professed having a strong need for silence and solitude. Having time and space to be alone was a very important part of their lives. What to Chinese may look and feel like loneliness is to Germans a precious time to think and feel.

> *"I need a lot of alone time to think, to weigh things and find out where I stand."* (Jonas K., Ger/Tw)

> *"I am not shy, but I feel good being alone and I don't like to have many people around me."* (Carola B., Ger/US)

> *"I always need a lot of time and space to be alone. I love visiting my daughter, but I dread the prospect of going with her family on vacation and staying with them in a small cabin. It means that there will always be people around me and I can't withdraw. The older I get the more I feel a need for silence and solitude."* (Hanne S., Ger/US)

> *"My mother had a sign on the door: <u>Stille macht stark</u> ('Silence makes you strong'). Germans crave silence. Germany has strict rules how late open air restaurants or bars can stay open in residential areas and compared to Americans they have a rather limited patience for noise, whether it's noise coming from an adjacent apartment or children's noise outside."* (Peter F., Ger/US)

> ⇨ *"For the vast majority of Chinese being alone, as in sitting alone on a bench in a park, spells loneliness. It's a negative feeling. For me silence and solitude are very important."* (Oliver K., Ger/PRC)

> ⇨ *"When I lived with my husband's family in Taiwan, I had to hide in the bathroom to be alone."* (Margaret M., Ger/Tw)

The German concept of <u>Gemuetlichkeit</u>, a word that does not easily translate into English, is central to German life. The term refers to a good feeling, usually generated by enjoying a quiet, comfortable and beautiful physical space, either alone or with a person who is close to you. It also includes the notion of having time, of not being in a rush to do something afterwards.

Expression of feelings

As inner selves, Germans are not particularly adept at expressing their feelings verbally. They may debate topics with enthusiasm, be passionate about soccer playoffs and championships, and act with cheerful abandon during carnival celebrations, but many, especially among the older generation, are hesitant to express their emotions. The younger generation is more demonstrative, but even they tend to be less expressive than their American counterparts. Whether arising from joy or sorrow or just as a mood, Germans consider feelings to be private and rarely share them outside of close, personal relationships, which leads Chinese and Americans sojourners in Germany to conclude that Germans are cold and unfeeling people.

> "Most Germans like to be factual. Of course, there are some emotionally expressive Germans, who may say something like, 'Oh, Marianne, you look simply gorgeous today!' but they make up maybe five percent of the people. The rest are factual, people who do not easily verbalize their feelings toward others. Even at home there is less demonstration of feelings than in the US. And yet, people may discuss their inner feelings quite freely with people they are close to. In America you go to a psychiatrist, which probably means that you don't talk about your true feelings either, at least not about negatives ones." (Arnold B., Ger/US)

> "Sometimes we hold back because we don't know how to express our feelings so well. It's true in my own family, so I am used to it. Last week several relatives came to visit because an uncle had just died. It was a very stiff affair. People just didn't know how handle their feelings. So out of embarrassment people were withdrawn." (Manuela M., Ger/US)

> ⇨"I think we display our feelings less than Americans do. It's not because we don't have strong emotions but we can't handle them very well and we are embarrassed to show them. Once I was part of little group of foreign students who were hosted in the home of a very nice American family. As we were getting ready to leave I noted that one of the girls among us thanked the hostess in a very American way. It boiled down to something like, 'Oh, it was so nice of you to invite us . . . ,' but she used a lot of words to say it in different ways.

She was great but I took note that I simply could not have said it that way. To me it was over the top. I think this difficulty to express our emotions verbally makes us Germans poor performers. I became aware of this recently when I attended a large gathering of international Fulbrighters in the US. As part of the program participants were asked to make some kind of presentation to introduce their country's culture to the group. There were Fulbrighters from many countries, most of whom did a very nice job performing various kinds of dances or songs. Our German group was the largest contingent, yet we were all rather bashful and did not present much." (Olga K., Ger/US)

However, when Germans do express feelings they tend to do so with honesty. For them a smile is an honest smile, coming from a happy person, not something that you put on your face to be polite or to appear happy when you are not.

"There is a little kiosk up the street from us where I often buy tickets for public transportation. The man who works there is sometimes friendly and pleasant. Other times he is grouchy. I think, that's the way most people are. It just depends on whether you catch them on a good day or a bad one. What's so bad about not smiling when you are having a bad day? Let him grumble if he likes it!" (Andre B., Ger/US)

⇨ *"As a professor at an American university I regularly receive student evaluations for my classes. One of the comments I recently got was, 'It would be nice to see the instructor smile.' I don't go around like Americans smiling all the time. If I am not smiling it means nothing but when I do smile it has meaning. It's not just a social smile, something that you put on your face because it looks good, because you want to appear happy when you are not, or to make others feel good. The way I look when I teach has nothing to do with how I feel. That is two different things. I like people who are a bit more serious, more honest, not hypocritical." (Rainer M., Ger/US)*

⇨ *"My own sadness, likes or dislikes are written all over my face and I like this same openness in others. We show our feelings more honestly than Chinese or Americans. In Chinese faces you don't see a thing, and Americans seem to only show positive feelings. For them it's: keep smiling; everything is wonderful, amazing. . ." (Regine F., Ger/US/Asia)*

Many Germans initially react negatively to the customary American display of smiles, enthusiasm, and exuberance. However, after a prolonged stay in the US most come to realize that the American smile is a social smile, a social norm. Others continue to feel uncomfortable with what they see as "frozen" or "permanent smiles" on American faces.

⇨ "When I spent a year as a high school exchange student in North Carolina, it was a good experience, but I discovered that I don't fit there. The women there were so exaggeratedly friendly, and they used a lot of exuberant gestures, which to me appeared artificial and hypocritical. It got on my nerves." (Julia B., Ger/US)

⇨ "I find Americans to be so over the top (überschwenglich) in their friendliness and praises. I can't stand that 'Oh, how wonderful! I love it!' It almost sounds hysterical. And all those kisses and hugs feel so exaggerated, so excessively emotional. For me it is hard to take." (Manuela M., Ger/US)

⇨ The constant smiling mask on American faces gets on my nerves. I find it suspect. It makes me wonder whether the need to always smile, to appear cheerful and to think positively has something to do with the high rates of depression in America." (Christina G., Ger/US)

Not all of my German respondents saw the American expression of emotions in a negative light.

⇨ "In my experience Americans laugh a lot and are loud, and emotions have to be expressed with gestures and interjections. American men can get passionate about sports and politics, which is not unlike us German men getting emotional over soccer, especially when drinking. For a year I had an American roommate who was exuberant and had an opinion about everything. But I did not see his exuberance as something negative. I saw it was genuine." (Jonas K., Ger/Tw)

⇨ I learned quickly that you are not allowed to look grouchy in America and that you need to have a lot of smiles for others. I learnt that it is not necessarily a mask, just a friendly habit of reacting to others they meet. Even if this kind of smile is not an invitation to a friendship, I found a lot of joy on a daily basis in being surrounded by considerate and friendly people. And sometimes when *they beam at you and give you that loving embrace, they actually mean it. At least at that moment. It's our problem if we read too much meaning into it." (Ilse F., Ger/US)*

Though both the Americans and Chinese tend to interpret the lack of social smiles in Germany to mean that Germans are cold and unfeeling people, in a broader perspective, the lack of social smiles is not unusual in other parts of Europe.

"We Germans may smile less than Americans but when we went to Lithuania we found the people's seriousness there to be extreme. Whether in private homes or in public places, people, especially older persons, were so very quiet and looked so very serious that it almost felt depressing." (Inge L., Ger/US)

"Americans say that Germans are somber people, who don't smile and don't laugh much. To put things into perspective, a Russian emigrant in Germany told me that many Russians in Germany complain that Germans smile too easily, that they smile even when they don't mean it." (Marie W., Ger/US)

Communicating

Honesty, directness and objectivity

German communication makes a distinction between the factual and the personal level, considering the message to be separate from the listener. This separation provides the freedom to be honest and direct without offending, allowing the speaker to focus on the content, on what you say, not on how you say it. In comparison both Americans and Chinese pay more attention to how the message is received by the other, while at the same time being more sensitive to feeling offended themselves. A few of my German conversation partners came to like the softness of indirectness they encountered in American and Chinese societies, but most confessed that they had a hard time with it. To the latter the nonseparation of message and listener meant sacrificing honesty, clarity, and objectivity in favor of being indirect and evasive. To them tailoring speech to please and appeal to emotions seemed not only cumbersome but also a form of self-censorship.

Honesty, in the sense of communicating with truthfulness, directness, sincerity and objectivity is part of being authentic, true to one's inner self. This makes it paramount to be honest about voicing one's views and calling a spade a spade. This strong regard for honesty and directness makes Germans highly sensitive to hypocrisy and vagueness, or to any form of misrepresentation or hiding inner thoughts and feelings.

> *"If I can't say what I think or feel I can't be myself. It would be like walking on eggs." (Susanne C., Ger/US)*

> *"When I talk to someone, I open myself, even though opening myself might mean I make a mistake or say something wrong. But to me not opening the self means being unapproachable and arrogant." (Nikki Z., Ger/Europe)*

> *"I could not imagine myself working in a culture, in which I could not say directly what I think. I would feel like wearing a mask." (Ernst K., Ger/Europe)*

> *"Even though indirectness can be a friendly habit of politeness, I intuitively react negatively to vagueness, thinking that I will have to watch out for manipulative ways. I like the German straight talk better and I find it a lot less stressful." (Elena M., Ger/Tw)*

> *"We Germans are straightforward in our talk. Americans call it blunt and sometimes rude. But in my mind I am not your enemy if I say things straightforwardly. In Germany we deal with people honestly, though we do have a tradition of arguing and fighting over who is right. So I argue a lot with my German friends and colleagues. It's very common and it's how I learn something. My good friend Heidi and I, for example, fight all the time. It may be over politics, sports or science, whatever. We enjoy our arguments. Yes, occasionally there is a point where things can be destructive; for example if someone just argues to show how dumb the other is. There is a line that should not be crossed with regard to personal issues, such as how to live your life or how to educate your kids. If your way of life is different and you have a missionary idea of convincing somebody else about it, then the issue may be personal and can lead to discord. But otherwise arguing with people is interesting and fun." (Rainer M., Ger/US)*

Germans in the US often complain that Americans don't mean what they say.

⇨ "American politeness or friendliness is superficial. People say things to be nice which means they often don't mean what they say. For example, I live in a beautiful home with a view over the ocean, where professionals like to take photos for magazines. 'We will send you the magazine,' they'll say when they leave, but they never do. What people say cannot be taken seriously. It's just being nice." (Arnold B., De/US)

⇨ "Americans often don't do or mean what they say. Just the other day my mother-in-law told someone on the phone, 'Oh, I'll be over in a few minutes,' but when I asked her a few minutes later whether she was going, she said, 'Oh, no, I am busy.' I think it would be proper to be honest and up front to begin with." (Anna K., Ger/US)

⇨ "Like so many other Germans in the US I also experienced people casually telling me that I should come and visit them any time. If as a result of this 'invitation' I really stood with my backpack on their doorstep, they'd probably close the door on me. It takes time to learn whether people mean they say." (Ilse F., Ger/US)

"I know it's idle to discuss which custom is better than another, because they all have their pros and cons; but being a German, I prefer not to be lied to. I like to know where I stand." (Andre B., Ger/US)

Germans in the United States also encountered an unaccustomed degree of indirectness. While a few liked it, most saw the American habit of stating things in positive terms to soften the impact or make things sound better than they are as whitewashing (*Schoenfaerberei*). This includes the various politically correct terms, such as calling someone 'mobility challenged' instead of 'physically handicapped' etc.

⇨ "I find Americans very indirect, and they pack one another in fluff all the time. We call a spade a spade. So I can understand that Americans may view our honest and direct communication style as bluntness and rudeness. We may sound blunt and rude to them, but it does not mean we are cold. Our feelings are mostly inward-directed, not so much outwardly expressed." (Olga K., Ger/US)

⇨ *"Americans are good at acting and beating around the bush, but I miss the German directness. In the US I have been called stubborn and opinionated. Maybe I am a stubborn German. But standing up for my opinions does not make me aggressive." (Andre B., Ger/US)*

One of my German conversation partners shared with me a list of British expressions he had come across. "They show a degree of indirectness that baffles the German mind," he told me. "Though the expressions supposedly describe the British, after having lived for decades in the United States, I know that they are just as common in the US." (Ingo R., Ger/US)

"I hear what you say" = I disagree and do not wish to discuss it further

"With the greatest respect" = I think you are a fool

"Not bad" = good, or very good

"Quite good" = a bit disappointing

"Perhaps you would like to think about" = this is an order, or, justify yourself

"Oh, by the way" = this is the primary purpose of our discussion

"Very interesting" = I don't agree, I don't believe you

"I'll bear it in mind" = I'll do nothing about it

"Perhaps you could give that some more thought" = it's a bad idea, don't do it

"Not entirely helpful" = completely useless

"You must come for dinner" = just being polite

Often Germans find that Americans may take things personally when according to the German way of thinking it was merely a statement of opinion or fact.

⇨ *During the year I lived in the United States I came to realize that Americans have a different way of communicating with each other. In Germany we separate content from the person we speak to, so we can be honest and direct without offending. That is not so in the United States." (Helga B., Ger/US)*

⇨ *"With my American colleagues in the university, I can't be myself. They have a totally different way of coming together. Here, everybody has to have a 'good time,' which means that when people start to argue they immediately move on to another topic. In Germany we deal with people honestly and among friends we enjoy the mental challenge. If I dealt with people here the way I deal with people in Germany I would be an outlaw and have lots of problems. So I have become much quieter. I've learned not say everything that is on my mind, but I miss the openness. For me life is easier when I can be direct, when I know where I stand. I'd like to be more diplomatic because sometimes I create unnecessary problems with my directness. But in my heart I get along better with people who say freely what they think and feel." (Rainer M., Ger/US)*

⇨ *"I think the average middle class American abides by political correctness regarding politics, religion and race relations more than his German counterpart. I have come to the point in America that when I am together with several people, I hardly dare state my opinion any more. In Germany I don't have to be careful." (Ingo R., Ger/US)*

⇨ *"Once, when we were discussing politics in a group of four, one person, whom I did not know very well, said, 'Let's stay away from talking about politics around this table. It makes me feel uncomfortable.' I was annoyed. 'You just censored my speech!' I told him." (Christa Y., Ger/US)*

⇨ *"In America even very small children are taught to watch out not to say something that might hurt others' feelings. A friend of mine, a kindergarten teacher, says she wants her children to learn good behavior, for example by teaching them not to say to another child, 'Oh, it's easy!,' or 'You can do it, it's easy!. . .' That sounds so American to me. If I can't say something simple like 'It's easy' because somebody else might find it not easy, I don't have much liberty anymore." (Olga K., Ger/US)*

⇨ *"I am often baffled when my sons, who grew up in America, are offended by various things I say. When I just state my feelings about something, they take what I say as personal criticism. But I don't mean it as criticism; it's just how I feel. I am just being German! People who are so easily bruised must have fragile egos." (Rosemarie N., Ger/US)*

The clash between German directness and honesty and the Chinese understanding of politeness and respect is equally pointed. Though the Germans who were living or had lived in Taiwan or China generally liked the customary politeness they encountered, they also reacted to it with ambivalence.

⇨ *"I usually like the Chinese politeness. The German philosopher Schopenhauer said it well, 'Politeness is like an air pillow. It has nothing but air in it, but one sits more comfortably.' I do feel that we Germans are impolite. Saying that form is not important, that only content matters, may just be an excuse for slovenliness." (Ingo R., Ger/US)*

⇨ *"I like the openness of the Chinese and their friendliness towards me, the white foreigner. However, I can see that people with darker skin, such as people from Southeast Asia or from Africa, face a much less friendly attitude." (Karl M., Ger /Tw)*

⇨ *"As their professor's wife, my husband's students treated me with great politeness. Yet, I could also see that they had no interest in who I was as a person. They rarely asked what I did or what my interests were. To them I had a certain status, a role to play, but I was not an individual person. So the politeness felt like a rather cold politeness." (Barbara S., Ger/Tw)*

⇨ *"I react negatively to the manipulative part of Chinese politeness, even though I have to intellectually admit that their politeness and attention also makes things very pleasant. I also realize that even though there are often ulterior motives involved, being nice and helpful is a must in Chinese society and becomes a habit, even when there are no such motives. Still, I prefer the German straight talk. It makes life a lot less stressful." (Marie G., Ger/Tw)*

Often the Chinese discrepancy between truth and what people said felt like an enormous reality gap. Not only did the Chinese appear to forgo truthfulness for politeness, lack of honesty also seemed to be tied to self protection and a perceived need to look out for one's own advantage.

⇨ *"When my Chinese friends want to decline an invitation they need to resort to a lie, maybe saying that they don't feel well or that they have another commitment. As for me, I might just tell people that at this time I just don't feel like being around people." (Susanne B., Ger/Tw)*

⇨ *"When you ask the Chinese to do or agree to something, they'll immediately say yes. But that does not mean that they will abide by it later. I am slow to commit. Because to me a commitment is an obligation that must be kept, I want to be careful before I agree to something. I prefer to underpromise and overfulfill, but for the Chinese it's the other way round: they overpromise and underfulfill." (Elena M., Ger/Tw)*

⇨ *"In China I had to learn to not tell the truth and to look after my advantage. Otherwise people would take advantage of me." (Anne B., Ger/PRC/Tw)*

⇨ *"The Chinese don't stick to factual truths and objectivity, neither in private, nor as a nation in the use of history as propaganda. It's a point that displeases me to this day, but it is inherent in Chinese culture." (Oliver K., Ger/PRC)*

German honesty also applies to praise and criticism. Praise must be valid and sincere and not be dispensed with for the sake of politeness. The inner self is expected to be independent and not rely on others for self-worth. Rob, my bookbinding teacher who was raised in America but in a strongly German cultural environment, did not believe in praise. "Don't be dependent on praise," he would tell us students. "Just stand back and admire your own work." He stood by his words. He neither praised nor criticized.

"Praise should be valid. If it's a distortion of the truth, it makes me feel uncomfortable. Better to arrive at a healthy sense of self-worth by being treated as a person in our own right. (Ursula L, Ger/Tw)

"In Germany we don't do much praising and we don't say to people, 'You look beautiful!' I want to be able to speak truthfully, not pretend, though I do make a certain allowance for etiquette." (Marie G., Ger/Tw)

⇨ *"Americans dole out a lot of praise, especially to children, to make them feel good and have self-esteem." (Christina G., Ger/US)*

⇨ *"The Chinese love to compliment and praise. I hear a lot of, 'Oh, you are so beautiful, so intelligent, so . . . .' Americans admire others more often for being popular or good looking, less for being intelligent. In Germany a compliment is less likely to address the external, how you look. Instead people would be more apt to compliment someone on having had a great idea." (Karin S. Ger/Tw)*

⇨ *"The Chinese think that praises make someone feel comfortable. But they make me feel uncomfortable. Usually it's such a distortion of the truth." (Anna E., Ger/PRC)*

When the message is considered to be separate from the listener, the individual is free to state opinions, aim for objectivity and express criticism without fear of endangering a personal relationship. Criticism that would be quite acceptable in Germany might not be so in the United States.

"To Germans criticism, including self-criticism, is seen as positive because it shows objectivity. In fact, rather than just saying wonderful things about someone, my family or myself, we give more weight if what we say is balanced, perhaps admitting to some weaknesses." (Marie G., Ger/Tw)

"I don't see criticism as negative. If I have my own opinion I will stand up for it even if I am attacked on it. I need to be able to stand criticism. Without this kind of freedom to speak you miss an important part of democracy." (Olga K., Ger/US)

"Correcting others' mistakes is not criticism. It assumes that they want to learn and improve and you just help them along the road." (Kirsten B., Ger/US))

"If people are annoyed by something I said, I like them to tell me directly and frankly. If done factually it's not an insult. It simply gives me a chance to know that I said something wrong. If they just hinted at it or used hidden criticism I might not even get their point." (Andre B., Ger/US)

⇨ *"At American scientific conferences everybody is very polite. To your face they may tell you something like "I admire what you do," but when you get the criticism through the blind review process and find out what they really think, it is rather shocking. Germans say exactly what they think even if it means hurting people's feelings. I have received some tough reviews but they were scientifically justified. If you get this kind of criticism you can improve, so you know what you have to do. Instead of clearly stating a criticism, an American scientist may say something like, 'Have you thought about this?' or 'Maybe you* could. . . .' In Germany we prefer criticism to be straightforward, because even with all this 'Have you thought about this . . .' or 'Maybe you could . . .' they still mean it's hogwash. People just don't say it that way." (Rainer M. Ger/US)

⇒ "The Americans I met when living in California say things more cautiously and they seemed extra sensitive to the feelings of others, more empathetic. Some Germans take it as lack of critical thinking or they call this kind of sensitivity superficial or fake, but I don't think that's what it was. I thought it was pleasant." (Lisa K., Ger/US)

Germans living in Chinese society quickly became aware that Chinese politeness meant avoiding all criticism. However, they also discovered that in some cases politeness did not apply and that Chinese could be even more critical, if not ruder, than people in Germany.

⇒ "Whereas in Germany people don't hold back criticism, here in Taiwan you can be as impolite as you want to be, and yet you will hear no criticism. On the other hand, Chinese do a lot of ridiculing people, for example for being different or handicapped. And yet, they themselves have an enormous fear of being laughed at!" (Karin S. Ger/Tw)

⇒ "There is a strong taboo in Chinese society about saying anything even slightly critical about your own family to an outsider. Several times when I said something less than complimentary about a family member of mine, perhaps mentioning the fact that my sister is an alcoholic, the Chinese reacted with an uncomfortable silence giving me a clear sense that I just violated one of their basic rules, namely to bring glory, not shame, to your family. And yet, within their own family Chinese can be extremely critical." (Barbara S., Ger/Tw)

⇒ "In my experience the Chinese don't have tact. My students may tell me, 'Oh, you have a pimple on your face!' and one colleague once told me that I had fat legs. She was right. I do have fat legs, but in Germany we would not point that out. There are things you don't need to say. As friends Chinese can say these things, though they wouldn't say it to a superior or to people they don't know well. I had a good relationship with my students, so I suppose they felt free to tell me. But on those topics we would be more cautious in Germany. Here in Taiwan people may also laugh at you when you make a mistake or fall." (Susanne B., Ger/Tw)

Importance of content

Given the high value attached to thinking and having a broad knowledge base, substantive and open-ended discussions on big topics are favorite pastimes in everyday German life. Commonly Germans enjoy meaningful conversations and animated discussions entailing an honest exchange of views on topics of mutual interest. Deeper conversations present an opportunity to clarify one's own thoughts and feelings, gain new insights into the topic at hand, and to get to know the other better.

"What I like best about Germany is our conversations about God and the world."
(Karin S. Ger/Tw)

"For me, a stimulating conversation, usually one on one, is the spice of life. My brother the other day said that to him it was like 'a refreshing rain.' A certain overlap of ideas sure makes for a sense of having found a kindred spirit, but equally important is the person's ability to generate ideas that are different, that teach me something new or challenge my view. Unless truly offensive in a personal way, conflicting views will not turn a relationship adversarial."
(Barbara S., Ger/US/Tw)

"In my circle of friends everybody wants to have an opinion. Especially we men will defend our view when others do not share it. When individual minds are allowed to be free, they naturally come up with different interpretations. To me, it's always been a positive sign that people are using their minds." (Uwe O., Ger/US).

"It would be horrible if after every discussion everybody came away with the same opinion. To me, that would be like a straightjacket. I will stand up for my opinion, but if someone comes along with a better argument I might change my view." (Amanda K., Ger/US)

"I have many confrontations, but I also feel free not to have an opinion and per-haps no interest in forming one. If someone tells me, 'Oh, you haven't yet read this or that book?!' I might tell them that I don't have the time or interest. To me it doesn't mean being poorly educated, though I know that some people demonstrate knowledge in order to show off." (Oliver K., Ger/Chin)

> *"I want to know about and be able to talk about a lot of different topics, so I can hold my own in conversations with others. I don't want to be considered ignorant." (Christel Y., Ger/US)*

> *"Currently talking about the Chinese I Ching [one of the Chinese Classics] seems to be a fad. For most this interest does not reflect their personal philosophy and has nothing to do with a spiritual feeling. Rather it means that one should know something about the topic if you want to belong and be able to talk with others about it." (Anne E., Ger/PRC)*

My German respondents voiced strong reactions to the American light way of communicating. Besides finding much of American talk to be trivial, superficial talk, filled with words that do not mean what they say, they noted a lack of interest in longer and deeper conversations. A common pet peeve of Germans in America is that American restaurants are too noisy and the service too pushy, both of which seemed to indicate that conversation among the guests was of secondary importance. Germans find it intrusive and impolite when a waiter, after having taken the order and served the meal, comes back to the table, often more than once, to ask if everything is okay, each time rudely interrupting the ongoing conversation.

> ⇨ *"In Germany Americans are stereotyped as being superficial, a perception which I think is mostly based on the content of their conversations. We don't have such a thing as small talk, which means we need to have something to say to someone. But because we shy away from talking to people we don't know, it's not a problem." (Karin S., Ger/Tw)*

> ⇨ *"American small talk is very troublesome for me because I don't know how to react. When someone asks me a question, I assume they need an answer. But then why does a stranger want to know my answer? It's a problem for me and is something that does not fit into my life. It annoys me when someone I don't know well asks me 'How are you?' It's clear that people are not really interested in knowing how I am." (Manfred B., Ger/US)*

> ⇨ *"In Germany we expect an honest response when we ask people how they are; so the American response 'I am fine' sounds terribly superficial. But as I see it*

now, it's mostly a language problem. It's a greeting, rather than a question. But it took me five months to understand that." (Olga K., Ger/US)

⇨ *"Americans talk a lot. We love conversation, but we hate empty talk. Here in Germany I go out to eat with a group of four or five guys once a week. We always have interesting topics. I did not have that when I lived in the US, where people mostly talk about what they are going to buy, what they just bought or what they might buy in the future." (Andre B., Ger/US)*

⇨ *"I have been in America long enough to know that at sit-down dinners I sin every time I get engaged in an interesting conversation with someone sitting next to me, because under those circumstances I will pay little attention to, or worse, even ignore, the person sitting on the other side of me. Usually I am vaguely aware that what I am doing is considered impolite, but I just cannot bear to sacrifice the opportunity and joy of a good conversation for some empty small talk." (Barbara S., Ger/US/Tw)*

⇨ *"After many years of living in the US I have come to appreciate many things about life in America, though I do miss the deeper conversations with people. There are Americans who like such conversations, but it's just so much harder to find them." (Ingo R., Ger/US)*

Over the years I have attended many social events, conferences or parties, where people from many different countries came together. At such gatherings it usually turns out that Europeans gravitate toward each other and end up in some corner carrying on sustained and animated conversations, while the life of the party goes on elsewhere. It appears that others had similar experiences.

"Sometimes we international students would go up to the roof of our dorm for parties. Initially there would be one large group, with us Europeans drinking beer and Americans cola. But then after ten minutes or so the Europeans would be congregating on one side and the Americans on another. We would talk about political and economic issues, films and literature, and the American students about sex. In my view Americans do not read much and though they see movies, they see Hollywood films, whereas we tend to see more serious films, which often are made in the US too." (Karin S., Ger/Tw)

Serious conversations and discussions do not play a prominent part in Chinese life. Though meals in a restaurant by a group of people are usually accompanied by a great deal of noise and laughter, the main topics tend to be food and family. Good will and relationships are confirmed, but rarely through sharing thoughts and ideas. Politeness, harmony, and self- protection rank above content.

When I met with Elena M., a German who had married into a Taiwanese family and had been living in Taiwan for eight years, she, like other Germans in Taiwan, described the Chinese style of conversation as dull. When we parted after our four-hour long conversation she had tears in her eyes. "I am missing you already!" she sighed. Though I had been a total stranger to her and we had just met for the purpose of the interview, she had clearly enjoyed the conversation and realized that it was a rare moment in her life in Taiwan.

⇨ *"I am homesick for my friends and others who enjoy intellectual discussions, who stand up for their opinions. Here in Taiwan everybody is very careful not to say anything that might be taken as an opinion. People want harmony, so they need to make sure that no one is offended." (Hans B., Ger/Tw)*

⇨ *"Here [in Taiwan] the children learn how to be part of a group. Thoughts and feelings of the individual don't count for much. Occasionally I try to engage the women in our church groups in a conversation, perhaps while we work alongside each other, but when I ask about what they think about a certain topic, more often than not the answer is, 'I don't know.' I am never quite sure whether the person has no opinion or does not want to say." (Erika F., Ger/Tw)*

⇨ *"I find there are very few people in Taiwan with whom I can have an intellectual conversation. Here people go and eat and talk about family." (Karl M., Ger/Tw)*

⇨ *"Our Chinese fellow graduate students always had lots of tales to tell about the relationships between various Chinese professors. Mostly it was about who did not get along with whom, rarely about their professional ideas." (Barbara S., Ger/US/Tw)*

⇨ *"When my Chinese fiancée and I were having an argument, she'd immediately question whether our relationship should be continued or not. So I would tell her, 'We are going to have different opinions, but that has nothing to do with whether we should have a relationship.'" (Juergen S., Ger/PRC)*

Relating

Differentiation between close and nonclose relationships

Germans think of relationships in terms of a connectedness that comes from knowing each other well by way of mutually sharing the inner self. A true relationship is a close relationship, one that entails honesty and commitment.

Because sharing the inner self is part of a relationship, Germans are particular about selecting the individuals they will engage with and include in their lives. Opening the self to strangers is clearly not appropriate and not done, but even casual relationships retain a certain distance. The common German saying *Dienst is Dienst and Schnapps ist Schnapps* means work is work, and private life is private life. The two are kept separate and to a certain degree coincide with the linguistic distinction between the familiar "you" (*Du*) and the polite "you" (*Sie*). Traditionally, *Sie* maintained a certain distance, preserving a welcome personal space, while *Du* was reserved for family, friends, and children.

One of my Chinese interviewees recounted his experience when he was invited to a *Duzen* ceremony, an event that marks the occasion of switching from the formal *Sie* to the familiar *Du*. He learned that the two couples had known each other for over twenty years. "We went through a lot together," they told him, "and we know a lot about each other." Yet, they had been in no rush to change to the familiar address indicating that to them the *Du* needed to reflect the reality of closeness.

Though there have always been some regional differences in the use of *Du* and *Sie*, over recent decades the distinction between the two forms of address has weakened, especially among the younger generation. At this point in time holding off with the *Du* for twenty years and then marking the occasion with a little ceremony is rather old-fashioned and no longer common. Nonetheless, the differentiation between close and nonclose relationships continues to be well defined.

Though Chinese culture also differentiates between relationships, it does so by relying less on personal closeness and more on the perceived standing in the social hierarchy. American norms, on the other hand, differentiate only minimally between close and nonclose relationships, preferring instead inclusivity and a light friendliness toward all.

> *"I would never invite my boss or my employees to my home. Nor do we invite our work colleagues. In Germany we separate work life and private life. At work, relationships are not so important to us, but in private life they are very important." (Rainer M., Ger/US)*

> *"I am not shy but I don't like to be inundated by too much company. It is important to me to be able to choose with whom I want to be in my free time. On my last birthday I celebrated with thirty people, but I selected them. I'd never want to invite a whole group, such as a class, everybody at work, or a group of relatives I am not close to." (Betty S., Ger/US)*

> *"In Germany I talk to very few people I don't know, but once I have developed a relationship with someone, we will often get together and talk. So I get to know them really well, and once they are my friends they will be my friends for life. In America relationships are different. It's not that relationships are less valued than in Germany, but they are different, less selective." (Rainer M., Ger /US)*

German newcomers to the US tend to be confused by the lack of differentiation between close and nonclose relationships, sensing insincerity behind the friendliness. Other times they mistake American friendliness for the beginning of a relationship and as a result feel disillusioned or "left hanging there" when there is no follow up.

Friendship

In Germany friends are more likely to be soulmates than playmates. Moreover, because friendship implies sharing one's inner self, making friends takes time. People need to feel the friendship before they will extend it. Once a friendship is established, however, there is a strong commitment and the expectation that both sides will nurture the relationship by frequently spending time together.

"For us friendship ranks very high in importance and is very fulfilling. To be accepted, liked or loved gives us extreme emotional security. And since friendships give you a lot, you want to nurture them, which means you can't have a lot of friends." (Lisa K., Ger/US)

"Friendship is a deep relationship, which means you must cultivate your friendships. So if I am away for a prolonged period of time I must make an effort to stay in touch. If after five years away I go back to a place where I once lived, I might take a look where someone I once knew lived, but I would not ring the bell nor call him. If you have not been in touch with someone for a few years it's over." (Marie G., Ger/Tw)

"In Germany my true friends are people who think like me or at least have some similar interests, people I can count on being honest with me. I nurture my relationships and there is a lot of give and take." (Gudrun S., Ger/US)

"What is great about the German way is our commitment (Verbindlichkeit). It's a certain steadiness. When friends share a basic common understanding there is no risk of offending. We can challenge each other and take different positions, without it affecting our relationship." (Karl M., Ger/Tw)

"I associate friendship with commitment, which to me means a mutual understanding of a stable foundation, something you can build on, that is there when you need it. So it does not matter when you disagree on things." (Karl M., Ger/Tw)

"I want my friends to criticize me. In fact I don't consider them friends if they don't. An evening when everybody has the same opinion is a waste of time. I have now lived in the US for over ten years, but I have had only one American friend. My other friends are all from Germany or from other countries." (Rainer M., Ger/US)

"During carnival people drink and have fun together. Some may even take the beer from somebody else they don't know that well and take a sip. That's okay during carnival time in some parts of Germany. But it's not done here in northern Germany and it is not friendship." (Helga B., Ger/US)

Because close relationships depend heavily on exchanging thoughts and ideas, conversations often lie at the heart of friendship. Unhurried conversations, sometimes for several hours and in a place that offers a comfortable surrounding, are a favorite pastime. Whatever the topics during these exchanges, Germans will disclose their views and feelings with honesty. Friends are not expected to be cheerleaders and do not look to each other for approval.

> *"For me, good conversations are the essence of friendship. I would starve without good conversations. Even when we do something together, like going to the movies, we enjoy discussing the film afterwards. With American friends it was mostly a matter of doing things together, which was fine though it felt shallow to me. I think it has something to do with sharing personal things. We are very open about our personal lives, which does not seem to be the case with American friends. In the US I had one person with whom I spent a lot of time. In a way it felt like friendship, but it was not very deep. There was no real person there!" (Olga K., Ger/US)*

> *"Friendship to me means to sit in some comfortable surrounding and talk about God and the world, or maybe about our grief and sorrow. To do this we must share honestly and have some mutual interests. I want my friends to inspire me, but also to be able to criticize me to help me know myself and grow. We don't verbalize our feelings for each other the way many Americans do by saying things like 'I like you,' or 'I will miss you.' In fact I react a bit negatively to expressions of frequent verbal admiration or to receiving presents." (Alex J., Ger/US)*

> *"For me friendship goes both through the heart and the mind. It has to be both. When you meet with a friend for a meal, it's to enjoy the conversation. The food is secondary." (Arnold B., Ger/US)*

> *"Friends tend to spend large blocks of time together. A dinner get-together in a restaurant probably means three to four hours; at someone's home it tends to go on into the wee hours of the morning. So any given friendship means a commitment of time, which is why I don't aspire to have many friends. I very much enjoy meeting new people, but it's difficult to add new friends and still maintain the existing friendships. I have only so much time and I can't and won't leave my current friends just hanging there. Still, occasionally I have to*

be ready to cool one relationship to make room for a new one. I do it, but it is not the norm." (Betty S., Ger/US)

"If I invite friends it can't be for just forty-five minutes. It's going to be at least two to three hours, more if a meal is involved. If I spend the whole day cooking for guests and then they come, eat and go home, it's not worth it. Unless you have a valid excuse, leaving too soon may create some ill feelings, because if I went to the trouble to prepare a meal, I expect a leisurely time with some interesting conversation to follow." (Albert T., Ger/US)

Though conversation is the primary glue in friendships, German friends also do things for each other or engage in activities together.

"In my experience it's quite common in Germany to ask friends for help when we move into a new place. In Berlin many buildings have no elevators, so we need bodies to carry our stuff up the stairs. My Dad's colleagues and friends all helped to build the house I grew up in, and my brother helped to convert a friend's apartment. And he built furniture for others. I must admit, I have never offered that sort of help to others—no boxes carried or walls painted— but I've proofread academic papers and scientific articles for friends. I guess that's what I know and like, and like to offer to do." (Olga K., Ger/US)

"My godchildren are all children of friends, not children of relatives. As a god- mother I talk to the children on the phone, take them to a movie, invite them to eat at my house where I talk with them at length and, if necessary, teach them table manners. Once in a while I send a little gift. For me it's not a godchild in the Christian sense. Rather I think of it as helping the parents, my friends, to see to it that their children get what they need." (Marion B., Ger/PRC)

"With our German friends we may spend days together on the beach, maybe switch diapering our kids, or even exchange our kids for a while." (Rainer M., Ger/US)

The intimacy and openness that are part of a German friendship means that friends are not shareable. Germans do not usually invite strangers to join their friends, and even if they do introduce someone to a friend, the interaction be- tween the friend and the newcomer tends to be minimal.

"Germans don't want to share friends. You can't transfer the feeling of soulmate. Introducing one friend to another is somewhat of a problem for me and I am not very good at it. In English you can just introduce them and chances are that one of them will initiate a question based on whatever little information they have about the person at that point. When we speak English it works okay, but in German it's not as common to introduce others. If I said, 'Erika, this is my friend Helga, Helga this is my friend Erika.' They would both say 'Hello' to each other and then nothing, at least if they are part of a larger group. At a later point they might cautiously approach that person, but very careful not to be too pushy. I think it's not disinterest, rather it's about giving it more time." (Olga K., Ger/US)

"I have many friends, but these relationships are either very personal or are geared toward a specific common interest. In either case it does not make sense to open up the relationship to others." (Andre B., Ger/US)

"When we go out with a friend, or a couple of friends, we don't talk with outsiders. We go out with our friends to enjoy each other's company, not to meet new people." (Lisa K., De/US)

Many of my German interviewees who live or have lived in America shared with me their disappointments and frustrations regarding the American style of friendship. "I love to have friends," Rainer M. said. "But here in the US, I don't know. Do Americans really have friends?" It is a common question and concern. My German respondents usually did appreciate the American inclusiveness and the ease of meeting new people, but the American eagerness to establish a quick familiarity and their noncommittal friendship was not in line with their expectations.

⇨ *"With Americans the welcome mat is always out. There seems to be this huge desire to be friends even when you have just become acquainted. You get to know them quickly but it does not make for much depth in the relationship. In Germany we are very selective, because treating everybody alike robs you of closeness."* (Rainer M., Ger/US)

⇨ *"I would rather go to a party alone in the US than in Germany. In the US if you make the slightest move, people will jump to include you. It's easy for them* because they rarely have deep conversations anyway. So it's no big deal to interrupt an ongoing conversation." (Olga K., Ger/US)

⇨ "When Americans introduced me to their friends, I was accepted right away as their friend as well. They would immediately ask questions and pay attention to me. It felt good, but in Germany that rarely happens." (Susanne C., Ger/US)

⇨ "Before I left the US, my friends at the university gave me a wonderful album as a farewell present. In it were lots of photos and comments that made me feel very special and welcome. But now when I read those comments I wonder. To be honest, I never felt very close to any of them. Yet, in the album they said so many good things about me and seemed to appreciate me so much. Yes, it feels good. Here in Germany we might never make the effort to show it that much. Here it's small things: a birthday present with a lot of thought behind it; or being there when needed, listening, talking, including talking about the friendship itself." (Olga K., Ger/US)

⇨ "American friends don't keep in close contact, but if you call half a year later and say that you are in the neighborhood, they'll be enthusiastic and may say, 'Come over and stay overnight if you can.' It's a different kind of friendship." (Anna K., Ger/US)

⇨ "Germans often complain that Americans are very superficial and can't maintain friendships. In the beginning I also thought that way. Americans are friendly to everyone and they use the same friendly tone toward everyone, plus they do certain things which we Germans interpret as a sign of friendship. So we think, 'Oh, that's a new friend and it will be a lasting friendship.' And then we are disappointed because it doesn't happen. So we label that behavior superficial. Actually the real reason is that we misinterpret their signs and actions. Many of those words or gestures are signs of a general friendliness or politeness, directed at anybody. It is not reserved for a special group of friends." (Olga K., Ger/US)

⇨ "I have lived in the US for fifty years. Looking at my own close relationships over the years, they were always with people who were born overseas. American friendship suffers from a superficiality regarding the expression of true feelings." (Ingo R., Ger/US)

Similar to the German experience in the US, Germans living in Chinese society felt a lack of personal closeness between friends, in part due to the fact that Chinese friendships are primarily group relationships. However, they also observed that Chinese friendships entailed more mutual help than is customary in Germany and that they were lasting even without ongoing nurturing.

⇨ *"I see Chinese friendship as a relationship between people who belong to groups that share a common experience, like classmates or university students, not persons they individually chose. Many continue to see each other on a more or less regular basis and these relationships remain for life. The Chinese may not like all of their classmates but they accept each other as they are. They have a group feeling and they don't see it as distasteful to do things together. Chinese classmates also offer each other more help, such as taking someone to the airport. In Germany that is less common. In Germany our friendships are more individual. We need to like our friends and we select them according to their personality." (Susanne B., Ger/Tw)*

⇨ *"Within their in-group the Chinese are there for each other, which is nice, but their curiosity and interest in the other also provides fodder for social gossip. If there is interest we Germans want the interest to be genuine, not tied to an ulterior motive. But in Chinese relationships you can't distinguish the true from the fake. He may be interested in me because he wants something from me: you pay in and you pay out. Often it's a quid pro quo. But people may also be nice without motivation, or be nice to strengthen the group feeling. The only place where I experienced something similar to the Chinese group feeling was in the German military, where there exists the command and a law that soldiers are to honor camaraderie, independent of whether people like each other or not. Even though the camaraderie is required because soldiers need to depend on each other, it ends up that they also help each other in daily life and it feels good." (Oliver K., Ger/PRC)*

⇨ *"My husband suffers from my many Chinese 'friends' here in Berlin. They come with a bottle of expensive whiskey and then they want to stay for a whole day or later ask us for some major favors. For us friendship has no agenda or purpose." (Friederike G., Ger/Tw)*

⇨ *"The Chinese can remain great friends even if they do not see each other for ten years. If all of a sudden someone comes back and says 'I went to school with you,' there is an immediate bond, strong enough to feel an obligation to help each other. In Germany that is not so. Either we are in regular contact or we are not. If we don't hear from each other for a couple of years, it means that there is no interest and therefore no friendship." (Elena M., Ger/Tw)*

⇨ *"Chinese friends continue to be friends for as long as they live. A Chinese may be a hundred years old and still have some kindergarten friends. In Germany it's more out sight, out of touch. German friendship is deeper and closer but Chinese friendship is longer lasting." (Susanne B., Ger/Tw)*

Thoughtful conversations, exchanging inner thoughts and personal feelings, which are such an important part of German closeness, seemed to be largely absent in Chinese friendships.

⇨ *"I have made friends here in Taiwan and it's a warm relationship, but it's different from my relationship with German friends. In Germany we share feelings and talk about problems or issues. We know how the other feels inside. Here in Taiwan you don't talk much about feelings or problems. It's usually about light and positive things." (Karin S., Ger/Tw)*

⇨ *"I noticed that when a group of Chinese friends get together, maybe several or all will talk at the same time! It appears to be an interaction process, more of a group feeling, a physical togetherness as a form of relating. It's not about discussing topics or ideas." (Karl M., Ger/Tw)*

⇨ *"It's hard for me to make Taiwanese male friends, because I can't enjoy their conversations. They mostly talk about food, money, or who is good at this or that. I like thinking conversations, discussions on topics, but the Chinese find those boring." (Manfred M., Ger/Tw)*

⇨ *"I had been very much looking forward to seeing a Chinese college friend of mine for the first time after nearly twenty years. But when we finally met, he suggested that we spend our time together visiting a museum in the area. So there was no reacquainting ourselves with each other. Not even over lunch, when the conversation was more about the food than about our lives. It left me feeling disappointed and empty." (Amanda K., Ger/Tw)*

Family relationships

As is true for friendships, German closeness within the family must entail a true emotional connection, be freely chosen, and leave ample freedom and space for the individual. The mere fact of being related by blood does not make for closeness.

> "In Germany we don't feel forced about blood relationships. We emphasize the individual and his liberation from the family and others. If our relatives are nice, fine. But if we don't like them we don't go to visit them. In China according to what I have observed, the obligation persists, even if you don't like them. In Germany we are in a relationship only if we care." (Gisela W., Ger/PRC)

> "In my family we often go for walks or hikes together on the weekends. Other families get together for Sunday afternoon coffee. But for many Germans it is very important to feel that they nurture their family relationships out of their own free will, that it not be an obligation or duty." (Lisa K., Ger/US)

> "I am grandmother by choice! I want to bring things that interest me into my grandchildren's lives: gardening, needlepoint, reading. I also always remind myself that they are not my children, that they are my son's children. So I keep my mouth shut when I feel the urge to give parenting advice." (Helga B., Ger/US)

Relationships between couples, whether as husband and wife or unmarried long-term partners, are expected to be close. This is the ideal but when this closeness is lacking, people usually separate or divorce. Those who do stay together tend to have a good relationship.

> "I wrote my Ph.D. dissertation on women and love. In Germany love is very important for men and women. For young people love aims for a good partnership with trust, independence and autonomy that allows them to fulfill their life theme which refers to a strong interest or interests that are usually developed prior to marriage. They may look to achieve self-fulfillment through the job, or for a while through child raising, but, whatever the life theme is, it should

be compatible with that of the partner. Marriage is seen as a piece of paper issued by the state authorities. Many people have children before getting married or don't get married at all, partially in rebellion against authority, an attitude hailing from the '68 generation. But partnerships without getting married are also an expression of a preference for authenticity over outer form. What matters is the love, the commitment. Couples who live together don't just make do; it means their relationship is good, because if the relationship is not good for a partner it's legitimate to leave." (Lisa K., Ger/US)

"Love, that is emotional closeness, is hugely important. It belongs to life. It is part of our European tradition as we know it from German literature and theatre which for centuries have used love as a central theme. Think of all the theater plays in which young women do not want to succumb to their parents' choice of spouse but instead make their own choices so that heart and mind are in line. I don't think Asian or Chinese literature ever produced such a wealth of literature on this single topic." (Olga K., Ger/US)

"Expectations for marriage or partnership are high in Germany. If you are not content you are likely to separate. It's about honesty and closeness." (Steven B., Ger/Tw)

"In my group of thirty- to thirty-five-year olds, only two out of eighteen are married, but the fact that there is a huge percentage of singles does not mean that these people all like to be alone. Many single women have just given up looking for a partner. They haven't figured out how to have both a career and a family. Also, once you are single and beyond a certain age it is hard to get out of it. ." (Manuela M., Ger/US)

Parent-child relationships were not a major topic in my conversations with Germans. Though parents aim to prepare their children for independence, hoping to make them strong and able to make their own decisions, the relationships with their children may be close, in a way similar to other close relationships. However, intergenerational conflicts between the young and their parents are also common.

"I tell my parents a lot, and after the year away in the US my relationship with them is even better. But many of my schoolmates of the lower grades didn't

want to communicate with their parents, maybe even try to evade them. But now my high school classmates also generally seem to have pretty good relationships with their parents." (Julia B., Ger/US)

"I have a good relationship with my parents and I tell them when I am sad or happy, pretty much everything. On the whole we Germans may not be very emotionally expressive, but I think we are more emotional within the family than people are here in Taiwan. In the Chinese family there is no place for thank yous or words of praise, and they don't know what goes on in the other person's life. However, an American family, provided it's a fully functioning one, seems to be more verbally expressive than a German family. There are more I-love-yous, kisses and hugs between parents and children, and also lots of 'dear,' 'honey' and 'thank yous' between couples." (Karin S., Ger/Tw)

Some of my German respondents noted that American inclusivity also seems to apply to family relationships. Even when the particular personal relationships may not be especially close, Americans, more than Germans, maintain contacts with family members and do so over long distances. They are also more apt to accept an outsider into their midst.

⇒ "Since Americans go where the job takes them, families are more scattered and may not be able to see each other that often. But I admire how they drive long distances over the weekend, just to see relatives." (Hannelore G., Ger/US)

⇒ "I liked the sense of family that I perceived among the Americans I came to know in California. By travelling far to be together, at least once or twice a year, they modeled for me a new importance of family. In Germany we don't try to keep the larger family together." (Anna K., Ger/US)

⇒ "I think American families are more likely to take an outsider into their family than a German family would. When I was an exchange student in the US, a couple of my high school classmates lived with friends because they had problems with their own parents. Perhaps they came from dysfunctional families or could not get along with a stepfather. So the parents of the friend took them in and more or less accepted them as an additional family member. One of those boys sent me a photo inscribed 'my brother and me.'" (Julia B., Ger/US)

⇨ *"My first host family in the US was terrible. But luckily I had made a friend in school during that first month so when my sponsoring organization wanted to send me to another place, I cried and called my friend. She told me that they were coming over to pick me up, and that I could spend the night at her place. But then they decided that I could live with them for entire ten remaining months. It definitely was not because of the money, because the host families receive only minimal compensation for hosting an exchange student. It was great for me, but in Germany I would not feel good staying with my friends for more than a night or two." (Kirsten B., Ger/US)*

The topic of Chinese family closeness elicited strong reactions in my German conversation partners, especially in those with a Chinese spouse, pointing to what—in their minds—German family closeness is not. As members of Chinese families, they missed personal freedom and alone time, close emotional ties between husbands and wives, as well as meaningful family conversations.

⇨ *"My (Chinese) husband is very filial. He respects his parents and when his father calls he goes without a moment's hesitation. I find it difficult to accept that the father-son relationship has priority over the husband-wife relationship. I also find it difficult to accept that family members, especially elders, can just appear in our home any time without asking and without advance notice. They don't ask whether we have time." (Elena M., Ger/Tw)*

⇨ *"My husband is Chinese and I have lived in Taiwan for almost fifty years. I see a lot of Chinese marriages that are primarily economic arrangements and agreements to carry on the family line. For a few there is love, for some it's more like a good friendship, but for many it's parallel lives, with a lot of affairs. That is normal. For example, one of my husband's friends, now in his sixties, lives in one apartment, his wife in another, both in the same building. They have no close relationship. Another of our friends is a man in his fifties whose wife lives with their two children in the US. He has a girlfriend here whom he brings along to social occasions. Initially it was very discreet, but now we all know though his wife does not. When we had conflicts in our own marriage, we could never talk about it. My husband is not communicative so that in the end I just gave in. For me this was a big problem, but for him it may not have been important. After we were first married and still lived in Germany I* knew everything he did, but after moving here he would go out to eat with his friends in the evenings at least three times a week. That was difficult for me, and at the time I resented it, because sometimes I would have liked to have gone along. But then our relationship was not bad and I gradually accepted it. Nowadays, I don't ask him where he goes and he no longer asks me where I go." (Ursula L., Ger/Tw)

⇒ "It strikes me how well my (Chinese) wife's family attends to me here. Recently when my wife went on a business trip to the US for a few weeks, an aunt called me suggesting that we go some place. Then an uncle called and said, 'You are home alone, let's do something.' I see this is as a mixed blessing. I am happy that they care about me, but I also would like to have some time to be alone. In Germany we don't want to impose on people and overdo the togetherness. Still, I want to learn that Chinese value of families spending time together. It is nice to see that they enjoy it." (Heino M., Ger/Tw)

⇒ "Chinese family closeness requires constant availability and there is no alone time. To me it's smothering, intrusive and draining. I have managed to maintain a positive image within my husband's (Chinese) family and I want to keep it that way. I won't be open and direct with them and I prefer to remain the outsider. I don't really know my sisters-in-law as persons, and they don't know me either." (Elena M., Ger/Tw)

⇒ "Initially we lived with my (Chinese) wife's parents, which worked well enough, though we never managed to have real conversations. For my parents and grandparents mealtime was a good time for conversation, talking about things that were of interest to us. This concept is not common here. There is a curious mixture of cordiality and superficiality in the family. Provided that I don't do some terrible thing, I am part of the family. It's fine to sit there brain-dead. And as long as I say it tastes good and smile, I am okay and accepted." (Hans B., Ger/Tw)

⇒ "Chinese families easily separate for years. One wife has gone to get a Ph.D. in Germany and comes home only for the summer. Her husband is here in Taiwan, but their children are raised by an uncle and aunt. In another family the husband works in China, while their two young daughters are overseas; one lives in a host family in America and the other lives in Canada. I would *want to be around to know what friends my children have and how they are doing. Chinese parents work and are into making money so that their children can study some place. For us our personal relationships and staying together is more important than making money." (Elena M., Ger/Tw)*

"When our children were little my husband was always there for the family giving up certain professional opportunities. So I am happy that he now has a chance to broaden his career, though we have mixed feelings knowing that it means separating for a year. My husband will stay in Taiwan, where we have lived for three years now, but I and my daughter will go back to Germany so she can finish high school there. I find it interesting that Chinese and Germans react very differently to my telling them about our situation. For the Germans it's a big thing, for the Chinese nothing at all. Marriage has a different meaning here." (Marie G., Ger/Tw)

Let a stranger be a stranger

Given the importance that opening the inner self plays in German relationships, there is relatively little interest in light, casual relationships. Occasionally a short encounter may have a profound impact and lead to a lasting relationship, but generally Germans do not anticipate nor desire that an acquaintance, even a prolonged one, will turn into a friend. Equally important is the German understanding of politeness as granting the other the courtesy of privacy by not being intrusive (*aufdringlich*).

Germans are content to let a stranger remain a stranger. Not wanting to be intrusive and lacking a tradition of small talk, a stranger starting a conversation is generally understood as a signal that the person needs or wants something.

"Our first reaction when a stranger approaches us is to assume that he wants something from us. If you want to talk with me about a certain topic, fine, but we don't have such a thing as light conversations without purpose." (Lisa K., Ger/US)

"Germans don't talk to strangers. It's not fear, it's deeper. It's not done. It would be considered impolite, intrusive, too curious. When I talk to someone, I open myself. We have no other way but to be direct and honest, but if you open

yourself to someone you don't know, you need some self-protection." (Nikki Z., Ger/Europe)

"For me it is a matter of respect for people. I can enjoy meeting strangers under certain circumstances, for example when the gathering is for the specific purpose of meeting new people. But in other contexts I would never go up to someone and talk to them, because I would not like them to do it to me. We don't want to bother you, impose on you." (Andre B., Ger/US)

"Not only is it awkward to start a conversation with a stranger we also find it awkward to break it off. We don't have the custom of saying something like, 'Nice to meet you, see you some time,' or at a party 'I think I'll get a drink' and leave without coming back. So we start out with a distance as an initial attitude and need a long warm up period." (Ernst K., Ger/Europe)

"When people hesitate to initiate contact with a stranger some of it maybe shyness or not knowing what to say. In Germany we have weak established signals—e.g., no social smile—to let the other know whether an approach is wanted or not, so there can also be a fear of possible rejection. Maybe that person does not want me to talk to him. But luckily we Germans are also more honest and direct than others. So you can always ask, 'May I come over and talk to you about how to raise bees, how to grow better vegetables or about what is involved in owning a horse?'" (Christina G., Ger/US)

Of course, Germany also has its extroverts.

"Where I come from people can ride in the same train compartment for five hours and never say a word to each other. But my mother starts talking to people before the train is out of the station." (Baerbel I., Ger/US)

"In my social circles people do talk to strangers. My father talks to everybody and so does my mother. And so do I. I talk a lot to people I don't know, even in the subway." (Ehrhard A., Ger/Asia)

Both Chinese and Americans have difficulty recognizing and adjusting to the prevailing German form of distance and politeness toward strangers and people they don't know well. "Germans are like machines," one Chinese respondent said, while an American described the Germans as "the coldest people on earth". Because in the German sense "meeting someone" refers to something more than a brief encounter, Germans have their own difficulties with the American quick familiarity and friendly inclusiveness.

⇨ *"I react strongly to the American custom of seeking friendly relationships with everyone, including with people who happen to be with you in the bathroom. They do so by filling the sonar void with idle chatter. Can't I let a stranger be a stranger? There is no need to establish a personal relationship with strangers. Maybe someone wants to be left alone." (Manuela M., Ger/US)*

⇨ *"When I lived in the US, one of our neighbors often came over at night, which I thought was annoying. Also, much to my disdain, I found that after a few visits to a certain boutique or restaurant, the owners started to ask me questions which were too personal for my taste. I was there to spend money for products or services and I would like my privacy to be respected. In my view, it is none of the lingerie boutique owner's business what I do for work." (Andre B., Ger/US)*

⇨ *"Americans seem to have a different private sphere. For example, someone I don't really know well may tell me that his mom died. For me my family or my illness would belong to my private sphere. Not so in America. Talk about illnesses is common. As a German I don't do that." (Rainer M., Ger/US)*

⇨ *"Even though Americans may share certain personal information, at the same time they seem to fear revealing any weaknesses. They don't bare their souls the way we do. When a relationship keeps a large area private there is little risk in entering a new one. But we Germans are basically very open, so there is more risk." (Marie W., Ger/US)*

After realizing that some of the American quick familiarity is form and cannot be taken at face value, Germans living in the US generally do come to like and appreciate the American friendliness and inclusiveness.

⇨ *"It took some getting used to the American friendliness, but now I like it and it doesn't appear to be hypocritical. Their smile may not be an invitation to a deep friendship, but it is more pleasant to live in a society with a lot of friendliness than in one full of grumpy people. When I lived in the US I derived a lot* of pleasure by being surrounded by attentive and friendly people who respect each other." (Ilse F., Ger/US)

⇨ "I like the way people deal with each other in the US. Their openness makes it easier to get to know people. Even though I sometimes do miss the German directness, overall I find this aspect of American life very positive and I will miss it in Germany when I go back." (Katharina N., Ger/US)

⇨ "I noticed that people in America are alert to help you. I could do it here, but we feel it would be intrusive, unless the person signals first. It's not a matter of lacking interest. You just don't get involved unless you are specifically asked." (Inge L., Ger/US)

⇨ "When a teaching assistant in my [American] university course asked me whether I wanted her to introduce me to the chair of the department, I told her 'No, it's not necessary.' The concept of being introduced was a strange concept to me. Why would someone want to introduce me to someone I did not know? Now that I know better—I think my reaction was funny. But I was not familiar with introducing people to others and even now after having lived in the US, I would not be as quick to introduce others." (Olga K., Ger/US)

Though the Chinese are known for their politeness, especially toward authority figures and others they deem to be important, they do not extend that politeness to everyone. Germans living in Chinese societies became familiar with both Chinese politeness and indifference toward strangers.

⇨ "It seems to me that the Chinese would rather want less communication with strangers than more. Unless they see some business or benefit in such a contact, they don't care about others." (Andre B., Ger/US/Asia)

⇨ "Here in Taiwan, the Chinese tell me that I should be more cautious about interacting with strangers. For them people talking to strangers are suspect. People need an introduction from a go-between." (Manfred M., Ger/Tw)

Germans commented extensively on the Chinese lack of concern for others in the public sphere and their disinterest in the common good, that impersonal kind of caring for the well-being of the society at large that is an important aspect of German culture. Chapter Four, "The World Around Us," will deal will this topic in detail.

From stranger to friend

The German reluctance to reach out to newcomers and their need to get to know a person slowly over time before extending friendship makes it difficult for outsiders to make friends. This holds true for both foreigners in Germany and for Germans when they move into a new and unfamiliar social environment.

> *"I once went to an aerobics class, where there were all sorts of little groups which made it difficult for me to have any contact. I think that is normal. If I brought a friend to an existing class or group, I'd take her under my wing, but we don't do that for people we don't know. People generally don't introduce themselves to strangers and others don't introduce them." (Ilse F., Ger/US)*

> *"A group of people who know each other will not pay attention to a newcomer, an outsider. If there is a clique of mothers with children on the playground, a new mother with a child does not belong and will not easily become part of the group." (Lisa K., Ger/US)*

Knowing the difficulty of creating a new circle of friends makes Germans less mobile in their lives.

> *"We Germans do not move much, partially because we are more attached to our homes than Americans, but also because we know that it won't be easy to get to know people in a new place." (Olga K., Ger/US)*

> *"Our politicians complain that we are not mobile enough. And it's true—we don't move easily for a job. It's because we like to stay close to family and friends and often we are anchored in our communities by engaging in various community activities." (Marie G., Ger/Tw)*

> *"For us it's difficult to make friends. We don't make them lightly, and once we have friends they are part of the reason why we don't like to move away." (Hanne S., Ger/US)*

So how does one go about getting to know people in Germany? From the above it is clear that the American way of engaging in friendly small talk, smiling and presenting oneself as an enthusiastic and optimistic person is not an effective way. Nor is a beer tent at an Octoberfest or during carnival a suitable venue to make connections. Though such occasions may be fun for the moment, that kind of German outgoingness, aided by alcohol, is unlikely to lead to a lasting relationship.

A more appropriate approach would be to engage in purposeful conversations or activities, which is why my effort to find Germans to interview for this book was so successful. Often we sat together for many hours during which time people were willing to share their ideas and happy to think along with me regarding the various topics at hand. This kind of conversation involved no small talk, no risk of rejection, and no commitment, just the joy of exchanging thoughts and ideas, and if by chance minds and souls did meet, the prospect of a friendship.

> *"For us friendships tend to start on the intellectual level. The emotional part comes afterwards." (Karin S., Ger/Tw)*

Doing

Work as expression of the inner self

Though a few Germans stated that the job defined them as a person, for most it was less about what they did, than about how they did their work. The old mantra from German grandmothers "If something is worth doing, do it well." still seems to be alive and well. In my postwar small rural family in northern Germany, the worst I could have done as a child would have been to do things haphazardly or start a task without completing it.

Pride in quality and workmanship, in line with Germany's traditional educational and apprentice systems, means that the majority of people stay with the kind of work they were trained for for the rest of their lives. With the quality of work as an expression of the inner self, motivation comes from within. It is less dependent on praise or money and more on finding joy in having done something well and achieved a goal. However, aiming for perfection also tends to generate a good amount of stress.

"I work for myself, not for recognition or for the boss, which gives me self confidence and motivation." (Jakob D., Ger/US)

"As for me, I have an intense urge to be perfect or at least very good at whatever I do." (Ingo R., Ger/US)

"My stress at work comes from taking too much time for everything in order to be perfect. My bar of perfection is high and may not be achievable, but it is worth pursuing." (Olga K., Ger/US)

⇨ *"I feel we are more stressed out by work than Americans because of our attitude toward work. We want to do it well, and are stressed out when we fall short of our own expectations. Americans are less harsh on themselves, more willing to experiment, more forgiving. Their ideals don't have to be reached one hundred percent. Just getting started is already a noble thing." (Anna K., Ger/US)*

Given this cultural background, Germans were struck by the different work environments and working styles they observed among Americans and Chinese. In the American working world, Germans noted more of an emphasis on practical training and a varied work experience rather than on broad knowledge and formal education; also more on speed and measurable results than quality. Moreover, they felt that when solving problems Americans let themselves be guided to a greater extent by intuition than Germans, skimping on planning and paying less attention to the broader implications of their projects.

⇨ *"In Germany factual knowledge is super important, more so than in the US. You need to know your stuff. For us it's the product quality that counts, not the service, or whether the salesperson smiles at me." (Manfred B., Ger/US)*

⇨ *"Germany stresses broadness of knowledge. Formal education is valued and even practical training programs include a general knowledge and an education in the arts. Americans put broadness into doing, working in many different jobs over the course of their lives." (Olga K., Ger/US)*

⇨ *"In Germany I used to look forward to going to work, but in the US I had a hard time finding a balance between the quality I expect from myself and the quantity that others demand from me. One time, when I was hired by a California*

company that sold services, I was told I'd have to tell potential customers who were looking for somebody to fix their specific problem that we had just the right person available who could do their job. The reality was that we did not have anybody and only would start searching for somebody after we had a request. The day they told me that I quit. That's my integrity, my honesty."
(Jakob D., Ger/US)

⇨ *"Americans dwell more on what to <u>do</u> about problems. In Germany people discuss the problems in detail without immediately considering how to solve them. The emphasis is on understanding the problem fully and it's our mentality to express it negatively, thinking in detail about all the possible complications that might arise. Here in the US the emphasis is on what needs to be done, how to make things better. It is more constructive. And yet, overall I think the level of productivity and results is pretty much the same in both countries. When it comes to accounting for mistakes I don't see much difference between Germany and the US. In both places people are relatively open to admitting mistakes, but the manner of dealing with them may be different. Americans have a better way of presenting them. When admitting mistakes they may at the same time present a new proposal, a way out or another way to move forward. We Germans tend to present our mistakes in a more devastating and pessimistic way, and without offering alternatives." (Rainer M., Ger /US)*

In the Chinese work environment Germans encountered a far more authoritative climate than they were used to at home. As a result the Chinese workers seemed to be less committed to their tasks and take less responsibility for their actions. Personal relationships also played a much larger role than in Germany.

⇨ *"Here in Taiwan applying pressure is the tool of choice to motivate workers. Teachers or bosses yell or shame people to make them perform. I am a member of a local choir, in which the leader frequently yells at people and puts them down. It has an effect. In Germany I am used to more positive motivation. In my view the best motivation is to take the individual seriously, so that he'll try again and perhaps find the fun in the work or pursuit. In Taiwan people don't seem to know about positive motivation." (Karl M., Ger/Tw)*

⇨ *"In Taiwan I saw that people are able to live their lives in uniforms. From a young age they are trained to obey, to accept and adjust. The work environment requires total loyalty to the boss. Don't state your point of view or make suggestions, because you must trust that the boss or management are always right. Anything less than full trust and loyalty is understood as criticism. To me it felt stifling." (Elena M., Ger/Tw)*

⇨ *"When working for others the Chinese maintain a narrow focus on the assigned task spending little time and thought considering what might be beneficial to the overall quality of the work or the well-being of the organization they are working for. Often this is due to caution and fear of being considered ambitious, which would affect their immediate relationships in the organization. People with ideas and ambition tend to be seen as a threat." (Ursula L., Ger/Tw)*

⇨ *"We internalize values, the Chinese do not. For example, a Chinese will not feel bad if nobody finds out that he has done something bad. They only get upset when others, possibly the boss, find out. For us, nobody tells us what to do. We take responsibility and we feel guilty if we don't give it our best." (Manfred M., Ger/Tw)*

The feel of life

The German feel of life is characterized by a certain seriousness, a preference for quiet pleasures, and a sense of yearning that adds a certain melancholic quality to German culture. The feeling of well-being is more about emotional depth than highs and therefore quite different from the American vitality with its enthusiasm and passion.

Mutual perceptions

Americans often perceive the German feel of life in negative terms. They fault Germans for not smiling, for lack of passion, for being pessimists and spending too much time brooding about serious issues. American jokes about the German lack of humor abound. One of these jokes asks, "Have you seen the section in the library on German humor? It's all empty shelves!"

⇨ *The Germans do a lot of introspection. They may sit there rather quietly, dwelling on the negatives in this world, a little bit depressed, maybe angry, probably a bit critical and disillusioned with it all. They convey a sense of feeling weighed down by something. And even if they are not depressed, they may take a deep sigh and when you ask them why they sighed, they say, 'Oh, I was just breathing.' There is a yearning and a melancholic quality to it."* (Mark R., US/Ger)

The Chinese impressions of the German frame of mind are similar.

⇨ *"The Germans are just too serious. They look grim when they walk down the street burying their heads in their raincoats and frowning all the way home. And I swear, even the babies in the strollers frown."* (Cheng A.L., f, Tw/Ger)

⇨ *"Germans always want things to be perfect, but that attitude collides with living life. I think the Germans think too much about the meaning of life. We Chinese don't think as much. We are much more practically inclined."* (Hsieh S. H., m, Tw/Ger)

On their part, my German respondents generally did not feel comfortable with the American display of enthusiasm and excitement. To them the American cheerfulness appeared to be more of a social requirement rather than a sense of well-being coming from the heart, while they perceived the Chinese sense of well-being to depend primarily on large boisterous get-togethers, food, and, above all, on making money. To Germans it looked as if neither the Americans nor the Chinese have or take the time for leisure and quiet enjoyment.

⇨ *"Americans look more cheerful in daily life, but it's expected of them, which means that much of it is form, manners, a façade. In Germany we do not need to pretend to be happy. Americans also tend to praise others to the skies, but by doing so they put themselves down. One of my friends told me several times that I had certain traits she admired that she hoped would rub off on her. Though saying so might have been mere politeness and modesty, I think it was also a lack of feeling good about herself. To me putting others on a pedestal reflects a lack of self-confidence."* (Olga K., Ger/US)

⇨ *"In my surroundings here in the Northwest of the United States, I have met many people who are so stressed out that they have a hard time to enjoy life."* (Else B., Ger/US)

⇨ *"During a vacation with my American girl friend I noticed that she didn't have much patience to enjoy just sitting quietly on the beach. She always needed to be doing something. It makes me think that in Germany we not only separate work and leisure more than in America, we are also better at enjoying leisure. It's why vacations are so important to us." (Manfred B., Ger/US)*

⇨ *"I think the highs of joy for the Chinese rest with having children, food and money." (Heino M., Ger/Tw)*

⇨ *"The rate of depression among university students in Taiwan is said to be about 25%, which is very high. I find that very strange, because for me my time as a student was a happy time. I derived a lot of satisfaction from the process of mental development. Maybe the depressed state of mind of Chinese students has something to do with their being so strongly focused on making money. Most of my students don't look for meaning in what they study or do. In Germany the individual self has more responsibility. We need to come up with a very specific way to realize ourselves, to become who we want to become." (Steven B., Ger/Tw)*

Seriousness, quietude and pleasures of the mind

Germans generally prefer serious and quiet forms of enjoyment, often related to thoughts and inner feelings. Generally, their sense of well-being is not expressed through external cheerfulness, nor does it depend heavily on monetary success. For many it is more important to look within and seek a broader context for their feelings. Several common concepts describe aspects of the German cultural mood. Though these expressions can be explained in another language by using several words to describe the general meaning, chances are that the feeling that goes along with the words is lost, or at least is not fully conveyed in translation. A few examples are as follows.

Gemuetlichkeit: A cozy, warm, comfortable place

Geborgenheit: A perfect mixture of feeling acceptance, trust, love, warmth, protection and security

Sehnsucht: An intense yearning for something far off and undefinable

Fernweh: A longing for far away places

Wanderlust: A strong longing to travel

Georg Haider, a German composer living in France, described the Germans as "more somber, heavier, less light" than the people in Paris. "Germany is more serious, like a solemn piece of music. But the seriousness is part of me." [4] My German interviewees agreed that their sense of well-being was a rather quiet form of contentedness, often generated by enjoying a *Gemuetlichkeit* in a certain place or by a feeling of *Geborgenheit* when spending time with family and friends.

> *"The German feeling of well-being is not a light hearted gaiety. To be jolly and lighthearted we might need alcohol." (Heike V., Ger/US)*

> *"I was born in Venezuela but I grew up with my adoptive parents in Germany. When I spent a year in Venezuela as au pair (a person providing household help in return for living in the family), I initially thought I'd never want to leave. The people were so much more alive, meaning more emotional and fun loving than in Germany. It seemed like a good fit for my genes. But with time it got on my nerves. In Germany we don't laugh as much and in comparison to Latin Americans Germans appear cold. We are not as party happy, we don't go out as much, and our enjoyment of life is quieter. Over time I found the Venezuelan boisterous life over the top and I looked forward to returning to Germany." (Gudrun S., Ger/US)*

> *"I feel really well when I am fine and the others I know are also fine, when I am surrounded by people I love, and have friends with whom I can talk until three o'clock in the morning. Then I feel a wonderful Geborgenheit." (Marion B., Ger /PRC)*

> *"Many of my highs and lows come with and on the job. But sitting at home with a book is pure well-being." (Christina G., Ger/US)*

My German respondents also spoke of the importance of the wider surrounding, human and nonhuman, for feeling well. This might mean enjoying the flowers in their back yards, a beautiful urban environment or the great outdoors. And it included the knowledge that others around them were also well and that there were no huge disparities of well-being in the wider society. Traveling and understanding the world has also long been an important source of pleasure for the German mind. For some it lies at the very core of feeling alive.

"I have a lot of friends who, when they speak about their feelings, talk a lot about how important it is to them to feel a harmony between their self and their surrounding. 'Surrounding' here means other people, society and nature. For me, too, my sense of well-being comes with living in a cared for environment, one that is beautiful, natural and healthy. It also comes from knowing that everybody else around me can live well too. The social differences should not be too great." (Lisa K., Ger/US)

"Germans have long had a yearning for far away places. Some of this Fernweh arose with the Romantic Period [an artistic and intellectual movement in Europe from circa 1800 to 1850] but it is also part of a long tradition of young craftsmen being expected to travel the country and apprentice with different masters. That seems to be coming back now. I love to see these craftsmen, for example carpenters, walk around in their traditional outfits. In the past Northern Germany also had a lot of seafarers and the emigrant ships left from northern Germany. So the far away was a part of daily life at least in that part of the country. Many Germans are intrigued with the exotic and we all like maps. Give me an atlas and I will be occupied the whole afternoon. Here in the US there is very little available in the way of good maps. The interest is not there. Perhaps the lack of interest in foreign language in America is part of it." (Regine F., Ger/US)

"For me living means searching and learning. I want to understand the world. When I was young I roamed the world. Now I do my roaming intellectually." (Barbara S., Ger/US/Tw)

"If you have lived your whole life sitting on one chair facing one direction, you don't know what is behind you and beside you. If you turn around you see more. You may not like what you see but it means being alive because you learn something new." (Nikki Z., Ger/Europe)

A melancholic quality

As evident from some of the difficult-to-translate words above, there is a melancholic quality to the German cultural mood, a feeling of yearning for something. It might be a kind of thoughtful sadness, thinking or dreaming of something good or worthwhile that is out of reach, at least for the moment, or it might be nostalgia for the past. Many of the traditional German folk songs sing both of a yearning to go out into the world as well as of dreaming of home and loved ones left behind. To some of my German conversation partners this wistfulness was a good feeling, to others it was not. Yet all seemed to agree that melancholy is part of German life.

> "Germans are in love with yearning and melancholy. We make it easy to be melancholic by putting the goal out of reach." (Erhard A., Ger/Asia)

> "While I lived in Hawaii I didn't actually miss the fall as a season, but somehow I did miss the melancholy that goes with it. I remember several of my friends and family in Germany writing about how the fog was starting to creep up late in the morning and early in the afternoon, how the cold was marching its way up the sleeves. And then I could almost grasp this strange, end-time feeling. Now back in Germany I am more aware than usual of the changes in the trees, in temperature, in the air. And I love it. I love the crisp air, the light melancholy and the wistfulness that makes you anticipate the long, dark winter days, and therefore appreciate even more a sun beam on a leaf or the sounds of the migrating geese in the sky." (Olga K., Ger/US)

> "I relish the fall with its colorful and falling leaves in Germany. It's a time that puts some people into a melancholic mood. Melancholy belongs to German life but in my view it is not a warm and fuzzy feeling. In fact, to me it's nothing positive." (Marie G., Ger/Tw)

> "Melancholy implies a yearning and to me it implies some sadness. I don't use the word and it doesn't speak to me." (Inge L., Ger/US)

Meckern and Jammern (M&J)

Germans like to dream of an ideal world (*eine heile Welt*), a world or society that is orderly, good and safe for everyone, which has the effect that they are quick to point to perceived shortcomings when things are not what they should or could be. Complaining, in the form of *meckern* ("griping, complaining") and *jammern* ("whining, bemoaning") is very much part of German daily life, so much so, that I have coined the expression "M&J" for this phenomenon. When I asked my German conversation partners about it, every single one of them agreed that Germans did indeed engage in a great deal of M&J. Much of it is directed at social conditions, because even though compared to the US, China, or Taiwan, Germany has an outstanding social service system, it rarely seems to meet German expectations. And yet, the M&J habit is less serious and less gloomy than a foreigner might assume. In fact, sometimes the complaining and whining creates a bond between people. It might even serve as a German substitute for small talk between strangers!

> "People complain and whine because they have inflated expectations. They don't know how privileged they are." (Jonas K., Ger/Tw)

> "We Germans do a lot of whining, especially when there are some reductions in our social benefits. We are spoilt when it comes to vacation time and our social safety net and people whine over any suggestion that our six to eight week annual vacation might be shortened. Sometimes I feel I have to remind people that we have a pretty good social system. When I take that role and point it out to my fellow Germans, they may even agree and say, 'Gee, you are right.'" (Olga K., Ger/US)

> "In Germany people always seem to need a problem when they talk with another person. Complaining and whining is a leisure activity. Much of the time the problems they talk about are not big—it's mostly about little things." (Ilse F., Ger/US)

> "Yes, we Germans do engage in a lot of griping and complaining and we are obsessed with negatives. It's almost a kind of superstition, fearing that if we anticipate an optimal outcome it won't happen. So if we gripe and expect the worst, a good or better outcome is so much more enjoyable. And yes, we are pessimists, though at least in my view our pessimism does not necessarily reduce our joy of life." (Ulla M., Ger/US)

> "In the US when something weighs on their minds people tend to be silent. In Germany we express it and when we do we may exaggerate. It's not that we are

in a bad mood when we gripe and complain. It's that our griping and whining has entertainment value and also makes people feel better afterwards. Some do it for a psychological cleansing effect. I go hiking instead!" (Christina G., Ger/US)

"In Germany we zero in on what is not working, and we are less prone to comment on good things. What I think is funny is that many young people are aware that Germans complain a lot and they complain about it! But we don't try to change it. Okay, now I'm complaining about it too! I think our free and accepted expression of griping and complaining may actually feed on itself." (Olga K., Ger/US)

"Even though our griping and complaining is not intimate—it usually deals with objective matters and is generalized—sometimes it can be a bridge to the other, a means to talk to people we don't know." (Nikki Z., Ger/Europe)

⇨ *"Germans in America often come to like the American light and cheerful interactions in daily life, but some of us wonder whether our own complaining and whining might not be a better way because it allows us to vent feelings and frustrations. If it has the same effect as the antidepressants that are prescribed in America to a huge number of people, ours might be a healthier way." (Olga K., Ger/US)*

Fears, insecurities and self confidence

Though the habit of griping and whining is not an indication of unhappiness, Germans do have broader fears and insecurities. Accustomed to seeing things within a larger context and in a longer time frame, German fears are not limited to what happens to themselves or their family in the future. Their worries include environmental concerns, such as global warming, acid rain, destruction of tropical forests, extinction of animals and plants, fears concerning other societies, and the state of world peace. The changing array of serious problems and dangers to mankind creates a constant sense of crisis, reflected in yet another untranslatable German term: *Weltschmerz* ("distress over the state of the world"). In comparison, Americans are more likely to end a discussion about a serious problem on an optimistic note, while the Chinese might not look far beyond the security of their family, much less fret over the collective well-being of their society or mankind.

> *"In Germany we immediately talk about* Weltuntergang *('the end of the world'), as soon as the accustomed well-being and wealth is being questioned." (Uwe O., Ger/Europe)*

> *"The focus of fears in Germany seems to change every few years; three or four years ago it was pedophiles, before that it was acid rain. It depends on the major news of the time." (Karl M., Ger/Tw)*

> *"Our holistic ideals are goals that are unreachable; so people get frustrated." (Rainer M., Ger/US)*

In spite of unfulfilled yearnings and a tendency to complain and whine even over small matters, Germans overall seem to be quite content with their lives. If that is indeed so, the reason may lie in the importance they attach to nurturing close relationships. According to an ongoing seventy-year-long Harvard University study on happiness, the most important ingredient of a happy and healthy life lies in the quality of personal relationships.

Notes

[1] Julian Marias, *America in the Fifties and Sixties. Julian Marias on the United States.* (University Park and London: Pennsylvania University Press, 1972), 74.

[2] Charles Hampden-Turner and Alfonsus Trompenaars. *The Seven Cultures of Capitalism: Value Systems for Creating Wealth in the United States, Japan, Germany, France, Britain, Sweden, and the Netherlands* (New York: Currency/Doubleday, 1993), 208.

[3] Andrew Clark, "Lunch with the FT: Sir Simon Rattle." *Financial Times,* September 6, 2008.
www.ft.com/cms/s/0/fb4b5fe8-5c52-11de-aea3-00144feabdc0.html

[4] Georg Haider, during an interview on German TV (Deutsche Welle, April 20, 2001).

III. The Chinese Relational Self

An identity

I am my relationships

THE Chinese self is a relational self, defined by relationships, primarily family relationships, which are unbreakable structural bonds based on blood relationships and roles. In return for loyalty and fulfillment of family obligations family membership provides unconditional acceptance, stability and existential security thereby giving the individual a sense of being securely rooted.

"People relationships are not only a big part of life, it's all there is." (Sun W. T., f, Tw/Ger)

"When I think of my life, of what I want to do with it, must do or must not do, I think primarily in terms of my relationship to my family." (Lu H. T., f, Tw/Asia)

"The single person is not understood as a person but as a part of a group, such as a family or a school. The Chinese self has a collective personality, which means we prefer to be in groups where we don't need to stand out. In the family a person may be father or mother, a son or daughter, an older or younger brother or sister, but not an independent personality." (Huang S. L., m, Tw/ Ger)

"We Chinese worry about our family identity, that is its reputation, not about our individual identity. Personal issues pale in comparison to family issues." (Matthew C., ABC/Tw)

"For us family relationships mean total reciprocity." (Hsieh S. H., m, Tw/Ger)

Family roles

Family relationships are roles that are designed to ensure the family's security, well-being and continuity. The role of an adult member entails contributing to the family's financial security, getting married, and having children. Emotional bonds, considered to be too weak and too unstable to insure the security of the group, are secondary.

The adult role

Maximizing family assets

Maximizing family assets is a vital part of the adult role. Family members are expected to work hard and seek either lucrative or at least safe and steady jobs, while foregoing frivolous occupations that respond to personal interests but do not benefit the family's financial status. The adult role includes expressing one's filial piety by giving money to parents and supporting them in old age as well as investing in the children's education in order to ensure future earning potential. Generally, parents also consider it part of their role to buy homes for their sons (and sometimes daughters) and leave an inheritance in order to be remembered as good ancestors. In Chinese society, more so than in the US and Germany, family status in the community is overwhelmingly determined by the exhibition of prosperity, which adds urgency to the pursuit of wealth.

In order to maximize income, families commonly opt for long-term family separations. Many Taiwanese take jobs on the Chinese mainland, leaving their families behind. In the past some families in Taiwan also separated in order to avoid military service for sons or to access higher education for children, who did not pass the local university entrance exams. More recently families, both in Taiwan and the PRC, send their children, even young ones, with or without a parent, to be educated in American schools, thinking that an English education will be a profitable investment for the family's future. Other families separate for extended stays in the US in order to qualify for legal permanent residence in the US.

The ease with which the Chinese opt for family separations reflects several basic Chinese values: The belief in unbreakable family relationships, the importance of wealth for family status and security, and the relative unimportance of close emotional bonds. Though the Chinese often say that family separations are a sacrifice for a better future, it is rarely the poor families who do so. When they learn that Westerners find such long-term family separations unusual, if not shocking, Chinese are surprised. In fact, they may be shocked to hear that Westerners might actually sacrifice a career or business opportunity in order to stay with the family.

"Family separation reflects our values and priorities: What matters is the family as a whole, not the individual person and his or her feelings. Chinese marriage is an economic arrangement and the children's education is more important than the marriage. Besides, family ties are unbreakable no matter where the individual family members reside." (Tu C. L., m, Tw/US)

"We Chinese think of family separations as a positive thing. It's good for the family's long-term benefit in exchange for only a minor sacrifice. Besides, the husband may simply be too busy, so that even if the family joined him, he would not have time for them anyway. So they might as well live apart." (Fang Y. W., f, Tw/US)

"Chinese spouses may not start out with love and don't expect it in their marriage, so that for some there may also be an ingredient of freedom when living apart." (Pang H. Y., f, Tw/Ger)

"I have a cousin who works in the PRC, while the husband remains in Taiwan and their two children live in two different cities in Canada. When it comes to family separations like that, the feeling is that it is a sacrifice for the next generation. We sacrifice family life for money and long-term security while

> *Westerners sacrifice money and long term security for close family relation-ships!" (Chiang Y. H., f, Tw/US)*

> *"Sacrificing income and career in order to be with the family is not a sacrifice. It's stupid." (Tsou P. Y., f, Tw/US)*

While family separation is acceptable for financial and certain other reasons, moving away from the family for individual independence and freedom is rarely condoned.

> *"When I moved out it was a big thing, even more so because I am female. Every-body in the family urged me not to do it: 'Why don't you live at home? You can save so much money and use that money to do this or that, and help the family. Renting your own place is such a waste.'" (Doris F., ABC)*

Getting married and having children

Equally important as contributing to family assets is the obligation to marry and have children. Necessary for family continuity, Chinese marriage is a family af-fair. It is about continuing the family line, not about love between husband and wife. In the past arranged marriages were considered superior to those based on emotional bonds, though for the fortunate ones a mutual fondness between the couple might develop over time. Even though most marriages are no longer arranged, many parents still have veto power over their children's decisions re-garding marriage. Because many of my Chinese conversation partners were in their late twenties or thirties, the topic of marriage aroused enormous interest.

> *"In my circle of friends, everybody seems to be getting married around the age of thirty. That's when it's 'about time' and the pressure from home starts mount-ing." (Ma C. H., m, Tw/US)*

> *"Single women are looked down upon. It's one of the things people don't talk about. I could not imagine myself not marrying. My parents certainly would want me to marry, and their wish would be a big factor for me, though not the only one. Society expects it. A woman who is not married is wasted. It's more okay for a guy to be single." (Tan S. T., f, Tw/US)*

"In Taiwan, marriage is an obligation. If you want love in marriage you need think of nurturing it after marriage. There is no love or affection between my parents. Some of my friends marry without love because they fear loneliness, but most Chinese women go by money. For men love does not matter much in their decision, because all marriage means is that you have someone to have your children and take care of the home. For exciting sex and maybe love there is a world of other women out there." (Pang H. Y., f, Tw/Ger)

"My friends in Taiwan still follow their parents' wishes. And my dad says: When my daughter gets married, it's a matter of the two families." (Tan S. T., f, Tw/ US)

"My sister's marriage to a Belgian man has created many problems. She married her husband for love, but now, if she had another chance she would choose differently. We Chinese know that if you marry a Taiwanese you marry not only that woman, but also the family and family friends. These are problems my parents predicted, and it has turned out that way." (Hsieh S. H., m, Tw/Ger)

Many of my Chinese respondents were amazed to observe that in the US and in Germany personal feelings played such an important role in marriage.

⇨ *"It was very interesting to learn that for Germans feelings are so important for their relationships. For us family relationships are too important to go by feelings!" (Ku H. J., f, Tw/Ger)*

⇨ *"For Westerners the partners' personal feelings are the one and only thing to consider. For us marriage is a strategic tie between two families, not only the two people. So a lot more people interfere in your decisions." (Tu C. L., m, Tw/ US)*

⇨ *"We don't idealize family life and marriage the way Westerners do, though nowadays many Chinese also do hope for love." (Yeh H. S., m, Tw/US)*

Extramarital affairs of Chinese husbands—now also of more wives—are common and taken for granted by some. A book entitled *One Country, Two Wives* describes the phenomena of Taiwanese men working in China (PRC) and establishing a second family there. [1] As long as family duties are fulfilled, meaning supporting the wife and children back home, few of the wives in Taiwan will divorce. As a result many couples live in separate worlds.

"Young men read about love and think they want to be faithful, but by the time they are forty, many have mistresses. Divorce laws favor the man and there are other financial disincentives to divorce, so wives often prefer to continue to play the usual family roles." (Tu C. L., m, Tw/US)

"I have not seen many divorces but I hear of tons of affairs. A lot of women don't want to divorce, for economic reasons, to maintain face, and also because they would not find another partner." (Ma C. H., m, Tw/US)

"The majority of people won't get divorced even when they don't have good re-lationship. Still, the divorce rate has been rising." (Yeh R. Y., m, Tw/US)

The child role

Filial piety

Even though many young Chinese nowadays may hope for love in marriage, they recognize that Chinese marriage has always been primarily about having children, specifically sons. Sons are needed to pass on the family name and, at least in the past, they bore the primary responsibility for taking care of aging parents.

To that end raising children means teaching them filial piety. For centuries an integral part of the Confucian tradition, filial piety consists foremost of obe-dience, respect, and gratitude in recognition of the unrepayable indebtedness owed to parents. In practical terms, filial piety means receiving good grades in school, gaining entry into a prestigious institution of higher learning, and preparing for a lucrative career.

Given the emphasis in child raising on inculcating filial piety, the years of in-fancy and early childhood hold little importance. Too early to teach filial piety, care during these years is considered a simple matter of feeding and dressing the child, which anyone can do, and therefore does not warrant foregoing a par-ent's earning capacity. If grandparents are not available to look after the child, a longstanding common practice has been to send the infant or child to live with a more distant relative. More recently many families are hiring outsiders.

"Here in Taiwan moms go back to work two or three weeks after giving birth. It's more important for the mother to make money than to raise the child. This means many children are taken care of by the grandparents or others." (Yang W. C., f, Tw/US)

"In Taiwan most parents don't take care of their own kids. If the mother did stay home, friends would ask 'Why do you stay at home? It's a waste. Go out and make money.'" (Tu C. L., m, Tw/US)

"Chinese families readily send their children overseas to be 'little foreign students.' The child may live with an older sibling, an aunt, or with an unrelated adult who is paid for having the child live in their home. No close supervision is expected or usually given, which leaves many children pretty much on their own." (Li K. P., m, Tw/US)

"The Chinese parents I know here in Southern California all work, so they send their young children to be taken care of by family in Taiwan. I know one couple who sent their child back to be raised by his grandma in Taiwan. They said it's more convenient and cheaper to go to a doctor there. The child is not sick, but they worry, just in case. This is common and nobody thinks about it. I've never heard of anyone finding it strange. And nobody thinks it matters whether the father is present or not. (Tsou P. Y., f, Tw/US)

"People have children so that they will take care of them when old. That is the purpose. We don't have a sense of their psychological development, of what they need." (Fan Y., m, PRC/US)

"We are all orphans and our children will also be orphans, because when we send our young children back to grandma she only feeds them." (Ma C. H., m, Tw/US)

"My grandmother told us that when she was a child nobody raised them, that they were street urchins." (Doris F., ABC)

Teaching filial piety usually starts with school age. From then on, commands, lectures, scolding and criticism are the norm, along with frequent reminders from parents and elders of how they worked so hard and sacrificed so much for the younger generation so that these must never forget this debt. In order to achieve optimal results, the dominant parental motto for raising children is: "You can never be strict enough." Children are expected to be obedient, concentrate on their studies, and through their conduct bring glory to the family. If the grades are good, it is a sign of a "good" child and the child may be given more leeway.

> *"In Taiwan we are taught to be filial and to study, study, study. It's difficult to follow your heart, because filial obedience and following the elders always overrule." (Yeh R. Y., m, Tw/US)*

> *"Obedience to parents is holy. If you don't obey you are a bad person and you have no worth. Since the entire society judges you in this fashion, if you don't obey, everybody will talk badly about you. You get it from all the relatives and all sides. So I am very careful about what I say and how I say things. I need to make sure not to show my anger." (Hsieh S. H., m, Tw/Ger)*

> *"From the time I was young I always heard people tell me, if you do anything bad, you do it for all of us, and that is terrible. We have sacrificed so much for you and you throw it all away when you do something that will hurt our family reputation. Never disgrace the name of the family. And if you don't know whether or not something will disgrace the family, don't do it." (Doris F., ABC)*

> *"Young Chinese children are loud and can be wild. They are not expected to be considerate of anybody. But those of us who are older have to be considerate of everybody." (Hsieh S. H., m, Tw/Ger)*

> *"Westerners use encouragement instead of beatings and they point to principles instead of applying arbitrary authority. The Chinese have no interest in the child as a person. They only want obedience which means that the children have no opportunity to develop a self." (Tu C. L., m, Tw/US)*

> *"For Taiwanese parents the child's success is for their own glory. They do a lot of comparing about whose child has the better job or gives them more status." (Tsou P. Y., f, Tw/US)*

Because the task of teaching filial piety is a communal effort, with grandparents, aunts and uncles, older siblings, and cousins all having their say, inconsistencies in the demands placed on the young are ever-present. Exposed to high levels of control as well as to individual favoritism, children learn early on to deal with multiple authorities.

> *"My mother says she was under the control of a tyrant sister. Later it was her brother who objected to her going to the university, and being the oldest, his word was law. Listening to authority and paying attention to seniority has stuck with me to this day." (Doris F., ABC)*

> *"My grandmother was the matriarch of the family. Everything she said was the law. My mom later told me that my grandmother liked me and told her that she wanted me to live with her. That's how I got stuck with my grandparents." (Sung M. K., f, Tw/PRC/US)*

> *"My parents favor my younger brother telling me that he is smarter. So even though he did not get good grades in school, it did not matter much. But when I got a 99 out of 100 on a test, that still wasn't good enough. They never put it into words, but I could feel it." (Fan Y., m, PRC/US)*

> *"One of my classmates complained to me that her parents liked one of her siblings better. But liking one child better than another is human nature. If I only have one toy and two children, of course I will give it to the one I like best. I think the parents can't help it." (Tsou P. Y., f, Tw/US)*

> *"My grandfather was very liberal and did not force his children into things but his family was exceptional. One of his sons liked drawing and eventually came to be a well-known painter, because grandfather let him develop freely. Since we often played together, some of it rubbed off on those of us in the extended family. During the summer vacations the older children taught the younger ones and we all had a good time, to the effect that our classmates envied us for having fun. That is the good side of a large family. If the patriarch is open-minded he has a chance to spread his influence, but a bad one does the same." (Lo M. L., f, Tw/US)*

A new perspective

Young people growing up in Chinese society are used to the prevalent authoritarian parental style and rarely complain about it. They know that it is the same in their friends' homes. However, after having lived overseas and witnessed a different kind of parent-child relationship, some began to question the Chinese way.

⇨ *"I saw how my American neighbors dealt with their children and grandchildren. They never hit their children. They just told them what they did wrong. There also was a lot more encouragement, something we never get. As an American child you don't need to be perfect." (Pai T. Y., f, Tw/US)*

⇨ *"American parents and children are more like friends. Parents are more emotionally involved and may have a good and free relationship with their children." (Chien H. M., m, Tw/US)*

⇨ *"Germans treat their children more like adults, asking for their opinions, something Chinese parents would never do. Chinese parents only tell their children to be 'good.' Nothing much else. With that sort of upbringing, we don't have a chance to develop self-confidence." (Pang H. Y., f, Tw/Ger)*

"Chinese parents have a problem: They think they are the elders and we are the kids, no matter what age. They send you overseas to study and then don't accept what you learned over there and don't allow you to do something different from what they envisioned for you. They look for a job for you, maybe ask someone for a favor to give you a job, even if you do not ask for it or positively do not want it. It's always an 'I have to.' Some young people may need it because they don't know what they want. It's only a matter of what others make you do. But I am strong. After I came back from the US, I let my parents know who I am, because before they had no idea what kind of a person I was. If there is any disagreement my parents will say 'We have the experience and you don't!' or they say, 'You are thirty, and we are sixty. We are set in our ways, so you should adjust.' For them that is the end of the discussion. I resigned a very nice job in the US and chose to come back to be near my parents, but they are not interested in hearing what I have to say. They don't appreciate my effort. Instead they keep criticizing me for a lot of little things." (Pai T. Y., f, Tw/ US)

"No matter what your personal plans may be for the day, if your parents ask you to take them some place, you drop everything else and go. Parents see that as obedience, but I ask myself, 'Am I a daughter or am I a servant?'" (Sung M. K., f, Tw/PRC/US)

138

Though many of my Chinese interviewees objected to their parents' communication style, they learned to deal with it, often by withholding information.

"Our family elders only lecture, they don't discuss. So we react pragmatically: Either with silence, or else we talk but don't tell them anything." (Fan Y., m, PRC/US)

"We just say what our parents want to hear. When you think they will disagree with something, you just don't say it, and as a college student you certainly don't mention that you have a boyfriend." (Tan S. T., f, Tw/US)

"Chinese parents talk to their kids and tell them what to do, but they will never enter into a discussion about anything. Yesterday in the supermarket [in Germany] I saw this girl aged about six speaking Mandarin with her mother. The girl kept talking while the mother completely ignored her. The only time the mother said anything was when the girl picked up the basket and the mother said, 'Don't pick that up! Put it down!' Chinese parents only talk to their children to give instructions or orders. When I observe conversations between Western mothers and their children I think to myself, 'There's no way my mother would've had these conversations with me!' I can see in myself that I did become more quiet and inhibited after the age of eight or nine." (Chu C. F., Tw/Ger)

Reaffirmation of filial piety

Several of my Chinese respondents shared with me how over the years their resentment over the Chinese parental style gradually mellowed. They came to realize that Chinese parental control, love, and concern were inseparable and that their own dissatisfaction lay primarily with the style, not with the principle of filial piety itself. They came to accept the values they had been taught with the effect that over time the required obedience morphed into a personal desire for parental approval.

"Now I want to get to know my mom, and not just the yelling one. It's been such a long journey and I have so much anger in me. When my mother came to visit me in the US, I told her how angry I was with her. Her answer was: 'Even if I am wrong I am right because I am your mother.' I told her, 'No, if you are

wrong you are not right. This is America!' Actually I really care for my mother and as long as she lives in China, I feel I have to go over and be with her even though the polluted air there makes me sick. I want her to have peace of mind and I have forgiven her totally. But I am now sixty-three years old, and it has taken this long before I could forgive. Actually, I admire her. She had to take a lot in her life. Her marriage was arranged and then after having three girls, her husband took another wife to have a son. I realize she has gone through so much emotional stress. So it's good to have her own daughter care for her, rather than an outsider. In fact, if I now did not go back to China to take care of my mom I would feel selfish." (Sung M. K., f, Tw/PRC/US)

"When the auntie who raised me wanted me to learn how to cook, she let our cook go and had me do every meal, even though in the beginning I didn't know anything about planning and cooking meals. 'What good are you if you can't cook? You won't be fit to be a wife!,' she said. In a way I am now grateful to her and can appreciate eighty percent of it, but her way of teaching me was awful." (Shao T. F., f, Tw/US)

"My sister no longer cares what other people think, so my parents feel grieved. I don't want my parents to feel that way about me. I want to communicate with them and I learned in the US how to do that. I want to be like my mom and have my husband be like my dad. I think they are good parents. I admire them and I like their views. By now I think my respect for them is an inner respect, not mere obedience, which it is for many others and which it was for me before I left Taiwan." (Hou F. L., f, Tw/US)

"My parents worked so hard to earn money to pay for my education. I understand that giving money is their way of showing love. But I could also say, my parents thought all I needed was money, when in reality I needed them more than money. Do I really need to go to a big name school? Maybe another school would be better for me." (Chien H. M., m, Tw/US)

"I will always be my parents' kid, no matter how old I am and because of that they will take care of me when I need it, but in return once they need to be taken care of I will have that responsibility. I accept that. Since I am the only son and the only male in the family including cousins, it's just me to take care of them." (Andrew L., ABC/Tw)

"I am now in my fifties and Hawaii has been home to me since birth. But this 'filial piety' thing is still alive and well. And even though my mom used the guilt card a lot, filial piety is ingrained in me!" (Susan E., ABC)

Ideal versus reality

In spite of the sincere reaffirmation of filial piety on the part of several of my Chinese conversation partners, they were also aware that in Chinese everyday life norms and reality concerning the relationship between aging parents and children do not always coincide.

"My father thinks and tells people he has a right to live with his son, even though my brother does not think so. He has told my mother that they expect a baby and that there is no room for my father. My father knows that but still tells others that as the father he has the right to live with his son." (Lu W .C., f, Tw/ US)

"My elderly aunt lives with her two daughters, both of whom criticize her a lot. To be filial often just means to preserve the appearance of filial piety. In daily interactions the elderly may be treated poorly." (Lo M. L., f, Tw/US)

"Both sets of my grandparents live with my uncle. Often I hear him talk about them, saying that these old people are so annoying. He may say so even in their presence." (Tan S. T., f, Tw/US)

"My uncle lives with his grandmother and pretends that he pays for her and cooks for her. In reality he is not treating her well at all." (Pang H. Y., f, Tw/Ger)

"After my father died, my mother was to be taken care of by my brothers. So Third Brother cared for her for a while, but only because he wanted her inheritance. After she transferred her assets to him he neglected her, cutting her down at every opportunity. Still, to her the boys continue to be everything, whereas we girls don't count." (Shao T. F., f, Tw/US)

Family closeness and harmony

Chinese family closeness is a sense of belonging, of unconditional acceptance and security based on unbreakable bonds and on each member fulfilling his or her role. Though frequent togetherness is the norm, especially over food, family bonds usually remain intact in spite of extended separations and internal discord. Family closeness does not depend on inner feelings or individuals liking each other and usually does not entail a mutual opening of inner selves. As a result, family members may not know each other well as individuals.

> *"Our Chinese family ties are like a rope that ties us together. When I lived with my uncle, he wanted me to tell him every time I went out, but I often did not do it and he did not like it. Because he is older, he thinks it is impolite not to tell him. A lot of grown children will ask their father and mother before making any major decision. It should be our decision, but still, we want them to approve."* (Pang H. Y., f, Tw/Ger)

> *"Compared to Americans, I am more family oriented. I am forty-three years old and live on my own, but on weekends I go home and pray before the family altar. I eat with the family either at home or we all go out to eat together. When there is a family gathering, everybody must be there. It's an obligation. Not showing up means that you don't care and it is disrespectful."* (Pai T. Y., f, Tw/US)

> *"I like the strong Asian commitment to family and marriage. The divorce rate is going up, but the commitment is still there."* (Ku H. J., f, Tw/Ger)

Because family ties are unbreakable, communication within the family is direct and dispenses with politeness. There is no need for thank yous or praises, as these would convey an undesirable distance. Many Chinese enjoy this freedom to be honest, which they do not have outside the family. Others, however, feel smothered by the constant criticism in the family, especially when they return home after having lived overseas.

> *"Within the family we don't say thank you. That's for outsiders, guests, not for family. Thanking each other for something would imply that one might have*

done otherwise, which in turn would mean that we didn't understand our re-spective roles or that we felt we could choose to not fulfill them." (Andrew L., ABC/Tw)

"Toward outsiders we are polite and don't say negative things, but among rela-tives or really good friends people may tell you that you are stupid, that you are fat, or that your hat is ugly. With my American friends I try to avoid more sensitive topics, such as the issue of weight." (Tan S. T., f, Tw/US)

"My aunt may call my mother and tell her that mom's hair looks ugly. Or she may say: 'Don't wear that hat, I am taking you out to buy a better one.' I know there is love behind this kind of criticism, but sometimes it's hard to take." (Tan S. T., f, Tw/US)

"Members of the extended family like to be together as a group. We get along, but we don't communicate. We eat and talk, mostly about food, money and other people. We do a lot of comparing and dispensing criticism. But there are also lots of family fights!" (Sun W. T., f, Tw/Ger)

"Within Chinese families people often yell at each other but they rarely listen to each other. It may just be positioning the self within the group. There are a lot of fights which stresses me out, but my mother does not think of these in-stances as fighting. For her we are just talking!" (Doris F., ABC)

"The constant criticism from parents and teachers has made all of us numb." (Pang H. Y., f, Tw/Ger)

Family harmony is an important Chinese concept, but it does not necessarily include the inner dimension that Westerners may read into it. In Chinese daily life harmony often simply describes an absence of open conflict, not a consensus or people getting along well. Since the head of the family usually makes the important decisions, yet not everybody agrees with these decisions, individual family members may just follow their own inclinations thereby causing family quarrels. Nonetheless, the ideal of family harmony tends to invoke a good feeling of being part of a stable social order. Most importantly it means to project harmony and a united front toward the outside world.

"Harmony does not mean consensus. Ninety percent of family harmony is about wanting to avoid conflict. It is not a meeting of the minds or hearts. There is so much hypocrisy, always carrying on as if there was a consensus. In reality they just beat around the bush and don't confront the situation. There is a big gap between reality and ideal." (Sung M. K., f, Tw/PRC/US)

"Harmony is based on power, it means everybody plays their role according to the power relationship." (Cheng A. L., f, Tw/US)

"Because of our need to maintain harmony, we can't have conflict and we have no skill in dealing with conflicts. So it festers inside and we resort to revenge and deception." (Jade Y., ABC/Tw)

"You never ever sully the family name. Toward the outside you preserve the image of family harmony, even though inside all hell may break loose. That's a responsibility, a duty, which takes priority over personal happiness or mental health." (Doris F., ABC)

The inner self

Because the primary task of the relational self lies in fulfilling his role in the human network, dwelling on inner feelings and thoughts that conflict with appropriate behavior is considered self-centered and lacking humility. Intentions and motivation are of little concern. It's what you did that matters, not why you did it.

Without an inner autonomous self, there is no need to reflect on what you want to be or where you want to go. When I asked my Chinese conversation partners about their relationship to their self, most of them looked puzzled. "It's a strange question," one said. "We don't look within. And we don't dwell on what we might want or think because it makes you sad and weak. It does not make you a good member of the group."

"As a self defined by relationships we don't have an individual self. There is no stable core to the self, so if you start looking for one you have a problem." (Pang H. Y., f, Tw/Ger)

"You need to be like others, which means there is no effort to know yourself." (Hou F. L., f, Tw/US)

"We don't engage in self-reflection because it's of no use. You are under the control of others; so your self-reflection would not get you anywhere and would not change your life. You'd just be depressed. You need to do what the elders tell you and they don't say 'Be creative! Follow your dreams.' So if they tell you to go to the US, that's where you go." (Su M., m, PRC/US)

"We Chinese don't go within, because for most people there is an inner emptiness. We are, or have become, a people who are empty inside." (Yang W. C., f, Tw/US)

"Since we don't look within, we don't know what we want or like and so we don't miss the freedom to express ourselves. We are free of that burden." (Andrew L., ABC/Tw)

Given the absence of an autonomous inner self in their own culture, the Chinese have mixed feelings when they encounter the importance of the individual self in American and German life.

⇨ *"Americans are self-centered because everybody thinks they are Number 1. Some people just go on and on about their personal life, or they write a book about the experience of having been abused as a child. I don't care about somebody's personal life. It's not community-minded." (Doris F., ABC)*

⇨ *"I have zero tolerance for people needing to find themselves." (Liang J. C., f, Tw /US)*

⇨ *"I was amazed to discover how important his inner world was to my European boyfriend. He did a lot of analyzing ideas and feelings which seemed to constitute an important part in his life. To me things on my mind are just subjective incidentals, not worthy of attention, and risky if discussed, but to him they seemed to constitute a real world, worthy of much attention and discussion. For us Chinese, dwelling on our ideas and feelings is not an issue and is never encouraged." (Han M. L., f, Tw/US)*

⇨ *"Germans pride themselves of their inwardness. But their narrow focus on ideas and thoughts makes them intolerant and unconcerned about other people." (Hsieh S. H., m, Tw/Ger)*

⇨ *"The German 'I' is a very big 'I,' though it's a more elegant 'I' than ours. In English it is even written with a capital letter. The focus is on the self, on what I like to be or what I want to do. We Chinese don't have that. To a Chinese that is selfishness." (Cheng A. L., f, Tw/Ger)*

Feeling

The understanding that the inner self not important is reflected in the absence of an autobiographical tradition and inner drama in Chinese literature, which is primarily didactic, dealing with how people conform to expected behavior. Though the field of psychology has recently become more accepted, in traditional Chinese culture there is no concept of an inner psyche, something that can or should be nurtured or can be hurt or damaged.

Thus Chinese forms of parental affection differ from those in the West. Modern Chinese authors who reminisce about their childhood years often recall parental love being expressed through small gestures, such as being allowed to carry the father's briefcase after meeting him at the bus stop upon coming home from work, or of being carried by a parent when sick. Such actions would seem normal in Western families but in view of the general non-expression of feelings they take on a huge significance to Chinese children.

"Affection in relationships is not verbalized or acted out. Parental strictness is seen as love. I often read the newspaper's family section and I remember that one girl wrote that she never saw her parents smile at her and that they never encouraged her. But one day, when a notice of her having won a competition was sent to her home while she was out, her father opened it and went looking for her at her friend's house. It was then that she realized he was proud of her. These little incidents mean so much to children, because they are starved for love." (Liu T. Y., f, Tw/US)

"I think as Chinese we are so hungry for signs of love that we attach an enormous importance to tiny gestures. Of course, we might be right in interpreting them as love. I have an uncle who is really gruff. But when he plays with children we can see his caring side." (Doris F., ABC)

"Chinese raise their kids with a lot of criticism and scolding. That is their love, and that is how I raise my two children here in the US. Children do get used to it and tolerate it without feeling hatred for their parents." (Su M., m, PRC/US)

"Parents don't verbally express affection or love, but they will worry about you, and take care of you until you can earn your own money. Usually people do little things for someone or give money to express caring." (Ma C. H., m, Tw/ US)

"My mother's way of expressing love is by doing things for you, whether you want it or not." (Sung M. K., f, Tw/PRC/US)

"Giving a hug to a parent means being Americanized. We can't do that, because it's not being respectful. Once when I put my arm over my dad's shoulder, he shrunk back. Nor is closeness expressed in words. So we don't say 'Thank you,' or 'I love you.'" (Pai T. Y., f, Tw/US)

"In a Chinese family we don't get emotional support. Success is expected, not rewarded." (Jade Y. ABC/Tw)

"In educating their children Chinese parents judge them by what they can see and hear, which means mostly grades and English. They ignore the rest. They do not see the emotional development. What you don't see is not important." (Tu C. L., m, Tw/US)

By growing up under the motto of "Act according to what is appropriate, not according to how you feel," and witnessing a limited expression of feelings the young learn that personal feelings are unimportant and uninteresting.

"Very few people say you need to act in line with how you feel on the inside, because actually what you think or feel inside may not be good. The Confucian way prescribes a certain behavior which, provided you follow those rules, does not allow you to become a bad person. Whatever your inside feelings and thoughts may be, don't listen to them. Follow the rules and you'll be fine." (Ma C. H., m, Tw/US)

"When something is the appropriate thing to do, I do it. It has nothing to do with how I feel about it. What I want is selfish." (Andrew L., Tw/US)

"There is this huge cultural denial of feeling, which comes out as repression of feelings and emotions. You are not supposed to have them, especially negative ones. So we don't learn to deal with them." (Jade Y., ABC/Tw)

"About the time I was going off to college my father died of a heart attack. I was devastated, but when I cried my mother said: 'Just get over it,' and my brother scolded me for being weak. We can never talk about these things." (Doris F., ABC)

"We are good at sharing food, but not at sharing inner thoughts and feelings. Private feelings are not interesting." (Sung M. K., f, Tw/PRC/US)

"We don't know how to express feelings and affection." (Cheng A. L., f, Tw/Ger)

"The Chinese pride themselves on their warm-heartedness (<u>renqingwei</u>), but in reality their way of communicating does not have any intimacy. The so-called warm-heartedness is a kind of surface warmth. It's a façade, a bit like American friendliness. It's nice to have it as a form of dealing with people, but there is nothing behind it. It's just a way to deal with each other, and good form is better than bad form. The problem is when there is no time, place and room for a more intimate closeness." (Tu C. L., m, Tw/US)

Overseas the Chinese are often surprised to find that feelings play such an important role in Western relationships and they marvel at American expressions of enthusiasm and passion, at their always appearing to be excited about something.

⇨ *"Americans express themselves and show what they feel. When Chinese speak you don't see what they feel. It's a bit like a poem: You use other things to symbolize or to represent what you really mean." (Lo M. L., f, Tw/US)*

⇨ *"Americans often talk about their feelings. We don't do it at all, and as far as I am concerned I don't care at all what you feel, only what you do." (Hsieh S. H., m, Tw/US)*

⇨ *"I find it difficult to navigate being Chinese and American. Even though my parents were both born here in the US, they remained very Chinese. At home we spoke Chinese and followed Chinese values. As kids we were expected to be obedient, lie low and not be heard. There were a lot of expectations. If you are having a rough day, you don't talk about it. Nor do you talk about your feelings. That's taboo." (Jade Y. ABC/Tw)*

⇨ *"I came to Germany because of Gisela, my German girl friend, and though we are no longer together, through her I became—and still am—very close to her family. I liked the expression of affection in the German family and it made a huge impression on me. In my Chinese family we never show affection. I will tell Gisela's mom about my inner feelings and what goes on in my life, but I'd never tell my own mom. The first hug I gave my mom was when I left for Germany." (Peter W., ABC/Ger)*

Not only is the expression of emotions in a Chinese context considered to be immature, because it means the person, like a child, has not yet learned to control them, showing emotions is also thought to be unwise because it gives away information that others might abuse. So when life deals a heavy blow, rather than revealing his pain to a family member or a friend, a Chinese might visit a temple, a monk or a fortune teller for relief. Some types of gossip may also be an indirect way to vent feelings. Other times, even a Chinese can hold in only so much.

"Chinese gossip a lot, but sometimes this gossip can be a way to gain your sympathy. Talking about your difficulties with your mother-in-law and how much you are hurting —in some sense this is a way of showing feelings, opening up." (Hope S., ABC)

"For us Chinese life is about fulfilling our role, to be the person I am expected to be. But at some point people boil over and when they do, they explode." (Sung M. K., f, Tw/PRC/US)

"Since the worth of the individual depends on being validated by others, there may be this sudden explosion of anger when a person feels humiliated. At that point all he knows is to explode." (Pai T. Y., f, Tw/US)

Among the younger generation some changes seem to be under way:

"I think Taiwanese women are becoming more open about expressing their feelings, but not so much about expressing ideas. Taiwanese men though have to pretend. They don't want to admit to feelings and weaknesses." (Pang H. Y., f, Tw/Ger)

Thinking

Much of Chinese thinking revolves around how to deal with people. Thus, compared to Western thinking, Chinese thinking is more a matter of sensitivity and intuition and less a matter of the intellect. In the Chinese language the Western concepts of mind and heart are covered by the single word *xin*. "The critical mind is too thin and too cold," wrote Lin Yutang, who had studied in Germany and lived in the US for many years, expressing the idea that a rational mind, while good for natural science, is not suitable for dealing with human relationships. [2] Neither clarity nor knowledge are virtues in Chinese culture. Instead, vagueness and ambiguity are positive values, since they allow a variety of interpretations and avoid disharmony.

But even when the subject matter is not human relationships, the Chinese tend to think relationally, meaning that their main interest lies in comparisons and the interconnections between things, not in their inherent properties or characteristics. In a study in which researchers presented the participants with a set of pictures showing a panda, a monkey, and a banana and asked them to assign group belonging, Asians were prone to group the monkey and the banana, while Westerners were likely to group the monkey and the panda. [3]

> "Thinking as in opinions is not encouraged, but we do think a lot about what the other person meant or said, and about how to deal with others. So the Chinese thinking component is channeled into a narrower direction than in the West." (Lo M. L., f, Tw/US)

> "Our parents taught us to repay our indebtedness to them by measuring up to others. Much of this instruction was done by way of comparisons. They might tell us something like: 'So and so went to Harvard'—meaning you should go —or after a music recital, 'So and so played so well'—meaning you were no good. These things did not need to be spelled out. We understood right away what was meant." (Tan S. T., f, Tw/US)

Symbolism, a ubiquitous feature in Chinese culture, goes well with relational thinking by looking at the world in terms of comparisons and providing space for feeling and imagination.

Being smart

In Chinese, the word clever (*congming* or more specifically *xiao congming*) usually refers to what in English is called street-smart. Smart thinking generally serves one's self interest, most often by devising strategies that would save
or make some extra money but frequently also by outwitting another person.
Smart thinking also takes the form of subtle manipulation by means of giving presents or treating someone to a fine meal with the intent to gain a more
significant benefit in the future. In Chinese life, this kind of smartness is a
positive, desirable attribute, considered worthy to be taught to young children
by playing tricks on them in a good-natured way.

Being smart enhances one's status and therefore is one of the few things a Chinese individual can boast about. On the other hand, letting oneself be outwit-
ted is shameful, a severe loss of face. Within the family a lack of smartness
on the part of a family member may lead to outbursts of criticism and anger
over having been so stupid to let oneself be cheated or taken advantage of. In
the conversations with my Chinese respondents smart thinking was a favorite
topic.

> *"You are smart when you reach your goal or obtain an advantage by outwitting
> others. This kind of smartness is a positive value. It gives you status and makes
> you popular, especially if you are willing to share your tactics with others." (Liu
> T. Y., f, Tw/US)*

> *"Outwitting the other is a positive thing. Not doing so, or at least not trying to,
> means you are stupid. If you bargain well, get a real good deal, or obtain an
> advantage by being cunning, that is admired. So people like to brag about it."
> (Tan S. T., f, Tw/US)*

> *"From copying homework to buying papers, for university students being smart
> means obtaining a good result with the least amount of effort." (Hu T. H., m,
> Tw/PRC/US)*

> *"If I outsmart somebody, I'll feel proud of myself and tell others about it, but when
> you are outsmarted by somebody else, that means losing face, so you don't tell
> anyone." (Tsou P. Y., f, Tw/US)*

"Being told 'You are stupid!' is one of the worst insults you can receive. It expresses total contempt. Being stupid is so bad that it deserves being cheated, being exploited or looked down upon. So if you make a mistake, don't admit it because it will make you look stupid. If I was cheated out of money, I will feel bad. But worse than having lost the money would be for others to find out and call me stupid." (Doris F., ABC)

By this measure of smartness the Chinese often find Westerners "dumb," meaning they are too trusting and can easily be fooled. In his book, *The Importance of Living* Lin Yutang notes that the Chinese forestall disputes by inviting people to eat. "In China, we bribe our way into the good will of everybody by frequent dinners. I do not think this is peculiarly Chinese. How can an American postmaster-general or chief of department decline a private request for a personal favor from some friend at whose home he has eaten five or six good meals? I bet on the Americans being as human as the Chinese. The only difference is the Americans haven't got insight into human nature or haven't proceeded logically to organize their political life in accordance with it." [4]

⇒ *"Americans don't have our street smarts. They can't deal with people and they let others take advantage of them. It's stupid to let yourself be cheated." (Tang P. H., f, Tw/US)*

⇒ *"My two months in the US were so relaxing. People are so simple, so straightforward and gullible." (Meng S. L., m, Tw/US)*

⇒ *"Germans think only in one direction. They are so straight, whereas we Chinese think five steps ahead and around two corners." (Yim M. S., f, Hong Kong/Ger)*

⇒ *"When Germans do something it's fully thought out. But they are not flexible and can only think straight." (Fan T. P., m, Tw/US)*

Chinese students overseas make ample use of Western gullibility, sometimes to bypass rules and get away with something they know is not right. Other times they do it just for fun.

"Chinese students often use the excuse of not understanding Western culture or language in order to get away with something they know very well is not right. Later they laugh about the stupid foreigner who believed them. For example,

when caught for plagiarizing college papers, Chinese students often manage to convince their professors that they did not understand the Western rules regarding plagiarism." (Cheng A. L., f, Tw/Ger)

"Taiwan universities are not very strict about cheating, but in the US cheating is very serious. There you need to do your own reports. I felt a bit of shame for the Chinese at the University of British Columbia (Canada) because the cheating by Chinese students is often a topic in the news, on TV and in newspapers. We Chinese consider it smart to get a good result with cheating. Our value system is not the same. Americans learn about their standards from the time they are little. It's important to them to be honest. But in China and in Taiwan, cheating does not feel wrong." (Wu J. Y., f, Tw/US)

"A lot of Chinese use their US credit cards to the max before they leave the country, knowing that once they return to their home country the credit card companies will never find them. Since a lot of people are doing it, word has gotten around, so that it has become more difficult for Chinese in the US to get credit. There are also many ways in which the Chinese use legal loopholes, doing something that is not illegal, but is something we might call unethical. For example, they may buy a nice dress, wear it a couple of times and then return it. Or exchange a new computer against one bought several months earlier, taking advantage of a liberal US return policy. We think it's okay to do that. If nobody watches me, I don't have a sense of guilt. Besides it's not illegal." (Yang W. C., f, Tw/US)

"I went on a delegation with the Chinese junior rotary community service club to the Netherlands, where public transportation is quite expensive but uses the honor system. I was the only one in the group who bought a ticket, and I am sure the others thought I was stupid to do so." (Rose C., ABC/Hong Kong)

"In Germany we Chinese students teach each other our tricks. It's a way to show that you are clever and it makes you valuable to others. They'll think you are terrific. For example, we let newly arrived Chinese students know that they should borrow another Chinese student's train ID (Bahncard) for free or cheaper train rides. Because even though these cards have photos, to Germans we all look alike." (Cheng A. L., f, Tw/Ger)

The Chinese commonly look at smart thinking as a matter of survival, a weapon of the weak against the powerful or of the poor against the rich.

> "The Americans I know here in California look down on taking advantage of others in order to get ahead, but we see it as survival." (Tu C. L., m, Tw/US)

> "I don't think you have to feel badly about taking advantage of others. With so many people in China, the world is so competitive. If you did not outfox others you'd be a fool and a loser." (Peng J. L., m, Tw/PRC/US)

Independent thinking

Chinese culture assigns a low value to independent thinking. Speaking one's mind is poor manners, discussions mean inviting possible conflict and asking questions risks embarrassing the other person if he does not know the answer. Unless in a position of authority or among family, Chinese rarely take a stand on issues, since this would be deemed disrespectful, arrogant, or invite conflict if the opinion was not shared by the listener.

> "Good intellectual conversations presuppose objectivity, but for the Chinese the answer depends on whom they speak to. Discussions where opinions differ are perceived as arguments, as conflict." (Huang S. L., m, Tw/Ger)

> "If our thinking is different from the people around us it gets suppressed. It's now less punished than before, but there is no encouragement for it. So it's not worth it to dwell on what you think." (Fan Y., m, PRC/US)

> "We Chinese don't feel comfortable with different opinions. If someone states strong opinions, we see it as aggressiveness, an attack, which makes us feel the need to self-protect." (Hou F. L., f, Tw/US)

> "If I have a very different opinion from people I interact with I would not say it. I also don't ask questions, because what if the person does not know the answer? It would mean causing embarrassment." (Lu H. T., f, Tw/Asia)

> "Our lack of independent thinking affects creativity. An idea needs to mature in the mind. But in Chinese society if you have a thought that is different, perhaps extraordinary, it is suppressed. Parents and teachers suppress it, or else they just don't pay attention to it. There is no need for punishment, because

lack of encouragement and peer pressure have a similar effect. The Chinese model themselves after others and our fear of making mistakes and being different from others stifles our creativity." (Tu C. L., m, Tw/US)

"One family in our large extended family network allowed and encouraged their children to think and talk about ideas and ideals. So when I was with them I was very happy and did not feel oppressed. It allowed us to not follow the crowd. But when I grew up there were very few families like that." (Lo M. L., f, Tw/US)

Those among my Chinese respondents who lived in Germany noted a pronounced difference with regard to forming and voicing opinions.

⇒ *"In Taiwan a person with an opinion easily earns the label of being opinionated which is a negative thing, whereas in Germany not having an opinion probably means that you haven't had a chance to make up your mind yet, or worse, that you haven't made the effort to be informed about the topic in order to have formed an opinion." (Chung C. Y., f, Tw/Ger)*

⇒ *"Germans always asked me what I thought. But I had never thought about those things and I didn't know what I thought. So it was very embarrassing." (Ku H. J., f, Tw/Ger)*

⇒ *"People here in Berlin tell me I should have opinions, but I don't have any." (Peter W., ABC/Ger)*

⇒ *"I used to dislike a lot of people, because their ideas and opinions were different from mine. But I learned in Germany that having different ideas does not have to mean conflict." (Ku H. J., f, Tw/Ger)*

"For us, thinking conversations have low value and consequently questions are generally not taken seriously. In Germany I would have to think whether what I say is really my opinion and perhaps examine why I think the way I do. In Taiwan the reaction to a question, serious or not, is: 'What does she want from me?' Even among Chinese university professors, it is less whether their opinion makes sense or contributes to the discussion, and more about being polite and friendly. I do see some change though: Compared to ten, twenty years ago Chinese academic conferences are more factual now. People have become better at stating opinions and more people than before really listen and take things objectively rather than personally." (Huang S. L., m, Tw/Ger)

Everything is relative

In Chinese thinking, meaning depends on the specific situation or relationship at hand, so that statements are always relative. Since change is to be expected over time and place, there can be no contradictions, no absolute truth, and no right and wrong that goes for all circumstances, a view that conflicts with the Western concepts of logic, truth, and honesty. Indeed, studies with Asian students have shown that they have more confidence in statements that contain contradictions. The assumption is that there always must be more than one side to everything, more than one possible answer.

> *"It's naïve to be stuck on certain beliefs or principles. We Chinese don't become trapped in one position." (Hsieh S. H., m, Tw/US)*

> ⇨ *"Westerners see good and evil as two separate things. Trying to stamp out the bad and striving for the good, America goes about wanting to conquer the world with goodness, missionaries and revolutionaries. We Chinese don't see it that way. Bad is just the other side of good. It comes with it." (Kuang S. K., m, Tw/US)*

One of my Chinese respondents who thought of right and wrong as universal principles recognized that in Chinese society she was in the minority.

> *"For me, truth or correct behavior are just out there. That's what I think and I often want to shout this out loud, for example, when I see people cutting in line in the metro station. But for many Chinese truth and correctness are not out there; they are bound to time or place or to a particular relationship." (Cheng A. L., f, Tw/Ger)*

According to Chinese philosophy man knows intuitively what is right and wrong under given circumstances. Some years ago, Professor Peng, a young and dynamic visiting faculty member from China at the University of Hawaii, discussed the topic in class: "The Chinese highest moral principle has no specific content and must be determined by the circumstances," he explained. Seeking more clarity, one of his students asked:

"At what point is a man's desire for a woman selfish?"

"You can't consider it in the abstract, only in a specific case."

"Can the killing of another man be condoned?"

"Yes, it depends on the circumstances."

"How about war?

"War too cannot be said to be bad in every case," Professor Peng explained. "It does not mean that there are no principles, only that the main principle is that the correct action be carried out under the specific circumstances. The human being is not capable to consider things in the abstract. But since human nature is perfect, we do not need specific rules and commandments."

"So is it because we in the West think human nature is not perfect, in fact that it is sinful, that we need rules and regulations to keep us in line?"

Despite the fact that the Chinese generally do not think in terms of absolute values, in daily life they are told on a daily basis what is right and what is wrong. Chinese speeches, political writings and newspapers are replete with specific mentions of what is right and wrong. Most often such labels or rules for the individual come through authority figures. For children, filial piety means obedience to parents who determine on a case by case basis what is acceptable and what is not. Specific do's and don'ts are also spelled out by elders, bosses, and other superiors. Since authority figures are endowed with the power to decide what is right or wrong, standing up for personal convictions is not an issue.

"It is foolish to stand up for an abstract idea when you might get your head chopped off for it. There is no right and wrong when you want to get things done. There is no such thing as integrity or opportunism either which only means sticking to some principles that are either made up by you or that you internalized from society. It's the belief in principles and integrity that is the problem because they make people fight with each other. It's much better to be pragmatic and go with the flow. Take the Taiwanese situation in the 1950s. At that time some Taiwanese cooperated with the Nationalists who had come to Taiwan from the mainland, while others who did not cooperate were killed. Among those who cooperated were people who then managed to bring about some change to Taiwan from within the power structure. They

were the ones to be more successful. Harping on principle does not lead you anywhere." (Sun Y. H., m, Tw/US)

"We are trained to be narrow in our thinking, not take a larger view. If we thought in bigger terms, we'd ask about the power structure. But we don't question power and privileges, assuming that everybody profits from it on their own level. It's a kind of naiveté and ignorance, which is not without risks because there is always the possibility that you create a catastrophe out of not knowing." (Huang S. L., m, Tw/Ger)

Self-confidence

Because Chinese culture does not attach importance to the inner self, self-confidence is not considered a positive trait. Instead, it tends to be viewed as attributing excessive importance to the individual, and as something that reflects arrogance and does not serve the group. Chinese with experience of living in Western countries, where self-confidence has a positive value, tend to describe themselves as lacking in self-confidence.

"I think the reason we are less self-confident than Westerners has to do with the way we were raised, especially my generation and the generations before mine. When we were growing up, we were not encouraged to think on our own or to be creative. We were told to memorize things taught in textbooks, and that the most important thing was to pass the college entrance examination. I think people whose minds are more active and who have their own opinions about things are more confident." (Lu H. T., f, Tw/Asia)

"We don't have the same self-confidence as Westerners. Chinese always are told what to do, and they want to be told what to do—including from fortune tellers." (Li K. P., m, Tw/US)

"We don't have self-confidence. We are more concerned about what others think of us. So we pay a lot of attention to others, because we don't want to offend people. At the same time we are very sensitive to being offended ourselves. With self-confidence you can listen to others' opinions without feeling threatened." (Yeh H. S., m, Tw/US)

"I think a lot about self-confidence, but I admit, I don't have it. I look for support from a group." (Lu W. C., f, Tw/Ger)

"As university students we Chinese very often don't do our assignments by ourselves. From copying homework, to buying papers, being smart by obtaining a good result with the least amount of effort—this is no road to develop a sense of achievement, which is what you need to gain self-confidence and dispel self-doubt." (Hu T. H., m, Tw/PRC/US)

⇨ *"German culture is a strong culture, one in which you can confront a problem and admit a mistake. It has something to do with self-confidence. I used to shy away from admitting mistakes, but in Germany I learned to admit my own mistakes and found that by doing so my own authority and self-confidence increased." (Chung C. Y., f, Tw/Ger)*

⇨ *"What I really like about Americans is that they are confident and positive when it comes to challenges. I see it in class. In Taiwan it feels different. There people will give up before they really try. They will be afraid to fail. Americans will take on the challenge. In the university they might take some classes that they know will be really difficult for them. And they will ask questions in class. We Taiwanese would be afraid to fail, and to be wrong is terrible." (Ma C. H., m, Tw/US)*

Nonfamily relationships

Friendship

Chinese society expects all personal needs to be met by the family and, at least in large families, friends tend to be cousins. Given the central role of the family in Chinese life, outside friendships rank second to family and should not interfere with family duties.

"In Taiwan, when someone moves or needs assistance in some other way help comes from within your family. In the US it probably comes from your friends, which means that for Americans friends are so much more important than for Chinese." (Matthew T., ABC/Tw)

"Before you are married friends are important for daily life. You go out with them during the week, but weekends are usually spent with family. Once married, friends become less important." (Tu C. L., m, Tw/US)

"When I was little my mom didn't let me spend much time with friends. So I did not really have any good friends at that time. Later when I was in college in California and had the freedom, I still did not go out with friends. I did not know how to make friends or how to hang out with them. So I never initiated contact." (Fu T. J., f, Tw/US)

Most Chinese friendships are group friendships which come with being a member of a certain group, such as a class, a school, or a church. The primary function of such friendships is to provide a sense of belonging and to ward off loneliness as the Chinese commonly equate being alone with being lonely.

"As a Chinese you have to have friends, because the single person is not understood as an independent person, only as a part of a group, a family, or a class. So you make friends quickly—more like in the US, not as in Germany—but it means that friends always come as a group. Given our collective personality, not seeking acceptance by the group is seen as being non-cooperative." (Huang S. L., m, Tw/Ger)

"You can't be friends with someone older or younger than you. It's got to be the same age, which makes classmates such an important group. Even the relationship between upper and lower classmen is hierarchical, because the younger need to listen to the older." (Yeh R. Y., m, Tw/US)

"The members of a group may not necessarily like each other, but during activities we do stay together the whole time because if I wanted to do something different, people would think that I am not considerate of the group and that would be bad." (Lu W. C., f, Tw/Ger)

"Wanting to be a part of a group is mostly a matter of fear of being alone. We like to be surrounded by people and have a lively time, because it gives us a feeling of security." (Lo M. L., f, Tw/US)

When a group of Chinese friends come together they usually do so for some planned activity. This may mean playing games, going for an outing, or maybe watching television. Almost always it involves food, rarely conversations of substance.

"Friends usually do things as a group, and most of the time there should be a leader, someone who will explain things and tell everyone what to do. No wonder we like group travel." (Lu W. C., f, Tw/Ger)

"As friends we are not really close, but we have fun. We usually think, the bigger the group, the more fun and lively it will be when you play games or sing karaoke. It's also easier to make fun of everyone else. Eating together is a big thing for a group of friends. Since it is harder to talk while you eat, we usually don't have content conversations, but there is always a lot of laughter." (Tan S. T., f, Tw/US).

"Usually conversations with Chinese friends have no content because people want to avoid conflict." (Lo M. L., f, Tw/US)

Chinese friendship entails mutual help and protection, especially when there is no family in the picture. It includes letting your fellow students copy your homework or covering up for a friend in trouble. Even when members of the group are older and no longer see each other regularly, if someone appeals for help, friends respond. Even without communication and staying in touch over the years the obligation and willingness to help remain.

"Real friends are for mutual protection, especially when the family is not there." (Ma C. H., m, Tw/US)

"For us friendship means mutual support, helping each other. When there is a need we help each other, but otherwise there is no need to be in touch." (Tang P. H., f, Tw/US)

"In Taiwan when you ask your friends for help with a move, all the friends will be there. If I am invoking that relationship, no matter what was on their agenda that day, they will come. American friends might say, 'I am sorry, but I am really busy that day,' without feeling bad about it. In Taiwan I would feel so bad if I could not be there and I would have to come up with fifteen excuses to make it sound true. Saying that I am busy is simply not enough." (Andrew L., ABC/Tw)

"The Taiwanese say they have a lot of friends, but most of these are very superficial friends. They do help each other, but only if it's a good friend do we go all out when necessary." (Pang H. Y., f, Tw/Ger)

Conversations among Chinese friends often revolve around family relationships, occasionally including difficulties they might have at home. Disclosing personal feelings or engaging in substantial discussions is not common.

> *"When we get together or meet by chance, we Chinese will immediately ask about the family. Americans don't ask." (Chien H. M., m, Tw/US)*

> *"In Chinese groups of friends we talk while we eat, but conversations are not important for social get-togethers. Disclosing personal information or feelings would always be one on one, and usually on the phone, and then only with a particularly good friend." (Yeh R. Y., m, Tw/US)*

> *"When I first came to the California Institute of Technology, I joined a Chinese group, all of whom except me had grown up in the US. So we spoke English together. But I am also a member of a Taiwanese group, which feels quite different. People in the Chinese speaking group have a different way of communicating. They talk more about their families at home and they like to make jokes by teasing and picking on each other. The Taiwanese group also feels more closed. It is us versus the outside world. In the English speaking group we don't feel as separate." (Tan S. T., f, Tw/US)*

For many Chinese the American type of friendship is not a good fit. From the Chinese point of view Americans are less available for company and when they do get together they engage in activities that the Chinese may not care for. American friends also appeared to feel less obligated to help each other, and their friendships, compared to Chinese friendships, seemed short-lived.

> ⇨*"I like spending my time with other Taiwanese. It's comfortable because we have the same values. So we talk about our parents, about how my mom wanted to have a boy, not a girl; or my classmate might tell us about all the pressure he gets from his parents because he is an only son. Talking about our families is a big part of our conversations. With my Caucasian friends we talk about things that go on in our lives now, not what has happened in the past. And when they do talk about families, it's probably about how the family celebrates Thanksgiving or what the family does for Christmas. It makes me feel like an outsider." (Tan S. T., f, Tw/US)*

⇒ *"Although it is easy to meet Americans, they always seem to hold back in some way. For example, when I cook something and give it to my American room-mate to try, he might say 'I like it' but then not eat it. He would need to say 'I love it' in order to mean it. Amongst my Chinese friends we can say that we think it tastes terrible." (Fan Y., m, PRC/US)*

⇒ *"In the US they have this thing about privacy, but we Chinese like intensive people interaction. Here in Taiwan there are always people I can call up and go out to eat with. In the US people live farther apart and they may not want to go out again after they get home from work." (Yeh H. S., m, Tw/US)*

⇒ *"I don't socialize much with Americans because they like to go for drinks or they want to go to the beach and get a tan. These are things I don't do. So I never take the initiative and say let's go for a cup of coffee or something. I don't even do that with my Taiwanese friends. I prefer to be in a group, because otherwise I may not have anything to say. We just don't sit together and talk unless it's for a specific reason." (Tsou P. Y., f, Tw/US)*

⇒ *"I find it difficult to make American friends. For Chinese friendship means a lot more: For example, friends will help you when you need money. Also, my impression is that American friendships do not last. For them, it's out of sight, out of mind." (Chiang Y. H., f, Tw/US)*

On the other hand, several among my Chinese respondents were critical of Chinese friendship, preferring the American style.

"We Taiwanese are not necessarily good friends. Now living in the US I prefer American friends. The quality of friendship is different. Taiwanese friends are not as genuine as American friends. Chinese friends also may have agendas, whereas American friendships come without conditions. Best of all, American friends are generous, while Chinese friends tend to be stingy." (Lo M. L., f, Tw/US)

"Friendship is a means for the Chinese. They tend to have an agenda, love gossip and do a lot of comparing. To me friendship means loyalty, truth, and moral-ity. I knew quite a few Chinese who were kind and friendly in front of their friends but then gossiped and created scandals behind their backs. So now I prefer American friends." (Sung M. K., f, Tw/PRC/US)

"Last week I was really upset about my Chinese classmates coming the night be-
fore our take home exam was due and wanting to copy my work. I had agreed
to sit with them earlier and work together, but they did not want to do that.
They said the exam would be easy and so they did not even start until the last
evening. In the meantime I worked the whole weekend on it. Here in the US
you are expected to do your own work. In the end I decided not to let them
copy my exam, which of course made them very angry." (Fan Y., m, PRC/US)

My Chinese interviewees had mixed feelings about making friends in Germany.

⇒ *"For friendship the Germans start out on the non-emotional factual level. The*
emotional comes afterwards. The friendships I now have with Germans all
started out with factual discussions. It seems you need to have that intellec-
tual basis as a foundation for further interaction." (Huang S. L., m, Tw/Ger)

⇒ *"Germans don't change friends or let new ones enter their lives easily. But they*
also invest more time in their friendships than we do. In Taiwan we work like
ants, so we don't have that time." (Fan T. P., m, Tw/Ger)

⇒ *"I was told that friendship with a German is like this: You give and you give and*
you give, and as soon as you stop giving the friendship is over. Then when I
lived in Germany some of the Germans I dealt with at work and in social situ-
ations indeed would take and take and assume that you're perfectly happy to
continue accommodating them until they got a firm 'No.'" (Hsieh S. H, m, Tw/
Ger)

⇒ *"When we had the big earthquake in 1999, many of my friends in America im-*
mediately wrote to me or called, asking whether everyone was okay. But I did
not hear anything from my German friends. I have various German friends
who are in academia and who always know how to find me when they need
something from Taiwan. Maybe they will write a card for Christmas but when
the earthquake struck no one seemed to care. I felt I meant nothing to them.
Another time, when after a ten year absence I was considering going back to
Germany for a year and wrote to some of my friends there telling them about
that possibility, I did not receive a response from any of them." (Lu W. C., f, Tw
/Ger)

Communicating with outsiders

Whereas a Chinese individual's identity and self-worth within the family are determined and assured by his roles, outside the family, identity and self-worth depend on a person's face, that is the respect and recognition received from others. Validation from others, important for people anywhere, holds additional significance for the relational self. Unlike Christianity based cultures that assume each human being to have inherent value, Chinese culture does not assign such value to the individual. With the worth of the relational self depending on how he is perceived by others, there is a great concern for enhancing and protecting one's image, even more so because face is a collective asset. Just as the achievements of a Chinese individual are not his own, a loss of face means bringing shame to one's family or group. Thus the ever-present reminders to the young: 'Don't disgrace the family.'

Given the importance of extending and receiving respect, the Chinese are careful about what they say and how they say it. This is especially important since in the Chinese view message and recipient are not separated which means that topics that might cause offense, worry, obligations or friction need to be avoided. Chinese speakers tend to be keen listeners and observers, alert for nonverbal clues, such as body language, voice quality, and implied meaning. Someone's eyes lighting up during a conversation might be understood as a sign that the person is feeling gleeful or superior. Or it might indicate that the person has a strong vested interest in the matter at hand, an insight that can possibly be used to one's own advantage. Nonetheless, in spite of good perceptional skills, misinterpretations and miscommunications are common.

Western and Chinese ways of communicating have been likened to a tennis match versus a bowling game. Whereas the tennis ball is being batted back and forth, the Chinese bowling style of speaking throws a ball and then takes time to see how many pins, if any, have been hit.

> *"For us speaking is all about the reaction by the other and the consequences for us. What will the other person do or think if I say that? Will he be mad at me or like me? It's not a matter of facts or truth or self-expression." (Fan Y., m, PRC /US)*

"We can't speak our minds because that might lead to conflict." (Chieh P. Y., f, Tw /US)

"When we speak we are careful because we don't want to offend people who are important to us. And because we Chinese are very concerned about what others think of us, we pay special attention to what others say and how they say it. We always fear to lose face, especially since there are a lot of Chinese who offend others by talking badly about them behind their backs." (Yeh H. S., m, Tw/US)

"We Chinese love food. Of course! But it has more value than that. Much can be achieved with food: It can generate face or serve as a strategy to get what you want or need. So when inviting someone to a meal in a restaurant, people will go to great lengths to be the one to pay. It's not generosity. We don't really want to pay, but we must for the sake of face." (Yang W. C., f, Tw/US)

"In the West, matters are matters. For us Chinese, all issues are people issues which means that people are easily offended and always afraid to lose face or be rejected." (Su M., m, PRC/US)

Politeness and indirectness

Politeness, which includes praise, flattery, stylized awe, and expressions of humility, is the primary way to show deference, that is, to "give" face (*gei mianzi*) to others. It is particularly effective and appreciated when demonstrated in the presence of others or in public. Although politeness in personal interactions is also a pleasant habit in Chinese daily life, showing deference applies first and foremost to superiors, people who are older than you, to persons who hold authority or power, or to individuals who are or are perceived to be rich and for that reason can be assumed to have power and influence.

Westerners often see Chinese politeness as insincere because what is said may not be in line with inner thoughts and feelings. However, to the Chinese, politeness responds to a sensitivity to the human hierarchical network and serves as a means to avoid conflict and maintain a proper distance through form. An inner dimension is not expected, which means that there is little concern over what Westerners would label hypocrisy or a gap between genuineness and appearance.

"When I speak Chinese I am more formal and more indirect. Especially in Chinese educated circles—I live in the academic world—I must praise and flatter to show respect and then the other person must do the same. Sincerity for the Chinese means acting in line with the expected Chinese behavior within a specific relationship, which sometimes comes close to meaning loyalty. The English meaning of honesty is broader." (Hope S. ABC/PRC)

"At work in Taiwan, you need to display respect with words and flattery, especially toward the boss and others who are senior to you." (Liu T. Y., f, Tw/US)

"For the Chinese praise is not flattery. It is to make people feel comfortable, though there is also a blurred line between deference and manipulation." (Jade Y. ABC/Tw)

"If someone pays you a compliment, for example, saying, 'You write beautifully!,' we shouldn't respond. Even saying 'You exaggerate' would mean that you took the comment seriously. Believing people too easily is a bad trait." (Tang P. H., f, Tw/US)

"We learn early on to be cautious, not to take people's words at face value." (Fu T. J., f, Tw/US)

Politeness ranks higher than truthfulness. Honesty is not a Chinese cultural value.

"Being polite ranks much higher than honesty. Politeness is the social norm, honesty is not." (Tan S. T., f, Tw/US)

"Nobody ever taught me to be truthful, and nowhere did I read that you have to be honest. But we did learn that a polite lie is more important than honesty." (C. H., Lin, Tw/US)

"We may think one thing, say something else, and do something else again." (Kuang S. K., m, Tw/US)

"I was told in China that I was too frank, which means being honest is not good." (Hope S., ABC/PRC)

"We laugh when others believe us. For us it's not about truth but about getting results." (He Y. Y., f, Tw/Ger)

⇨*"Westerners have more honesty. In our society we are concerned with harmony, not honesty." (Huang S. L., m, Tw/Ger)*

Indirectness is part of politeness and has a high positive value in Chinese communication for avoiding conflict and loss of face. For example, when wanting or needing to respond negatively to a request, the Chinese will rarely come out with a "No." Instead they might say "I'll think about it" or use one of numerous vague expressions that stand in for a negative answer. The common use of indirectness has trained the Chinese to always be alert for what might be implied.

> *"My mom will say 'no' in a very indirect way and all her friends are like that. Especially women are trained to be indirect." (Sung M. K., f, Tw/PRC/US)*

> *"People like indirectness because it avoids open conflict and loss of face. But it also leads to a lot of misunderstandings because it's difficult to read someone's intentions. Still it's safer not to reveal yourself." (Lo M. L., f, Tw/US)*

> *"Unless it's family or friends, in China we do not say things directly. For example, if I asked a guest in my home whether he would like something to eat, I'd expect the person to say, 'No, thank you,' even if in fact he is hungry and really would like something. Since we know that, we don't ask, but simply put things out on the table for them." (Tang P. H., f, Tw/US)*

> ⇒ *"If my American friends ask me whether I want to go to a movie with them, I tell them that I'll think about it, rather than 'No, I don't want to go.' But then they'll call me again later to ask whether I have decided. My Chinese friends will know right away that saying 'I'll think about it' means 'No, I don't want to go.'" (Andrew L., ABC/Tw)*

> ⇒ *"Germans don't understand our indirectness. If I say neither yes or no, a Chinese knows that it means no. But in Germany people didn't understand my signals. On the other hand their directness makes life simple. With Germans you do know what they mean. There is no guessing there, which makes life more relaxing and consumes less energy than our Chinese way of communicating." (Chu C. F., f, Tw/Ger)*

Chinese politeness includes a high level of attentiveness. The larger the power imbalance, the keener the attention and effort to elevate the other, and to lower the self through humility. But since even basic politeness entails a certain level of attentiveness, not receiving sufficient attention, or worse being ignored, is likely to be understood as a willful act of humiliation. This can be a problem for Chinese living in Germany, where nonintrusiveness is part of politeness and people show little inclination to be inclusive for the sake of politeness.

⇨ *"When I studied in Germany I signed up to help with the renovation of the bar, thinking it would help me meet German students. When I showed up on time, only Astrid, a girl from Frankfurt, was there doing some varnishing. She had me do some simple cleaning. Then when Christoph came in, he talked with Astrid and pretended not to see me. I just smiled, wondering how they could be so impolite, and not at least ask who I was. Even though I continued to volunteer there, for a long time nobody talked to me. To me their behavior said 'I am not interested in you.' But later Christoph told me that he was afraid to approach me. We Taiwanese may also ignore others and we may even talk about them behind their backs, but when face to face we are attentive and polite. But in this case the Germans pretended they didn't even see me!" (He Y. Y., f, Tw/Ger)*

⇨ *"When I studied in Germany I shared an apartment with several roommates. When one of them injured his leg and had to spend several days in the hospital, another roommate suggested that we go and see him in the hospital. So he and I went, but then the two of them just talked to each other, and let me just stand there. When after an hour or so I said I'd leave, they just said 'Bye' and let me go. I thought they were very impolite to ignore me like that." (Hsieh S. H., m, Tw/Ger)*

⇨ *"At the German university I found it very difficult to make contact with Germans, not so much because of the language barrier, but mostly because Germans are so closed. Yet, when we organized an event designed for us foreigners to meet Germans, a lot of Germans came and it was fun and cheerful. " (Fan T. P., m, Tw/Ger)*

⇨ *"Our Chinese politeness is a bit of a mask, but it's a matter of respect. I miss that in Germany." (Chung C. Y., f, Tw/Ger)*

Withholding criticism

The nonseparation of message and recipient in Chinese speech means that all criticism is taken personally. Criticism within the family or by authority figures, even though hard to bear, is considered normal, but criticism toward or by outsiders is perceived as arrogance or intentional humiliation. If it takes place before others or in public, it is ever so much more serious and likely to cause a long-lasting animosity.

> *"We Chinese do not criticize others. In Christian societies human value is inherent; you don't lose it by being criticized, but we Chinese need approval from others to have worth, so we don't criticize others." (Huang S. L., m, Tw/Ger)*

> *"Criticizing is naïve. It only antagonizes people and doesn't bring about change. Chinese society has never been after justice. People don't expect it and they don't ask for it. There is no truth, no right or wrong, only the other's feelings and reactions to contend with." (Cheng A. L., f, Tw/Ger)*

> *"Most Chinese are offended if they hear a criticism, though they wouldn't tell you. They cannot or don't want to look within. So when someone criticizes them, they feel that they are being looked down upon. Once, when I suggested to a Chinese friend of mine—someone who was rather passive—to be a bit more assertive, she reacted badly, saying she would always remember that I wanted to hurt her and that we could never be really good friends again. So even between friends it can be a problem." (He Y. Y., f, Tw/Ger)*

> *"Even though I grew up in the US, I definitely feel more Chinese than American when I am with other Chinese. But when I lived in Hong Kong, there were certain occasions when I felt American. One area was dealing with confrontations. For the Chinese there isn't such a thing as 'Don't take it personally.' Everything is personal." (Rose C. ABC/Hong Kong)*

> *"We Chinese are afraid of being laughed at. Yet we frequently laugh at others. If you are wrong or make a mistake people laugh at you, which is why we don't answer questions in class. In elementary school teachers commonly ridicule kids and shame them that way. But Chinese also laugh at cripples, people who have fallen down, or if someone runs much more slowly than the rest. Basically it's a strong person laughing at a weak one." (Fan Y., m, PRC/US)*

> ⇨ *"When people criticize or ignore me, I feel they look down on me. Americans are more thick-skinned and criticism does not bother them that much. But to*

us criticism is really devastating. I was shocked when I heard one professor criticize another in front of students." (Tan S. T., f, Tw/US)

⇒ *"Americans feel superior and pick the faults of others." (Fang Y. W., f, Tw/US)*

⇒ *"Germans don't criticize their friends behind their backs, but they do a lot of finger pointing in public. With us it's the opposite." (Cheng A. L., f, Tw/Ger)*

Occasionally the Chinese do criticize, but when they do, it may hardly be recognizable, at least to Western ears. When I was working in a Buddhist charity organization in Taiwan, I was struck by one of its songs, which started out with the words, "In my world there is no one I do not love, in my world there is no one I do not trust." Both the melody and the words sounded beautiful to me. But since in the Chinese world I had come to know things were not this way, I asked a coworker to help me understand the meaning of those words. "When we hear something like that," he explained, "we Chinese intuitively know that there is a problem. Otherwise it wouldn't be said. Words that make an unrealistically positive statement draw attention to a problem. In this case the song criticizes people for not trusting others. But when you state things positively like that, nobody can blame you for criticizing anybody; and yet you have just criticized somebody."

Self-protection

Equally important to granting face to others is protecting one's own face. Warding off loss of face is a common concern when communicating with outsiders. It means not divulging family secrets or personal weaknesses, saying less rather than more and guarding against giving away information through body language. Self-protection also includes not admitting mistakes or guilt or lowering yourself through apologies.

Keeping family secrets covers any information that might tarnish the family's reputation, such as a son having failed his exam, an aunt having contracted a contagious disease, or a cousin exhibiting a mental health problem. Those who write about their family history find that they need to omit anything not complimentary. The shame and stigma attached to negatives might be partially due to the Buddhist belief that a person's ill fate or disability may be punishment for a wrong committed in a former life.

"We have to protect our image, so we don't self criticize or admit mistakes." (Huang S. L., m, Tw/Ger)

"If we made a mistake we never admit that we were wrong. We may say that we are sorry, but that would only be a required outward verbal humility. It is not an apology. I know that in Tianjin (a city in the PRC) there is an Apology and Gift Center which is thriving. Clients want to apologize but not do it them-selves, because they worry that they might lose face. There are many other similar services in other Chinese cities." (Fan Y., m, PRC/US)

"Outside the family we hide anything negative and pretend to be happy, but even within the extended family we don't talk about bad things—though we prob-ably have one or two people with whom we can share negative information. I have a lot of uncles and aunts, but most don't know what's really going on in the family. When we meet for family reunions, people don't talk about things that make people feel bad, and yet people are not as happy as they seem." (Teng T. Y., m, Hong Kong/Tw/US)

"I may have big fights in my family, but if guests come, I am humble. Toward the outside you pretend everything is normal, so both humility and face are important in communication with nonfamily." (Ma C. H., m, Tw/US)

Holding back on negative information also avoids burdening others with worry or the obligation to help. For the relational self it is a self-evident truth that any assistance or help received requires a payback of some kind, whether that be in a material way or as loyalty. While having others indebted to you feels good and adds to a sense of security, being indebted feels uncomfortable by creating undesirable obligations.

"I very rarely share my difficulties with others, because that would mean that they must help. We Chinese think we are responsible for the feelings of others, so we should not burden others." (Peng Y. F., f, Tw/US)

"We don't share difficulties with others because we fear that others will worry, that we will impose on them, or that they will gossip about it." (Tu C. L., m, Tw /US)

The Chinese also tend to be reticent about volunteering information that is not specifically asked for. They share the view that too many words just get you into trouble, especially since the content of conversations is viewed as public property and gets freely passed on to others. Holding back with information, especially any potentially negative information, not only wards off loss of face it also prevents others from using the information to their advantage. Assuming the outside world to be an untrustworthy place, the Chinese often marvel at how easily Westerners give away information.

⇨ *"In America you can't ask people whether they are married, how many children they have, or how much money they make and you can't ask a woman how old she is. For us these are silly taboos because we commonly ask these questions when meeting someone. Yet, on the other hand, Americans have too much trust and foolishly give away too much information." (Peng J. L., m, Tw/PRC/US))*

⇨ *"In the academic world Westerners disclose more about their research than most Chinese would. Perhaps Americans do so as a warning so that you will not work on the same problem, and they may control the information up to a point, not giving away all the information. But the Europeans tell it all, almost too much. The Chinese won't do it. They are afraid that others will copy. They want to protect themselves, which means that in the field of scientific research Taiwan is very closed." (Tu C. L., m, Tw/US)*

Communication is stressful

Given the importance of granting face to others and protecting one's own, many Chinese see communication as stressful, not as a pastime. Talking spells trouble, which is why less is better than more. Staying in a group and having the television turned on also ease the discomfort by reducing the need for having to think of what to say.

"In Taiwan people do not sit together and talk. They can't do it because they need to self-protect in order to avoid trouble. And since what you say is considered public property, people often don't know what to say. So they feel safer in a group setting. Americans can be more open because they don't expect others to abuse that information. The core problem is that the Chinese don't respect

each other. They find themselves in a narrow pyramidal hierarchic system, where you don't trust anyone." (Tu C. L., m, Tw/US)

"We experience a lot of stress from protecting face and seeking approval from others." (Huang S. L., m, Tw/Ger)

⇨ *"At many college parties in the US, you walk around and have one minute conversations and then you switch. You are expected to go and meet people, be social, to be a good conversationalist. We Chinese are not good at that." (Matthew C., ABC/Tw)*

⇨ *"Chinese conversations usually contain a lot of complaints about people which means that Chinese talk is not happy talk. It's very rare that they would talk about what they would like to do or are excited about. When my husband's German family comes together it's very different: They usually have a good time talking which makes their family gatherings more joyful." (Pang H. Y., f, Tw/Ger)*

⇨ *"After having lived in the US for several years, I now find the Chinese way of speaking very rigid. Not expressing feelings, always acting constrained and being so fearful—isn't it a huge burden to live like that? Why do I need to go to such effort to find out what people really mean? It is very exhausting for me." (Sung M. K., f, Tw/PRC/US)*

Work and money

Work

Most Chinese work very hard and take little time off to engage in activities that do not impact the bottom line. Yet, interest in the particular job is often low. Work per se has little inherent value, as its worth lies in the result: the monetary award.

"If you like what you do, that is a bonus, but people are taught not to expect it. The important thing is to make money to provide all the status symbols within and outside the family that are necessary to make the family proud." (Rose C., ABC/Hong Kong)

"Nowadays the salary expectations of Taiwanese are high. Many young people go without jobs, when they think the salary is too low. They don't have to worry because even if they don't take a job, they will still have a place to live and food to eat (in their families). In America, when you are eighteen, you want to be independent and your parents want you to be independent. Work does not define the Chinese the way it defines Americans." (Pai T. Y., f, Tw/US)

Relationships, so important in the Chinese relational world, also determine the character of the work place. Instead of job descriptions spelling out the duties and responsibilities of an employee, most Chinese work places do not make a clear distinction between official and personal business. Employees are commonly expected to run private errands for their superiors and their success and promotion at work is largely determined by their loyalty to those in power, not by their work performance.

"We learn loyalty, not responsibility. All through life things are decided for us: At home our parents tell us what to do; at school it's the teachers or the program; and at work the boss will tell us. Our responsibility is to please. Because of all this external discipline we don't know how to take responsibility or to make decisions ourselves and we don't develop self-discipline." (Ma C. H., m, Tw/US)

"In America I learned that in life others may help me tangentially but my success is the result of my own work and so is my failure. In China we need others to move up the ladder. So you need to create connections and relationships, usually by means of submission and flattery. If you flatter your boss, the boss will know that this is phony behavior but nonetheless he will promote that person over someone else who does a good job but does not flatter. As a medical doctor I wanted to do good work and not like most other doctors in the hospital use patients for drug trials without their knowledge and consent. In China that is very common because doctors get paid for it. So when I realized that I could never have gotten a promotion on the basis of my work, no matter how long I stayed, I left and changed professions." (Fan Y., m, PRC/US)

"Actually it's easier when the boss tells us what to do, because that way we are not responsible for the result." (Tang P. H., f, Tw/US)

"In Germany, if an assignment is undertaken by a team, someone is in charge of distributing the work. Here in Taiwan we may have three or four people

working on a given project, but each of them thinks the others will do it, or that someone else will divide and distribute the work. It's never clearly defined who is responsible for what." (Pang H. Y., f, Tw/Ger)

"In my view less than half, perhaps forty percent, of the Chinese take responsibility for their actions. Greedy businesses may ask for accountability from their workers but they don't have any accountability themselves. You can see it in so much deception and poor construction. It's a one way street for the powerful and rich. There is no accountability or responsibility." (Sung M. K., f, Tw/PRC/US)

"An important finding during my trip back home was that in Taiwan people like to blame others. Whenever something goes wrong, they immediately start thinking about who's to blame instead of seeking a solution. As a result when something happens everyone clears out and claims innocence. I call this 'persecutory delusion.'" (Cheng A. L., f, Tw/Ger)

"We Chinese work long hours and we are not stupid, but we are not very productive. In my office we all work until ten o'clock at night. But people don't work efficiently. It's only for the boss to see. In the US people are more self-motivated, whereas in a Chinese company much of the work time is done for show." (Ma C. H., m, Tw/US)

Chinese employers rarely encourage their employees to think beyond the immediate assigned task or to take the initiative, which has the effect that showing interest in the broader issues of the organization, or simply doing extra good work, is suspect.

"I can't think about things not directly delegated to me. If I suggested anything that might be good for the company or even just asked my boss about the visitors I just had to brief about our company, I would be perceived as too anxious, too ambitious. Doing too much, being too efficient or being too good generates envy among coworkers. They will assume that there is something in it for you personally or else you would not do it. In reality, the Chinese work environment is highly competitive, but it must not look that way." (Li K. P., m, Tw/US)

"I love teaching. And though I was hired only as a part-time English teacher, when the lead trainer came to observe my classroom, she liked how I taught and said, 'You are a natural.' I took it as a compliment, but apparently other teachers heard about the comment and did not like it. The Chinese cannot tolerate it if someone is good." (Sung M. K., f, Tw/PRC/US)

⇒ *"In the US saying someone lacks ambition is a negative statement. In China it is bad to be ambitious. It means being selfish. Say, I would like to have a certain position within a couple of years and want to work toward it—in the US I can say it. In China I cannot." (Tsou P. Y., f, Tw/US)*

"During staff meetings our boss often tells us that we are a team, like a family, in which everyone is equal. 'So if you have suggestions, speak up,' he says. In reality we all know that it's words only and that it would be very risky to speak up. So nobody ever does." (Lu H. T., f, Tw/Asia)

Several Chinese who returned to their home country after having lived and worked in the West, commented on the lack of a cooperative spirit among the Chinese.

"Chinese workers are not interested in keeping records of their work for the next person who might hold their job. The thinking is: I don't want to share my intellectual property. Let others find out for themselves." (Chien H. M., m, Tw/US)

"For my scientific projects in China it is difficult to get quality data because the team members don't cooperate. It's not that they don't know how to do the work. That problem could be solved with more training. But it's that I can't change the Chinese human software." (Chao J., f, PRC/US)

"I came back to Taiwan after I retired from my academic career in the US hoping that I could help raise the standard of graduate research here. But now after a year I feel disillusioned and I resigned from one project because I felt I could not accomplish anything worthwhile. Chinese relationships are just too complicated. People are always suspicious of your motives." (Wei H. J., m, Tw/US)

While Chinese workers have little opportunity to develop self-motivation and responsibility, they learn the virtues of acceptance and resilience.

"My supervisor in the office, who has been on her job for nine years, criticized me beginning with my first week, saying things like: 'You are stupid,' or 'You are an idiot, how can you not know such and such?' I realize that this criticism is her way of challenging me, her way of encouraging me and making me resilient." (He Y. Y., f, Tw/Ger)

"We have a saying in Chinese which literally means something like 'Rubbing an iron rod results in embroidery.' It refers to perseverance, meaning that you can take a steel rod and rub it until it's thin enough for a needle. It's a pretty way of saying it and, like so many other pretty sayings in Chinese, it accents the positive. However to my mind, the process of training the young in perseverance is often harsh." (Tan S. T., f, Tw/US)

"There is an old saying, 'If you are around long enough, you will get the best seat.' At work it's the same. It takes resilience and patience, which is a strength if you grow up in a harsh social environment. I am quiet, but I am tough. At work they made things difficult for me in order to get me to leave, but I was still there after the others were all gone. I think we Chinese have an ability to cope with what is handed to us. It's the result of all the practice and experience we've had in this." (Lo M. L., f, Tw/US)

Money

Maximizing family income and assets is a Chinese adult's primary obligation, while preparing the next generation for that role is the main parental concern. For centuries Chinese families effectively pooled resources to allow a member of their extended family to study for the civil service examination. If successful and subsequently obtaining an official position, it was understood that this individual would then support his extended family. Education of the children continues to have that meaning.

"The job of a person is to take care of their parents when they are old. And you can't do that if you don't have a good job, and you can't get a good job without studying. So it's the parents responsibility to make sure the child studies hard. If I say to my mom I want to go out and run, she will say that you can't make money with that, that it's no use, just a waste of time." (Ma C. H., m, Tw/US)

"Our parents paid so much for us and worked so hard for us. We are their investment and are expected to pay them back in old age. So as a parent you want to make your children psychologically dependent, so that your investment won't run away." (Fu T. J., f, Tw/US)

"For Taiwanese parents the child's success is for their own glory. Even if they have saved for retirement and don't depend on their children for support in old age, many children still will give money to the parents to express their filial piety." (Tsou P. Y., f, Tw/US)

"You need a lot of money to fulfill family obligations, both as a child and as a parent. If it weren't for these expectations I might not aim for the highest paying job. But our families want us to help them, so we carry a heavy responsibility." (Tu C. L., m, Tw/US)

Apart from the role money plays toward fulfilling family obligations, wealth translates into being treated with respect, i.e. having face, an identity. "Being rich is glorious." For a while that was an official slogan in China and even though politicians may not use these exact words any more, the idea that being rich is glorious is a thread that has run through Chinese life for centuries. The following paragraph taken from *The Dream of the Red Chamber*, a famous eighteenth-century Chinese novel, which is read by nearly all Chinese at some time during their youth, reflects the importance of money for the Chinese relational self, then as well as now.

"The loser (at the gambling table) scolded them for hanging around the winners hoping for tips and favors. The boys kneeled and said coaxingly: 'Please don't be angry with us, Uncle. We are only boys and act as our master has taught us, which is to act nicely only to those who have the most money. If you don't believe it, just win a few big hands and see how nice we can be to you.' Everyone laughed at the guileless speech." [5]

Because money is the prime measuring stick for things in life, the Chinese are preoccupied with the accumulation of wealth.

"Chinese worship their gods of prosperity because everything is perceived in monetary value." (Sung M. K., f, Tw/PRC/US)

"My mom told me that if I didn't know that money is the most important thing in life it's because I hadn't grown up yet." (Yang W. C., f, Tw/US)

"Love is money. We don't kiss and cuddle like foreigners. Instead we buy things for our children and leave an inheritance for them." (Pien Y. F., Tw/US)

"For years we Chinese thought every white person was rich. If tomorrow Ethiopia became the strongest country in the world, we would admire them and consider them divine, and all of a sudden we would think that all black people are the richest and the best." (Cheng A. L., f, Tw/Ger)

"When it comes to money, we fret a lot about the little things: How to save twenty cents by taking the subway in another more cumbersome way, or spending a long time to bargain something down by a few dollars. This sort of thing gives us pride and something to brag about." (Chieh P. Y., Tw/US)

My Chinese respondents became aware that Westerners seemed to have a different attitude towards money. They would talk less about it, work not as much and spend money on frivolous things, such as comfort, convenience and travel.

⇨ *"The local Canadians in Vancouver are very uncomfortable with the lifestyle of the Chinese there, their ostentatious display of wealth, their huge houses, and their teenage kids with fancy cars." (Fang Y. W., f, Tw/US)*

⇨ *"From living in the United States I have come to see that people's priorities in life are quite different. There are a lot of other focal points, not just money. In Taiwan it is not what you do or whether you like what you are doing. Money is what counts. Americans may not have much savings but they can be happy without it." (Hou F. L., f, Tw/US)*

⇨ *"Americans spend a lot of money on travel. Even students do so and they may start families before they are economically secure. These are risks we Chinese don't take." (Liu T. Y., f, Tw/US)*

⇨ *"In Germany people talk less about money. Also, more mothers stay at home, because for them money is not number one." (Ku H. J., f, Tw/Ger)*

Apart from its function of fulfilling family obligations and generating respect and status, money represents power and security. While the money-power connection holds true everywhere, in Chinese society money and power—and therefore money and security—are considerably more intertwined than in the US and in Germany. This aspect of money will be addressed in the next chapter.

The feel of life

"It's okay, I don't hate it"

When my American friend Helen came to visit Taiwan, we spent an afternoon in one of the teahouses in Mucha on the outskirts of Taipei. As we sipped our tea and delighted in the view over the tea plantations, we watched several Chinese families enjoying themselves nearby. While the adults were talking boisterously over tea and food, their small children were having a great time noisily running around, bumping into tables and chairs. That evening Helen, who had never been to either Taiwan or mainland China before, remarked: "After this one day in Taiwan I can tell that the Chinese are a loud and happy people." Later during my interviews I asked several of my Chinese conversation partners whether they thought Helen's remark was a fair description. While they agreed on the noisy part they overwhelmingly rejected the idea that the Chinese were a happy people.

> *"There is little question that the Taiwanese are loud but they are not as happy as they seem. When Chinese get together they don't talk about negative, troublesome things. You hide those and pretend to be happy. If you ask any deeper question people avoid answering." (Teng T. Y., m, Hong Kong, Tw/US)*

> *"People are not happy in their hearts. Our financial burden makes life stressful, not happy." (Ma C. H., m, Tw/US)*

> *"There is so much fear in the Chinese psyche: Fear of failure, hopelessness, fear of the future, fear of arousing the wrath of ancestors which would make them reappear as ghosts. My parents always expect the worst and can think only of money that would get you out of that pigeon hole." (Sung M. K., f, Tw/PRC/ US)*

> *"So many young people are depressed these days. We call them the 'strawberry generation,' meaning that they are crushed as easily as strawberries. These people are weak and don't know what they like, because all they have learned is to study for school. So when they start working and find that they are not making enough money, they are unhappy. That is especially true for those who come from financially well-to-do homes." (Chiang Y. H., f, Tw/US)*

"I think it's an illusion to think that the Chinese are happy. Most Chinese don't have any imagination and they have no wishes. They just think about working to make money. I love to draw. So when I come home from my teaching job, I want to do something creative, something that is not done for money. But my mother keeps urging me to teach evening classes in one of the cram schools for extra income. 'Why dream about drawing?' she says. 'You can't earn money with that!' But I am happy when I am alone and have time to myself." (Yang W. C., f, Tw/US)

"Do we Chinese enjoy life? Except for one uncle I don't know anybody who enjoys life. All the others, including my dad, are simply consumed by work and stressed out. But that one uncle does enjoy life. He loves gardening and has other interests." (Hu T. H., m, Tw/US)

Yet, those Chinese who never left their country and are unfamiliar with other lifestyles are unlikely to think about happiness. Aware that they have limited control over their lives, they see little use in thinking about what they might want or like to do. Better to be satisfied with an attitude of "It's okay, I don't hate it" (*hai hao, bu taoyan*). I first took note of this phrase when I asked one of my husband's family members who was pursuing an advanced degree in biology how she liked her field of study. "It's okay, I don't hate it," she said. At the time I felt it was rather sad for someone to start a career in a specialization that did not seem to hold much interest. Later I explored the topic during my conversations with other Chinese.

"We don't know what we like or want, and so we don't stand up for what we want in life. If it's good enough and we don't strongly dislike something, it's okay. I think eighty percent of the Chinese share the attitude of 'It's okay, I don't hate it.'" (Hu T. H., m, Tw/US)

"People don't think about what they like and don't like. They don't know that there is another world. It's a plain vanilla life. They are not unhappy, since there is no comparison. You obey, you study hard, and you'll be okay." (Yeh H. S., m, Tw/US)

"If you spend time thinking about what you would want to do with your life, you might end up dissatisfied and feel depressed. That's not how you want to be.

You need to be strong. Thinking about those kinds of things is also self-indul-
gent, and means you are making yourself more important than the family."
(Doris F., ABC)

⇒ *"The Western way of looking for happiness is selfish. It goes against the family."*
(Jade Y., ABC/Tw)

Over the years I have often marveled at Chinese grandmothers who take full-time care of their grandchildren, often caring for several children and for several years. So one day I asked Grandma Yeh, who after spending six years taking care of her daughter's three children and then was doing the same for her son's two children: "Do you enjoy taking care of the children?" Her answer was simple: "It's not a matter of whether I like it or not. It's what I should do." Grandma Li, who for several years cared for five of her grandchildren, all at the same time, responded in the same way: "It has nothing to do with whether I enjoy it or not."

Acceptance and simple pleasures

In a world where the individual is defined as a member of the group, subject to various layers of authority and having little control over his life, acceptance, balance, and hardiness are cardinal virtues. Indeed it appears that the Chinese generally accept fate with equanimity. As the famous Chinese philosopher Zhuangzi said over two thousand years ago: "Happiness is the absence of the striving for happiness."

The Chinese blend of Confucianism, Buddhism and Taoism includes the belief that the world is constantly changing and that things move between opposite poles. This awareness calls for moderation and balance. Several of my Chinese conversation partners reminded me of the well-known Chinese tale of the lost horse, a story that illustrates the wisdom of acceptance, because what is good today may be bad tomorrow and vice versa.

As told by Chin-Ning Chu the story goes like this: A man named Sei Weng owned a beautiful mare which was praised far and wide. One day this beautiful horse disappeared. The people of his village offered sympathy to Sei Weng for his great misfortune, but Sei Weng said simply, "That's the way it is." A few days later the lost mare returned, followed by a beautiful wild stallion. The village congratulated Sei Weng for his good fortune. He said, "That's the way it is." Sometime later, Sei Weng's only son, while riding the stallion, fell off and broke his leg. The village people once again expressed their sympathy for Sei Weng's misfortune. And Sei Weng again said, "That's the way it is." Soon thereafter, war broke out and all the young men of the village except Sei Weng's lame son were drafted and subsequently killed in battle. The village people were amazed at Sei Weng's good luck. His son was the only young man left alive in the village. But Sei Weng kept his same attitude: despite all the turmoil, gains and losses, he gave the same reply: "That's the way it is." [6]

Just as good fortune may turn out to be bad fortune as in the story of the lost horse, and therefore requires a dispassionate response, the Chinese saying of "Too much happiness generates sorrow (le ji sheng bei)" implies that intense emotions, such as passion and excitement, are best avoided.

> "According to the Confucian Doctrine of the Mean, which we all learned about in school, in life we should neither like nor dislike anything too much. So an attitude of 'It's okay, I don't hate it' is all right. It means I am not happy and I am not unhappy." (Ma C. H., m, Tw/US)

> "Our belief in fate relieves us of anxiety and gives us a sense of equanimity. I won't be frustrated, but at the same time I won't try to go against fate." (Lo M. L., f, Tw/US)

Instead of self-confidence the Chinese stress the need for resilience, which is sometimes likened to a bamboo that bends with the wind. As such it represents a positive image of strength. While acceptance of fate provides them with a sense of wise detachment, resilience and hardiness protect them against disillusionment and endow them with the strength to persevere in the face of difficult situations. Expecting no constancy, the Chinese excel at reconfiguring themselves according to the needs of the moment while enjoying the simple pleasures that come along.

Most commonly these simple pleasures come in the form of a good meal. In his book *The Importance of Living*, Lin Yutang aptly described this aspect of

Chinese life: "How a Chinese spirit glows over a good feast! How apt is he to cry out that life is beautiful when his stomach and his intestines are well-filled. From this well-filled stomach suffuses and radiates a happiness that is spiritual. . . .The Chinese idea of happiness is, as I have noted elsewhere, being 'warm, well-filled, dark and sweet'—referring to the condition of going to bed after a good supper." [7] Now, decades later, food continues to be the mainstay of Chinese pleasure along with shopping, karaoke and gaming.

> *"People's interests are very narrow: It's mostly eating, playing mahjong and gambling. People don't have hobbies, because it would take time away from earning money." (Teng T. Y., m, Hong Kong/Tw/US)*

> *"For us fun is either eating or shopping." (Lo M. L., f, Tw/US)*

> *"We are expected to always be considerate of relatives, the boss, coworkers, of everybody around us. That drains energy. So we go to karaoke bars to relieve stress." (Hsieh S. H., m, Tw/Ger)*

> *"In Taiwan, if you find yourself alone one night, you can always call people and easily round up five or six friends for company. In America there is less spontaneity. They need to invite people ahead of time, maybe even alert neighbors about an upcoming party. In Taiwan we just bring food and descend on somebody's home and have a good time together. In the US you can't do that. It would encroach on the other's privacy and freedom." (Tu C. L., m, Tw/US)*

Nonetheless, many of those who lived in the US or in Germany came to appreciate the variety of opportunities to enjoy life that they found there.

> ⇨ *"In Taiwan students only study and people only work. In the US people work AND enjoy life. In Taiwan we work long hours and the pace of life is very hectic. We don't know how to enjoy life and take care of ourselves. I think in America people live healthier lives, and have fun in a lot more natural ways. My fellow American students had a social life and played sports. They liked going to the beach, swimming or skiing. In Taiwan our activities are less varied and mostly inside. We sing karaoke, play group games, and we spend a lot of time playing online games." (Fang Y. W., f, Tw/US)*

> ⇨ *"Before coming to the US I thought I just needed to study and so I started out just focusing on my studies. But as time went by I realized that there is more*

to life than studying, that there are many other things one can do in life." (Hou F. L., f, Tw/US)

⇨ "When I lived in the US as a student I noticed that many of the cars in the student parking lots had baby seats in them. And if I asked my class mates after class 'How about lunch together?' they might say that they had to go and pick up their son or daughter some place. A lot of these students were my age, but they had a life besides being students. That would not happen in Taiwan or in Hong Kong." (Teng T. Y., m, Hong Kong/Tw/US)

⇨ "The German enjoyment of life is less visible. I think Germans are more in touch with nature and more concerned with a healthy lifestyle. In Germany, if you don't want to, you don't have to deal with the hectic city life. At night or over the weekend the cities look as if there was nothing going on. Here in Taiwan everything is visible in the streets: People eat, meet friends or go shopping." (Hsieh S. H., m, Tw/Ger)

⇨ "In Germany I saw that everybody had their own life, and much of their time was spent being alone. Germans have interests and hobbies; maybe they are into exercise or sports—and it's not necessarily soccer. In Taiwan we have no personal interests. Everybody's goal is to go to graduate school, but it does not matter which subject you choose, or whether you like it or not. I graduated a year ago with a degree in German. 'How come you are interested in German,' people often ask me, but in a negative way. Some even told me—supposedly as a joke—that I must be mentally deranged to study German. The Chinese just stick together, mostly because it feels safe. They are afraid to be alone and face themselves." (He Y. Y., f, Tw/Ger)

Pursuit of respect

Rather than seeking personal happiness or looking for purpose the Chinese relational self pursues social respect, the core ingredient that determines his worth.

"Westerners ask themselves 'Who am I?' or "Why am I here?' They look for purpose. But for that you need freedom and choice, because different answers are possible. For us Chinese there is only one goal: The pursuit of respect from *others (<u>zhuiqiu bie ren de zunjing</u>). And for respect you need money." (Chiang Y. H., f, Tw/US)*

"For the Chinese the pursuit of respect from others is a constant task. For them happiness depends on what others think of them. Yet, when they get older, many have regrets over not having gone beyond that." (He Y. Y., f, Tw/Ger)

"Whatever goals in life we might have, it would be in addition to making money. Happiness is not an issue. It is about social status and face." (Sung M. K., f, Tw /PRC/US)

Unfortunately, the good feeling that comes with respect and wealth has a parallel in a deep fear of not having sufficient money. Being poor, or just having less than someone else, means shame. In the strongly relational Chinese society in which people engage in a great deal of comparing, having less than others is an ever present worry.

* * *

Notes

[1] Qiu Zhang, Lin Tsuifen *One Country, Two Wives* (Xidai Press, 1994).

[2] Lin Yutang, *The Importance of Living* (New York: John Day Company, 1937), 63-64.

[3] Richard E. Nisbett. *The Geography of Thought: How Asians and Western-ers Think Differently … and Why* (New York, NY: Free Press. 2003). For a brief discussion of the book see Kate Volpe, "Geography of Thought," *Observer* (Vol.16, No.5 May, 2003). www.psychologicalscience.org/index.php/uncategorized/geography-of-thought.html

[4] Lin Yutang, *The Importance of Living*, 44-45.

[5] Tsao Hsueh-Chin, *Dream of the Red Chamber*. Translated by Chi-Chen Wang (New York, Twayne Publishers, 1958), 482.

[6] Chin-Ning Chu, *The Asian Mind Game: Unlocking the Hidden Agenda of the Asian Business Culture – a Westerner's Survival Manual* (New York: Macmillan Publishing Company, 1991), 182.

[7] Lin Yutang, *The Importance of Living*, 46.

IV. THE WORLD AROUND US

According to Chinese thinking, human bonds humanize and civilize by restraining people's selfish tendencies, making them conduct themselves properly. Thus the Chinese look to relationships for trust while freedom, primarily perceived as freedom from relational obligations, is understood to overlap with selfishness. This means that beyond family and other personal relationships, the Chinese wider world is a rather inhospitable place.

The belief in the inherent worth and equality of the individual human being, along with the Christian teaching to love your neighbor, allow Americans and Germans to view the world as somewhat kinder. In addition the Western value of truthfulness means that interactions beyond personal relationships are more transparent and therefore less stressful.

In his book *The Importance of Living*, Lin Yutang compares Chinese and American perceptions of the world, "The Christian believer lives in a world governed and watched over by God, to whom he has a constant personal relationship, and therefore in a world presided over by a kindly father. . . . On the other hand, the pagan lives in this world like an orphan, without the benefit of that consoling feeling that there is always someone in heaven who cares and who will, when that spiritual relationship called prayer is established, attend to his private personal welfare. It is no doubt a less cheery world. . . . And yet a pagan can come to the point where he looks on that perhaps warmer and cheerier world as a more childish world." [1]

The Chinese world

Distrust and fears

Chinese trust and security are based on personal relationships—primarily blood relationships—which entail loyalty and mutual obligations. This means that outside of relationships, distrust, vigilance and self-protection are in order as there is little expectation of goodness or fairness.

> "We Chinese are always afraid that others will take advantage of us. In a world where you expect deception and craftiness, you won't trust. If you were cheated once, you'll be all the wiser." (Su M., m, PRC/US)

> "If people don't know somebody, they assume that he is a bad person, someone who is out to deceive them." (Ma C. H., m, Tw/US)

> "I don't trust anybody and I don't trust the system. Rich and successful people can play the system and those with power create rules which they want others to follow but which don't apply to them." (Chien H. M., m, Tw/US)

Several of my Chinese interviewees reported having been initially fearful of the openness and trust Americans display toward strangers. Only gradually did they discover that it was harmless.

> ⇨ "We need to be polite only to the people we know. But here in the US people may start chatting with strangers. Initially, when people at the beach or in a restaurant came over and started talking to me, I was afraid. But over time I found out that they had no bad intentions." (Tsou P. Y., f, Tw/US)

> ⇨ "When I lived in the US I was taken aback when the young people in my building whom I didn't know at all said hi to me and smiled. I noticed that people also talked to strangers in the elevators. And once at the swimming pool an older woman started talking to me, asking me all sorts of things, what subject I was studying, what kind of work my father did, etc. I thought that was very strange and it made me feel uneasy." (Teng T. Y., m, Hong Kong/Tw/US)

> ⇨ "I now can talk with strangers and meet new people. When I go to a restaurant I can start talking to people I don't know. But I was not always that way.

Before I lived in the US, if someone started talking to me, I would immediately think, what does he want from me? But I don't have that feeling anymore because I saw how people interact with others in the United States. While there, I learned to say hello to people I pass in the street. However, I would still be afraid that others might take advantage of me." (Hu T. H., m, Tw/PRC/US)

The fear of strangers also accounts for the Chinese reluctance to travel alone as well as for their custom to accompany and take care of visitors, especially foreign visitors, to a degree rarely encountered in the US or in Germany.

"As a Chinese, when you are away from your family you are constantly worried about who is going to take care of you." (Sung M. K., f, Tw/PRC/US)

⇒ *"Westerners take more risks than we do. For example, they travel more, sometimes even alone!" (Liu T. Y., f, Tw/US)*

⇒ *"When I visited my German friend Uta in Shanghai, she told me that she was very busy and asked me whether I could go alone to visit a temple that day. In Taiwan we would not do that, especially when people from another country come to visit. We would take the time to accompany them." (Lu W. C., f, Tw/Ger)*

Chinese fears are primarily people fears, meaning that the Chinese spend relatively little time worrying about accidents, earthquakes, tsunamis, pollution, and other non-people related dangers and risks. Thus they tend to be surprised to discover that American fears are often about safety, concerns over roads or hiking trails that might be dangerous, toys with a loose screw or lead paint, or that Americans worry over the remote possibility of an accident, such as a child falling off a swing on the playground. Nor do the Chinese have the kind of *Weltangst* (worries about the world) that might preoccupy a German mind.

⇒ *"Americans see dangers lurking everywhere. They are particularly worried about children getting hurt. American homes have all sorts of safety features for young children. Their playgrounds have soft padding under each piece of equipment, and swings have disappeared for safety reasons." (Chien H. M., m, Tw/US)*

⇒ *"When I first got to Germany I was surprised to see German pedestrians wait for the traffic light to change, even when there was no car coming. They must feel very insecure." (Hsieh S. H., m, Tw/Ger)*

While the Chinese were astonished to find Westerners preoccupied with issues that seemed minor to them, Westerners, and Americans in particular, appeared to be incognizant of the true dangers in life, a competitive world in which cunningness and falsehood are rewarded. Instead of preparing their young for what they will face in the real world, the Chinese marvel at Americans raising their children with nursery tales in which the morally good is pitted against the bad but in the end, the good invariably prevails. Some of my Chinese conversation partners, however, took a more ambivalent view of their own society.

⇒ *"The American world is nicer, but Americans are unrealistically naïve. They think they can find security through control and planning." (Peng J. L., m, Tw/ PRC/US)*

⇒ *"In the US I felt more optimism. The world is not that bad. Here in Taiwan, there is a lot more fear that my actions will offend others or, if I am too successful, that others will feel jealous. So we are very cautious and hold back before we do or say something." (Pai T. Y., f, Tw/US)*

⇒ *"German society is well-planned, which means Germans don't need other people to the same degree we do. Ours does not give the individual that sense of security." (Cheng A. L., f, Tw/Ger)*

Security

Not surprisingly the Chinese look to meet their people fears with people security. Their first line of defense against the inhospitable world lies with the extended family. In return for loyalty, sacrifice, and sharing resources, family members derive a sense of security and protection against the outside world. Any loosening of family ties means insecurity, being out there alone in a world where no one will help you or care about you. In her book, *The Chopsticks-Fork Principle*, Cathy Bao Bean describes the discrepancies she felt when straddling the Chinese and American worlds during her childhood. "American parents got anxious if the children failed to make good friends who would be worthy confidantes. My own warned me against such a breach by 'aliens' . . . with tips on how to best form a tight circle of the family's wagons." [2] My Chinese conversation partners described their own sense of security in similar terms.

"My mom says that one's own family members are the only people in this world who would never hurt you." (Hsieh S. H., m, Tw/Ger)

"For us, the outside world is dangerous, so the family is our protected harbor (bi feng gang), which keeps the cold winds out. Within the family people are always there for you, even if there are no close feelings." (He Y. Y., f, Tw/Ger)

"In Chinese culture the concept of fairness does not exist, because that would imply an equality of the in- and outgroup and that simply is not the case. It's the lack of fairness and hostility out there that makes the family world feel so warm. The family is your defense group for facing and countering the hostile world." (Fan Y., m, PRC/US)

"Individualism has never been a value in Chinese society, but doing things as a group is related to feeling more secure." (Lu W. C., f, Tw/Ger)

The second line of defense against a perilous world is wealth. Though money represents security to people everywhere, in Chinese society its importance is hugely magnified. Money not only ensures a person's livelihood, accords social status, and makes life more pleasant, it also serves to circumvent inconvenient laws and provide access to persons with special skills and influence. Such connections are crucial in a world where personal power, not laws, decide whether you are right or wrong, or, in some circumstances, whether you live or die. "Money is the most important thing in life" was a phrase I heard many times during my conversations with Chinese.

"We seek family wealth and power for maximum security in an uncertain, hostile world. China has no concept of human rights and no ideal of equality, or even of fairness. I accept that. There is nothing I can do about it and it won't change. So the best thing is to accumulate wealth and with it power. Then you have control over certain events and people, which gives you some wiggle room." (Fan Y., m, PRC/US)

"In Chinese society the law does not protect you and does not give you rights. Money does. Taiwan is more capitalist than either the US or Germany. In Germany, and even in the US, the life of the individual person is better secured by the state. We lack that security from the social system, so we need to be more flexible." (Huang S. L., m, Tw/Ger)

"It's a one way street for the powerful and rich. There is no accountability for them. Even in the family, you can tell who has money. The person with money is more powerful than the others. The Chinese idea is that money will take care of everything. Many Chinese cannot think outside the box. They only see that money can do things." (Sung M. K., f, Tw/PRC/US)

⇨ *"In China, much of our social hierarchy is based on wealth, which means that the gap between rich and poor is blatant. In the US you don't see it as much." (Peng J. L., m, Tw/PRC/US)*

⇨ *"Once, when I shared a house with three other foreign students in the US, I remember finding a bank statement of one of my two German roommates when I was cleaning the house. It showed that he only had forty-two dollars in his account. I was shocked that a foreign student might have that little of a reserve. What if there was an emergency? We Chinese don't have that sense of security. We cannot rely on the government or any other assistance, which means we always need to have extra money for emergencies. For us this is very serious. Money means security." (Chiang H. Y., f, Tw/US)*

While it is painful to be exploited by the powerful, a common experience in Chinese society, several of the Chinese I talked to readily admitted that if they had power they too would make full use of it.

Freedom and selfishness

Overwhelmingly concerned with security, the Chinese traditionally have had little interest in individual freedom. Independence from others means isolation and insecurity. Moreover, because independence implies an absence of restraints through relationships, freedom is assumed to give rise to selfishness. Thus the Chinese concept of freedom has a negative connotation that is quite different from the American liberating sound of "Let freedom ring." Their understanding of freedom helps explain why the Chinese often say: "We don't think about freedom." "We don't want more freedom." "Freedom means selfishness."

*"I know we don't have freedom in China, and I don't care much about it. It's im-
   possible to have it, because we are all so tied into a web of human relationships. There is no point in pondering freedom or human rights." (Fan Y., m,
   PRC/US)*

*"In Chinese society the individual is defined by relationships with others and his
   worth lies in the role he plays in his relationships. There is no basis for freedom
   and human rights and the people are not ready for it." (Huang S. L., m, Tw/Ger)*

*"My sister has lived among Westerners for so many years now that she has lost
   some of our Chinese ways. What I most miss in her and regret is that she does
   not like to fit into the group. She wants to be free and independent of others.
   That to me is selfishness." (Doris F., ABC)*

⇒ *"There is too much freedom in America. We don't want it. It's the Wild West."
   (Wu J. Y., f, Tw/US)*

Nor is freedom of the mind an issue. One day, on my way to an interview
with a Taiwanese graduate student at the California Institute of Technology
in Pasadena I passed a sign in front of a church which read: *The freedom of the
mind is the beginning of all other freedoms.* "What do you think of this phrase?"
I asked my conversation partner after we sat down to talk. He did not hesitate
to answer. "Freedom of the mind? We don't have it." Not only do the Chinese
receive little encouragement to think independently, speaking one's mind would
also be impolite and self-centered.

*"I don't remember ever thinking about freedom. I feel perfectly free to think what
   I please, but of course, I wouldn't say it out loud, because if it wasn't what people want to hear, it would only create ill will." (Lu H. T., f, Tw/Asia)*

Though the Chinese have no basis for many freedoms, there is one kind of
freedom that they expect and take liberally: this is the freedom to disregard
impersonal rules. Some of my Chinese respondents maintained that in many
ways they were freer than Westerners, less hemmed in by rules and laws. For
centuries the Chinese have described their society as one that is ruled by men, as
opposed to societies ruled by law. Several Chinese reminded me of the anecdote
that tells of a policeman catching a man after he ran a red light. "Didn't you

see the light," the policeman asks. "Yes, I did," the man answers, "but I did not see you!" The story expresses two Chinese key ideas: That people need to be obeyed, not rules or laws; and that being caught is bad luck, not a reason to feel guilty. Over the years I myself have often witnessed the Chinese casual attitude toward rules. Even after years of living in the US, my Chinese companions are apt to happily disregard public rules. For example, when coming across a sign that says "No trespassing" they are likely to feel justified to ignore it, saying, "The sign does not make sense. Somebody just made up a rule. So let's just go!"

> *"People in Taiwan think that they are freer because in the US they have all the laws that they need to abide by. In Taiwan nobody follows them." (Pai T. Y., f, Tw/US)*

> *"Chinese society is chaotic. There are no rules, and that gives people freedom." (Sun A. T., m, PRC/US)*

> ⇒ *"In Germany you abide by rules. It's pretty rigid. We Chinese are more flexible. We don't challenge the rules. We just try to avoid them, go around them. Instead of asking for permission to do something, we simply don't ask." (Fan T. P., m, Tw/Ger)*

In some way the freedom from impersonal restraints represents the Chinese culture's version of the American doctrine of the individual. The scamp is a popular figure in Chinese literature. Lin Yutang idealized the rogue in his books because, as he writes, "The spirit of the scamp alone will save us from becoming lost as serially numbered units in the masses of disciplined, obedient, regimented and uniformed coolies. The scamp will be the last and most formidable enemy of dictatorships." [3]

Feeling powerless in an inhospitable world, Chinese look at guile and secrecy as a weapon of the weak against the strong. The pursuit of self-advantage is deemed a justified strategy for self-preservation in a competitive and unjust world. While some of my Chinese interviewees thought that Westerners were selfish because they did not care for their aging parents, others arrived at a new understanding of the meaning of freedom and selfishness, to the point of becoming critical of what they perceived as a pervasive selfishness in Chinese society.

"I think we Chinese are ruthlessly selfish. Perhaps it's because when most every-thing in your life is controlled by others, selfishness and manipulating others are the only ways to eke out a sphere where you get what you want." (Chien H. M., m, Tw/US)

"The Chinese people are so selfish and they will never ever change!" (Sung M. K., f, Tw/PRC/US)

⇒ *"Before I went to the US I thought that Americans were selfish because they don't take care of their parents and because they want all that privacy. Actu-ally, the Chinese people are more selfish. They first think of themselves. Many Chinese don't see that religion sets limits in the West, that the belief in God reinforces the value of self-discipline. Maybe Americans can have so much freedom because they internalize the authority of God." (Pai T. Y., f, Tw/US)*

⇒ *"I had heard about American individualism and understood it as selfishness. But actually it is very nice. It isn't selfish. For example, we have a fridge in our university lab which is too small for several milk containers; so my lab mate tells me to just help myself. No need to pay. I find Americans to be generous, often ready to help others. At least that's true for the people here at Caltech who are all well-educated." (Ma C. H., m, Tw/US)*

⇒ *"When people do something in Germany, it's usually for the 'I,' the <u>ich</u>. Still, it's mostly with an awareness of being a member of society and with a consider-ation for others in mind. The kind of selfishness I discover among the Chinese is rather unpolished and primitive. Every time I become aware of this, I sigh over the failure of education in our culture." (Cheng A. L., f, Tw/Ger)*

⇒ *"Western individualism does not mean selfishness. Instead our group-think-ing means lack of responsibility." (Huang S. L., m, Tw/Ger)*

The greater good

Though in Chinese culture the individual is thought of as less important than the family, he stands above the society at large. Many Chinese show little re-gard for the public good. Expecting to derive little benefit from society they are disinclined to contribute to it. Riding buses or trains without a ticket, not pay-ing taxes, disregarding copyrights are all commonplace and considered smart rather than selfish. Many of my Chinese conversation partners, whether from the People's Republic of China, from Taiwan or American born Chinese, had much to say about what they saw as a lack of social consciousness among the Chinese.

"If there is a greater good for the Chinese, it stops at the family border." (Doris F., ABC)

"The Chinese just think on a small scale. They don't think of the broader social or global well-being." (Tu C. L., m, Tw/US)

"The Chinese are very considerate when one on one, but not when they are in a group. As a group in a restaurant, an airport or some other public place, they can be out of control, showing no discipline whatsoever." (Hou F. L., f, Tw/US)

"We cooperate only if there is an ingroup, but not with outsiders. The Chinese saying 'Fertile water does not flow into your neighbors' fields' means keeping all the good stuff for yourself. This attitude bothers me. We are not raising the overall level of society. It's an obstacle to the development of the whole." (Andrew L., ABC/Tw)

"When I read Chinese materials in our local American library, I often find pages or pictures torn out. This is not true for materials written in other languages. It's a sign that the Chinese readers have no concern for public property." (Sun Y. H., m, Tw/US)

"When there are no personal obligations, people abuse others and use society to their own advantage. We see it in sweatshops, in human trafficking and in hospital ambulances waiting outside the execution grounds to harvest hu-man organs." (Fan Y., m, PRC/US)

"Evading taxes is a national pastime because people assume that much of this money goes into the private pockets of politicians, not into providing social services for the people." (Cheng A. L., f, Tw/US)

"I cannot put up with the emphasis on the family and the way of exploiting soci-ety for one's personal advantage. The Chinese have no concept of first come *first served. For example, when getting on the bus or train they use their elbows to push you aside in order to get a seat. They don't care. I am for myself, they think. People have little sense of community and no consideration for the common good. It's not at all the harmonious society Confucius advocated."* (Sung M. K., f, Tw/PRC/US)

"Our problem is with the ratio of people who will abuse society's rules. If ten out of a hundred do it, it might sustain itself at that level; but if fifty out of a hundred do it, then the other fifty will also start doing it to self-protect. If the number is large enough it becomes a vicious cycle." (Tu C. L., m, Tw/US)

The strong focus on the family also limits interest in public affairs. Chinese families like to remind their members that they should not pursue interests that do not contribute to the family bottom line or get involved in matters that are not relevant to the family well-being. To some, diverting interest and time away from the pursuit of the family good is selfish. To others, public matters are simply not interesting. If criticism is voiced it is mostly directed at specific officials or politicians, not at the social or political system.

"I am a social activist working with an environmental non-profit organization in Taiwan. My mom does not want me to do this. 'Take care of the family first,' she tells me. 'You can't worry about what other people do or not do.'" (Matthew T., ABC/Tw)

"The Chinese have lots of opinions on private affairs, how you should teach your children, what you should eat and not eat. But when it comes to public affairs people don't care and don't have an opinion, mostly because they assume it's of no use anyway. No matter how much talking you do, there won't be any results." (Pang H. Y., f, TW/Ger)

⇨ *"Americans love to debate rules and policies. When there is a new law they sound off, saying nobody can tell them not to do this or that. On and on they go, harping on 'It's my choice, it's my choice . . .'. This is so boring. It's a waste of my time. I need to preserve my energy."* (Doris F., ABC)

⇨ *"Germans often pick on people in public even when it is of no benefit to them personally. Being a crusader trying to change the world is naïve, because it only antagonizes people and doesn't bring about change. Getting involved in something that has no impact on me or my family is arrogant. What business do I have to tell other people what to do?" (Chu C. F., f, Tw/US/Ger)*

⇒ *"I don't understand why Germans can get so excited about politics. I have no interest in politics, because there is nothing I can do about it." (Lu W. C., f, Tw/ Ger)*

When talking about the lack of concern for the public good, my Chinese conversation partners liked to point to China's overpopulation and long-term poverty as the reason. Some concluded that the country having been poor for so long has had the effect that the entire society is based on self-interest as a matter of survival.

"I don't think it is a hostile world. Rather it is a world of limited opportunities, so you look for advantages and opportunities to get ahead." (Hope S., ABC/PRC)

Whatever the strength of that argument, the focus on family and personal relationships, which is an integral part of Chinese culture, almost certainly contributes to the lack of commitment to the public good. For example, the Confucian tradition of distinguishing between five sets of relationships (ruler/subject, father/son, husband/wife, older brother/younger brother, friend/friend), each with clear moral obligations, implies that there are few obligations toward fellow citizens who fall outside these five relationships. In addition, Chinese relational thinking, which elevates the personal over the impersonal and the specific over the abstract, does little to encourage the idea of contributing to an impersonal goal, such as the public good.

Strong family ties mean that there is little social cohesion above personal relationships. During the May Fourth Movement, a political movement in the early twentieth century, Chinese reformers unsuccessfully tried to spread the idea of democracy in China. At the time, they referred to the Chinese society as a "sheet of sand," pointing to a lack of supra-family cohesiveness that might hold the country together. Though many political changes have taken place since then, the concept of the greater good continues to be weak. Benevolent individuals may and do use their personal influence and power within their families or local communities for compassionate purposes but they are unlikely to have an impact on the society's overall attitude toward the public good.

Even though their personal contributions to society are limited, the Chinese feel strongly about wanting to see their country's image protected and its international status validated by wealth and power. Criticizing or exposing negative aspects of their society, especially vis-à-vis foreigners, is perceived as collective shame and not welcomed.

> *"'You have become so American, my mother told me when I returned to Taiwan after several years in the US. 'Stop bitching about things that are wrong in our society.'" (Liang J. C., f, Tw/US)*

> *"Even when we fight amongst ourselves, we do and need to stand up against an external enemy, for the glory of all Chinese." (Doris F., ABC)*

On an institutional level, the government and individual politicians are also prone to refrain from acknowledging social problems or other negative aspects that might tarnish the reputation of the country. The People's Republic of China has gone to great lengths to enhance the country's image by rebuilding historical monuments and places in Xi'an, Datong, Lijiang and elsewhere, less by preserving the authenticity of their historic character than by reconstructing them in a manner that idealizes and glorifies the past.

There are indications that certain sectors of Chinese society are beginning to show more concern for the society at large. Charitable organizations, often Buddhist in nature, have emerged and more people, especially individuals who earlier lived abroad, are willing to become engaged in social issues, such as helping the disadvantaged or caring for the environment. One of my respondents talked about his own involvement:

> *"I learned about working hard and helping people in need when I was in the US. So now I donate money to a non-profit that helps young girls who are abused, raped or are in danger of being sold into prostitution." (Wang R. Y., m, Tw/US)*

Undoubtedly there are many other individuals in both Taiwan and the PRC who, like Mr. Wang, think beyond their own family well-being and personal relationships. Yet, strong traditional forces, including the lack of ascribing value to the individual human being, continue to impede more widespread changes that would lead to a civil society, i.e., a community of citizens linked by common interests and collective activity.

The German world

Trust

Unlike in Chinese society, in which trust is based on mutual obligations and loyalty, German trust is strongly associated with truthfulness and honesty, thereby allowing trust to extend beyond personal relationships. By lessening distrust and the need for self-protection the individual feels more comfortable to move about in a wider world. Given the different bases for trust, both Westerners and Chinese judge each other by their respective standards. "Westerners don't have loyalty, so they can't be trusted," a Chinese may say. "The Chinese cannot be trusted because they do not speak truthfully," a German or American might respond.

Though my German conversation partners did not dwell on the topic of trust in German daily life, they were taken aback by the lack of trust and the disproportionate fear of danger and hostility in Chinese society, thereby indirectly describing their own society as not being so.

⇨ *"In Chinese society there is no trust toward people with whom you are not in a relationship." (Sabine D., Ger/Tw)*

⇨ *"The Chinese generally don't trust people outside their social net. Compared to what I am used to in Germany, the barrier is much higher to get to the same point of trust. On the other hand, I have also seen Chinese make very quick judgments. I was in Chicago last week where I interviewed people for possible employment in our Taiwanese company. After the owner of our company saw me interview one potential candidate, he told me: 'I do not trust him. He is too skinny.' This is a very external thing and I wondered whether that was his real reason. But during my years of working in Taiwan, I have learned that the appearance of a person relates to certain convictions. I know that my (Chinese) father-in-law thinks that if someone is too thin he can't be a good business person. Nor is a small nose a good sign 'because all important managers have big noses.' For me such convictions are very strange and hard to accept, but among the Chinese they play a greater role in judging and trusting people than I like." (Heino M., Ger/Tw)*

⇨ *"I see a lot of things in Chinese society that seem to be based on the assumption that the outside world is a hostile world. It explains why trust is the most important thing and why Chinese networks are so strong. One aspect of life that stood out to me when I came to live in Taiwan was that people here go to a lot of trouble to make it safe and convenient for others, especially for guests and visitors. In Germany you may have a guest room, but not feel that you have to be with your guests every minute. You may tell them to just take a taxi from the station whereas here in Taipei they drive through the whole city to pick someone up. When Chinese travel for business to the US or to Germany, they expect to be met at the airport and be taken care of every step of the way. Why do they worry so much about someone taking a taxi? Why make it so super convenient for people? We Germans are more practical. We ask more from the other. Our way is not better or worse, but we don't want the other to go to the trouble and do all that for us."* (Steven B., Ger/Tw)

⇨ *"Here in Taipei (capital of Taiwan) we, that is my husband's family, have four brass locks on the door and a chain. When inside we always lock ourselves in. We don't say goodbye on the balcony or wave goodbye when others can see it, and we don't turn off the light when we go out. There is a huge fear of thieves."* (Elena M., Ger/Tw)

Freedoms

Compared to the American view of freedom, the German understanding of freedom is less singularly directed at the freedom to do. Instead, it is more concerned with other types of freedoms, such as freedom of the mind, as well as bodily and spatial freedoms. Most importantly, my German conversation partners overwhelmingly viewed personal freedom as being inseparable from social justice.

Freedom of the mind

Freedom of the mind refers to an inner independence, feeling safe to express thoughts and ideas without needing to run with the crowd. It also means to have the space and time to search for one's personal meaning in life.

"Freedom to me means feeling free and comfortable to be on your own, to entertain yourself, to feel at ease exploring the mind and feelings and finding meaning in your life. I know, in comparison to the difficult lives people live in many countries, it is a luxury to think about meaning and self-realization. But that is my freedom and independence here, that I can think about it." (Olga K., Ger/US)

"Inner freedom means that I am less in need of feedback from others. It leaves me free to follow my heart, my abilities and interests." (Marie W., Ger/US)

"To me freedom means being free to find my own way in life. I want to be open to everything new and not have a fear of the unknown. Learning things, finding out how the world works in other places makes me feel free. It also makes me feel good because it gives me the sense that I am growing." (Nikki Z., Ger/ Europe)

Several of my German interviewees with living experience in the US commented on a lack of independent thinking amongst Americans and on the need of many Americans to be and think like others.

⇨ *"Supposedly Americans are more individualistic than Europeans. They don't want publicly enforced standards, because it might curb their freedom. Yet their crowd mentality is so much more pronounced than in Germany. I care a lot about being free to speak my mind, not having to tiptoe around people so they won't feel offended. That cramps my style and my personal freedom. Compared to what I felt in the US, we live in a less hypocritical world and we have less need to sound politically correct. For me that kind of freedom is very important." (Olga K., Ger/US)*

⇨ *"For me the most important part of freedom is the freedom to say what I think. In general we are more critical than people in the US. In America freedom is more about the opportunity to advance, rising from being a dishwasher to being a millionaire. It's more action oriented and more money based. Perhaps it is also more a belief than reality." (Katharina N., Ger/US)*

Bodily freedom

The German freedom to be who you are extends to feeling free with regard to your body. Being comfortable with nudity is part of it. In the US, Germans are baffled when they encounter a very different attitude. They are particularly dismayed to discover that what they perceive as excessive prudery even applies to small children.

⇨ *"The US is the greatest producer of porn, yet baring a breast in public is a huge deal. In the former East Germany we always went swimming naked, and if you grow up like that, nakedness is nothing special. I want my daughter to grow up without feeling ashamed of her body." (Manuela M., Ger/US)*

⇨ *"In Germany, especially in the eastern parts, it is common for people to swim naked. Even elderly women do it. I can't imagine that happening in the US where people take offense even when you just change your clothes on the beach." (Manfred B., Ger/US)*

⇨ *"Some years ago when visiting some friends in the Midwest I was shocked when their five- and six-year olds told me, someone the age of their grandmother, 'you must leave the room before we get undressed.'" (Hanne S., Ger/US)*

Spatial freedom

To many Americans the German casual attitude towards nudity feels strange and seems to stand in contradiction to what they otherwise perceive as an over-regulated and therefore rather non-free German society. Interestingly, from the German point of view there is an equally puzzling American counterpart: an America that calls itself "The land of the free," yet is full of "Private property" and "No trespassing" signs. Limiting free movement in this way clashes with the German expectation of spatial freedom.

"For us, the feeling of being free in nature is very important. Even though we don't have as much freedom as in Scandinavia where you can pitch a tent anywhere as long as it's two hundred yards away from somebody's home, to

be free to take walks in the woods and on paths between farmed fields is very important." (Olga K., Ger/US)

⇨ *"We want the natural environment to be open and accessible. When I lived in the US state of Oregon I often took my bike to enjoy nature, but there were signs saying 'Private Property' everywhere. It made me feel very unfree." (Lisa K., Ger/US)*

⇨ *"When we lived in Seattle we took our bikes on a ferry intending to explore the countryside on the other side. But it turned out to be an area with lots of private luxury homes and roads closed to the public. To me it felt very confining. Outside the national parks, there is limited freedom in the US to move around. In my view this private property thing makes America less free." (Regine F., Ger /US)*

Freedom and security

In the minds of my German respondents, individual freedom was inextricably linked to economic security, social justice, and a safe environment. Many felt strongly that there could be no freedom if these were lacking. Given that freedom and security are defined this broadly Germans look to society and its institutions to provide a protective security umbrella.

⇨ *"Social justice provides freedom. Freedom without social justice does not exist. It's a matter of social peace. Yet, in the US freedom comes first, not security and not social justice. There is this belief in America that if somebody doesn't have enough money in life it is his problem, his lack of will." (Lisa K., Ger/US)*

⇨ *"Our values include contradictions. We want both freedom and equality, but there can be no equality without social justice and for that we have to sacrifice some freedom. Americans don't see that you cannot be free without economic equality. To them it's only about freedom. They seem to think that what is good for me is good for all. We call that selfishness." (Regine F., Ger/US))*

⇨ *"I feel very free in Germany, but it is a different kind of freedom from the freedom Americans talk about. In the US freedom is more about, and limited by, money. In Germany there is more social justice, a better social security net. In*

America, if you are at the bottom of society, it is very difficult to move up. The educational system too is very unjust. The split between public and private education is huge, and to me it is unacceptable that students graduate with so much debt." (Katharina N., Ger/US)

⇨ *"When I lived in Texas I realized that all of my Texan friends had at least one gun, if not several. When I told them that we don't have that many guns in Europe they asked me what would I do to defend myself. When I said, 'Well, I'd run,' they burst out laughing. It was funny, but I suspect that they feel a lot more insecure than we do. We feel quite safe in our cities." (Olga K., Ger/US)*

Germans living in Chinese society noted that by relying on the family and other personal relationships for security, the Chinese gave up individual freedoms.

⇨ *"The Chinese derive their security, status and self-confirmation from the family or sometimes from a patron. Even if bad, the more powerful the patron is the better. I don't like the cronyism in Chinese society. It takes away the freedom of the individual, his emancipation and liberation from family and others. I control my life and I am responsible for it. We don't want to be dependent on someone else for security." (Gisela W., Ger/PRC)*

⇨ *"In Chinese society protection comes in the form of the family and relationships. Because there is no structure above the family that provides protection, people need to nurture their connections to be safe. In return they lose freedom." (Steven B., Ger/Tw)*

⇨ *"The people who work for us in our Taiwanese family business receive pretty good salaries but they have no security. They get only five days of vacation per year. If they are sick for more than five days, they have money deducted. The higher salaries make up for the fact that they have to take responsibility for themselves and that they can be fired any time. But the need to be responsible for unforeseen emergencies also gives them positive energy. That's how it is here. From the economic point of view it works, but in other areas it falls short. It is not my value model. The Chinese have put all their eggs into one basket, the family, which makes it paramount that the family is stable. The family is their life insurance which allows them to take risks, to take jobs without security or even engage in gambling." (Heino M., Ger/Tw)*

Germans also include a healthy environment in their concepts of freedom and security.

> "We Germans have very strong feelings about the environment. We want it to be beautiful, natural and healthy. This is necessary to feel secure." (Lisa K., Ger/US)

> ⇨ "Americans don't want to be told to curb emissions, to save energy and other resources. For me, maintaining a clean environment is part of freedom. I am not free if I have to breathe polluted air! Being free and unfree can happen on so many levels. It's not just what I am allowed to do." (Olga K., Ger/US)

> ⇨ "In the US I miss foods without an endless list of ingredients. Take the example of sour cream. It makes me feel sick to read the long list of ingredients which have nothing to do with sour cream. I miss the European regulations regarding the food supply." (Manuela M., Ger/US)

Though there is a fundamental difference in the German and American understanding of freedom versus security, many Germans acknowledged that the US offers more freedom in the realm of action and they admired the American readiness to take charge of their own economic security.

> ⇨ "In the US freedom in action is the number one priority. Americans have a larger scope for free action. In Germany there are many laws: you can't mow the lawn at certain times of the day; you can't wash the car at home because some oil might spill onto the driveway and get into the environment; and if you want to fell a tree in your backyard, you need a permit. That limits our freedom." (Marie W., Ger/US)

> ⇨ "If you want to start a business in the US you can be spontaneous and just start it. Bill Gates did it in his garage. Here in Germany if you want to start something there are thousands of conditions and you have to study the relevant laws for at least a year. It's cumbersome." (Heike V., Ger/US)

> ⇨ "In the US you won't be taken care of by the state, which means you need to depend on your own initiative. You need to plan for the college education of your children and for your retirement. But nobody goes around complaining. To me there is a wonderful optimism in America along with a high degree of personal responsibility." (Susanne C., Ger/US)

The greater good

Given the German broad meaning of freedom and security, no amount of family cohesiveness, personal relationships, or even money can provide adequate protection. Thus the Germans look to the state and society for a broad protective umbrella, one that provides a social safety net with affordable health care and free education and also takes responsibility for protecting the environment. Though the expectations are high and not always fulfilled, my German conversation partners displayed a strong sense of communal spirit and a willingness to do their part by paying high taxes and actively engaging in social issues.

> *"For me the ideal world is a just world, which makes it a much bigger thing than my backyard. That's why we talk a lot about expectations and the system's injustices." (Marie G., Ger/Tw)*

> *"Deep inside me I believe that it is good when society has a safety net for its weaker members. In this way those who receive help do not need to feel indebted or grateful to anyone in particular. They have the same rights as people who earn a lot of money. Our system is imperfect, because those with money still have advantages, such as having the option to pay for private health insurance which tends to provide better service." (Manuela M., Ger/US)*

> *"To Germans security means having access to employment and the social net with its social benefits. It is not a sacrifice to abide by certain restrictions imposed by the system. It's a contribution to insure freedom and democracy for all of us. Our security is less about guarding against other people, and more about larger impersonal issues. We fear global warming, the loss of rainforests, and the deterioration of the environment. With less water, the earth will be a less healthy place to live." (Olga K., Ger/US)*

Though both Chinese and Americans tend to see Germans as being obsessed with order, rules and regulations, sometimes interpreting their law abidance as a kind of slave mentality, my German conversation partners understood their system quite differently. Instead of thinking of rules and regulations as limiting their freedoms, they viewed them as giving them freedom by ensuring rights, equality, and neutrality. They agreed that regulations were sometimes excessive, but overall considered them to be a means towards everyone getting the same treatment, warding off favoritism due to personal relationships or in return for bribes. Most of my German conversation partners felt a strong sense of social justice and they shared the idea that as individuals we can only be free and secure if all of us are free and secure.

> *"Americans think that German freedom is taken away by rules and regulations, but for me laws give me rights rather than take them away. It's something I want to have, because it actually gives me freedom." (Jakob D., Ger/US)*

> *"To me human rights and the value of the individual human being also mean having obligations to the whole. I want those rules, because they protect me by ensuring my rights." (Oliver C., Ger/Tw)*

> ⇒ *"America is idealistic and tries to reconstruct whole regions of the world in the name of freedom. It does not work. Freedom can't be a privilege, something that is given to you. It requires certain attitudes as underpinning and needs to be earned, balanced by a certain kind of responsibility." (Ingo R., Ger/US)*

Viewing laws and regulations as ensuring rights and order for everyone, Germans do not shy away from reminding others that they too should abide by the rules. Both Chinese and Americans note, often with a good amount of dislike, a great deal of German finger pointing in public, telling people to fall in line and behave appropriately, whether that means not crossing the street against a red light, not running the vacuum cleaner during midday rest time or keeping an orderly yard.

> *"Interest in instructing others is very German, but at least it means people continue to behave reasonably well in public. There is less chewing gum on the ground, because people will be talked to. Or take the duty of <u>Kehrwoche</u> (in certain apartment buildings residents are responsible for cleaning the stairwells at given intervals). When it's your turn to sweep the staircase, you'd better do it perfectly, or else someone will knock at your door and tell you so." (Jens K., Ger/Tw)*

> *"I think it's a good thing when people voice their views about something that they don't like, whether its politics or someone throwing away the gum they just chewed. How should others know that a certain behavior is not appropriate? Some of that is necessary so we can have a decent public life." (Uwe O., Ger/US)*

Apart from following laws and regulations that would benefit society as a whole, Germans also expect members of society to contribute to the common good by paying high taxes and by being informed and engaged in public life. Several of my respondents noted that this public spirit is slowly eroding in German society. However, in comparison to Chinese and American attitudes it still seems remarkably present.

> "Our sense of being part of a larger community is not experienced through relationships with specific people. It's more an awareness of a larger whole, a kind of cosmic, existential whole. This sense leads us and other Europeans to feel that it is worthwhile it to give up a certain amount of personal freedom for the greater common good. Much of my money is taken away—too much—yet, I am willing to pay those taxes for the system to work. I do believe in our common responsibility. Though it's a rational thing it also includes an emotional sense of belonging to the world." (Jonas L., Ger/Tw)

> "The state takes a large portion of people's salaries and it gives much back. We Germans are fine with that. Giving up certain things for the greater good does not feel like a sacrifice to me. I've seen posters on the train saying that if you cheat by not buying a train ticket you cheat society. Our cultural norms expect you not to lie and not to cheat in that way. We think this is the most natural thing, part of human nature, not realizing that this attitude is really a cultural thing, that people in other countries do not think the way we do." (Olga K., Ger /US)

> "I know that some people abuse the system, but if the social welfare system helps those who really need it, it is worth it. In that case even if some people abuse it, that is okay with me. It does not change my own sense of solidarity." (Katharina N., Ger/US)

> "As an artist I am familiar with the German world of art. I know that for those artists who combine art and nature, their art usually goes beyond being simply inspired by nature. For many their art is a political statement, an expression of their concern for the global environment. I see a lot more political engagement in Germany than here in the US where it's mostly about money." (Regine F., Ger/US)

When my German conversation partners spoke about Chinese attitudes toward society, they were quite critical. Instead of exhibiting a public spirit they observed the Chinese to take advantage of others in public and to have little regard for laws and the environment.

⇒ *"The Chinese are well-trained in catering to relationships and connections, but outside of that they are very inconsiderate, especially in public places. They shove and push people and when there is a line, people just cut in in front of others." (Elena M., Ger/Tw)*

⇒ *"Here in Taiwan doing something nice for people with whom you do not have a relationship is suspect. In my apartment house I clean the stairwell every week and once I painted it. So now some of the residents, who are all university professors, are embarrassed to run into me and avoid contact with me." (Karl M., Ger/Tw)*

⇒ *"I can't imagine experiencing the same disregard for the law in Germany as what I see here in Taiwan. With that I don't mean to say that there are no illegal things happening in Germany. There are, but the disregard of the law does not have the same naturalness to it, and it does not pervade society to the same extent. There is no feeling of it being wrong here. Illegal behavior, including corruption, is viewed as a certain kind of accomplishment, on the government level as well the individual level." (Jens K., Ger/Tw)*

⇒ *"There is little urban planning in Chinese towns and cities, no effort to create a pleasant environment, to consider the vision of the whole. " (Anne B., Ger/Tw/PRC)*

⇒ *"When travelling in China I once spent several days and nights on the train. During the trip I stored the garbage I generated in a plastic bag intending to dispose of it later at a station. I never had the chance. My Chinese fellow travelers routinely threw their own garbage out the train windows and they thought nothing of grabbing my bag and throwing it out as well. The area along the tracks looked accordingly, strewn with litter. There is no concern for preserving the environment." (Barbara S., Ger/Tw/PRC)*

Instead of being informed and engaged in civic life my German conversation partners also found the Chinese to have little interest in larger social issues. Often there was an outright denial that certain social problems existed.

⇨ *"We Germans may be busybodies and admonish people in public, for example, by criticizing them when they cross the road against a traffic light, but here in Taiwan nobody says anything. We had a neighbor with a dog that kept barking every morning at five o'clock. All the other neighbors were angry about it, but I was the only one to say something to the neighborhood official in charge. It will take a lot before a Chinese person will speak up on a public matter like that." (Amanda K., Ger/Tw)*

⇨ *"There are no social problems in China: no gays, no cockroaches, no death! Truth and accuracy are not important, though sometimes the Chinese seem to think that saying so will actually make it so. That goes for both good and bad. It's like pasting up those scrolls or couplets by the door for New Year's, 'Good fortune has arrived.' In the same vein, the Chinese deny or don't talk about negative facts. So Chinese politicians and newspapers will say or write, 'We don't have unemployment'; 'Nobody died at Beijing's Tiananmen'; or 'We don't have a drug or AIDS problem.'" (Marion B., Ger/PRC)*

⇨ *"Chinese society is not a civil society. In Germany there is a very strong consciousness to be part of society, to participate in citizen initiatives on a national or even an international level, such as in Amnesty International or Green Peace. Here in Taiwan the interest does not extend beyond the family." (Steven B., Ger/Tw)*

Germans who lived or had lived in the US described Americans as generous and helpful toward strangers on a personal basis. However, the degree of inequality, insecurity, and lack of institutional empathy in American society left them in disbelief. Whereas to the German mind these broader social concerns were an integral part of a citizen's freedom, security, and responsibility, Americans seemed to neither expect nor trust their government to be effective in these areas.

⇨ *"I think compared to Americans the German people are more politically engaged, which is our way of showing empathy. Europeans demonstrate more easily than Americans. When I tell my American students that they should demonstrate for free college tuition, they have an interested look on their faces, but that is all. Revolution is not for them. The same goes for accepting social inequalities. 'Why demonstrate?' they ask. 'Everyone has the chance to become a millionaire!' In my view social circumstances often lead to crime in a society. That's why I think the responsibility for criminality by the poor often lies with the rich, the government or the society at large." (Ingo R., Ger/US)*

⇨ *"Germans expect a lot from their government while the Americans do not. About eighty percent of Americans I met did not trust their government. I don't blame them, but it's a sad state of affairs. The German reaction to the American government's handling of the aftermath of hurricane Katrina in New Orleans was one of disbelief. How could the richest and biggest country allow such inequality to persist, leaving so many black people without assistance? It seems that American society, which defines itself as being free has no room for institutional empathy, empathy for people who lack the possibility to attain the American dream. On the other hand, Americans are great about volunteering, which I see as their equivalent to the German sense of solidarity. However, volunteering is temporary, in most cases meaning a limited time commitment." (Olga K., Ger/US)*

⇨ *"Since I live in the US now and look at Germany from a distance, many things that I used to complain about in Germany I now see in a more positive light. For example, in Germany people have to pay for having television. But if I compare German and American TV programs, I think that German television is actually quite good, more objective than all the propaganda and privately supported views that we get here. Overall Germans seem to me much more politically conscious and engaged. Here in the US it holds true for only a very small minority with very specific interests." (Regine F., Ger/US)*

The American world

Americans, at least until recently, viewed the world as a place of opportunities, in which the individual can succeed and feel secure provided he applies himself. The American understanding of trust, freedom, and security is closely tied to faith. Faith in the basic goodness of the individual human being, faith that freedom is written into human nature, faith in the individual's ability to take responsibility for his life and, at least for many, faith in the protection by God.

Trust

The belief in the basic goodness of the human being translates into a view of a fair and benign world, suitable for the individual to pursue his dreams and opportunities. Used to the assumption that most people are honest, trustworthy, and will act with a sense of fairness, Americans living in Chinese societies discovered that the Chinese look at the world with quite a different sentiment.

⇨ *"The major difference I see between Americans and Chinese is how they relate to outsiders. For us Americans the starting point is trust. We assume that people are generally trustworthy. In Asian societies there is no such assumption. For example, when you go to buy things, you go to people you trust, because basically you distrust everybody else. That vendor you patronize will not cheat you, maybe even give you a little discount. But with others you need to watch out. Once when I had a typewriter repaired I just packed it up and paid the repair bill, as I usually do. 'Didn't you first open it up and look inside to see whether they removed any parts?' a Chinese friend asked me afterwards. 'You can't trust people, you know!'"* (Harry M., US/Asia)

⇨ *"My first year in Taiwan was definitely the most life-changing. Twice I was sexually assaulted. I did not know then that the people I was with that day were part of a gang. I had been told that I could trust them, and at the time I was still ignorant and arrogant. If a person said I would be okay, I believed it. That was the first time I got a slap in my face. Even being from Detroit, I trusted people. I think there is a big difference in reading people in different cultures. You can't use the same points of reference as at home."* (Julie L., US/Tw)

⇨ *"We value truth, which to me is saying, don't ever lie to me. If you do, there will be a long-term consequence. My trust will be gone. But in China honesty is not a value and not the basis for trust. Blood relationships are."* (Nellie W., US/Tw/PRC)

⇨ *"My brother worked in a Chinese family-owned restaurant for ten years. But then he was terminated because the owner wanted to hire a relative. When they close down the place at night, the owner or a relative must do it themselves because they don't trust anyone outside the family."* (Jonathan L., US/Ger/PRC)

⇨ *"The Chinese world divides into family and society. The dividing line between 'us' and 'them' is harsh. Look at all those iron bars over the windows, even on the twenty-second floor! It's their mark between the family and the outside world. In America, we do it with picket fences and shrubs. I live by a golf course, and as far as I am concerned, the golf course is part of my house, except that others are responsible for mowing the lawn. The Chinese are afraid that others will look in. For me it's important to be able to look out!"* (Douglas T. US/Tw)

⇨ *"For the Chinese, the outside world is fraught with danger. For me the world is a place to explore."* (Rose C., ABC/Hong Kong)

In comparison, the difference between America and Germany in terms of trustworthiness appears minor. One of my American respondents who had lived both in Asia and Europe described it this way:

⇨ *"I found the people in Germany and in Northern Europe to be very honest, in what they say as well as with money. In China people might well attempt to cheat you and if you caught them in the act, they might shrug their shoulders, turn to the crowd and smile, as if to say, 'I tried but did not succeed.' In Chinese society, when you get your change back you have to check to see whether you got the right amount. In Germany you can just take whatever change they give you because the people are very honest. The reason is probably their social attitude. If a German was caught being dishonest it would be seen as a disgrace by others who become aware of it. They would strongly disapprove. In my estimation I might have a 75% honesty rate in the US, but one close to 100% in Germany or in Sweden."* (Richard F., US/Ger/Asia)

Freedom versus security

I do not choose to be a common man.

It is my right to be uncommon . . . if I can.

I seek opportunity . . . not security.

I do not wish to be a kept citizen,

Humbled and dulled by having the State look after me.

I want to take the calculated risk,

To dream and to build,

To fail and to succeed.

Excerpt from "Common Sense," written in 1776 by Thomas Paine

Given the assumption of a trustworthy, benign world, Americans are more pre-occupied with freedom than with security. Though there are different kinds of freedom, freedom in the American context is most often thought of as freedom of action. As one of my American respondents defined it, "Freedom is to be able to do what I want to do when I want to do it." Taught to be self-reliant and feeling free, Americans do not like to be restrained, not by family, not by others and not by the government or its laws.

In Chinese and other Asian societies, Americans felt stymied by a lack of freedom due to family and relationships.

⇨ *"The Chinese family is a straightjacket. When I was taken in by one, it felt like a return to the umbilical cord, warm but stifling." (Elizabeth W., US/PRC)*

⇨ *"I had Asians tell me that we Americans are lazy, because we are too casual and don't pay enough attention to how we represent our family, our school or our group. For example, my host family in Japan told me that I should not chew gum when I am wearing the school uniform because I represent the school and it makes the school look bad.' Why can't I just do my thing, be myself instead of having to think what others think or how things look? Why try to impress others? It made me feel stressed out. So are we lazy or are we rebels?" (June M.., US/Japan/Asia)*

Though my American respondent who married into a local family on the Pacific Island of Palau recognized the family system there as a straightjacket, she also viewed the American independence and freedom in a somewhat critical light.

⇨ *"In Palau the extended family wants you to be part of the group and they just envelop you. It's a straightjacket, but you can miss the stability and it's not a burden all of the time. There is a correct way to live and it's authoritarian, but in return you feel a sense of belonging. For example, if my son went fishing and afterwards shared his haul with everybody, his relatives would go around bragging to others, 'Oh look, he brought me fish . . . .' He would get recognition and praise. In America we have no such stable foundation of a watertight personal web, a group where you feel totally secure and taken care of. Instead we have a lot of isolation." (Mary V., US/Palau)*

Americans living in Germany felt hemmed in not by family ties but by excessive rules and regulations.

⇒ *"When I lived in a German research institute I found a thick folder in our apartment explaining the rules of the facilities for the residents. I didn't read any of it, because the rules would rob me of my freedom and make me fearful that I might transgress some of them. So I chose not to know them." (Jack H., US/ Ger)*

⇒ *"Here in Germany there are so many rules to break. We don't always know what they are and they seem to be very random. So I shirk some of my responsibilities in terms of doing my part for the public good. I have given up sorting my trash according to the many different bins put out there. I will no longer waste my time doing it and so I put my cans into the regular bin, not the one specified for cans. The German system is very wasteful of time." (Jenna H., US/Ger)*

⇒ *"One day soon after I moved to Hamburg (a city in northern Germany), I had just crossed a side street without traffic when a policeman whistled at me. My first reaction was that something was happening elsewhere, but then he looked at me and said he was whistling at me, because I had crossed the street against a red light. I told him that I had looked, and that there had been no cars coming. Still I was rebuked and lucky to not get a ticket. To me the important thing is to use my judgment, but in Germany the important thing is that you follow the rule. To me, laws are guidelines, suggestions, reminders. They are not absolutes, and you do no harm by not following them. In Germany rules are not a matter of personal interpretation." (Richard M., US/Ger)*

In contrast, other Americans, often individuals of European heritage, were critical of the American perception of freedom and security.

"In the US it's all about freedom, not about equality or security. It's a place for winners. But not everyone has the same chances, the same luck. If you fall on hard times, your world can collapse." (Jenny S., US/Europe)

"We are naïve, because we never had to be afraid. I have never lived in a place where I had to be afraid." (Beatrice A., US/Asia)

"Like Europeans I think that rules and regulations give freedoms rather than take them away. For example, as a high school teacher I gave my class clear rules that let the students know how to stay out of trouble. That way I could provide all students with an orderly environment which gave them the freedom to learn. I get irritated when people don't follow rules and I usually abide by them. But most Americans assume that people will not follow them." (Jane M., US/Europe)

"The word freedom makes me cringe. I see American freedom as just thinking of oneself, not thinking of the consequences for others. Everybody is for himself. If the other person can't make it, tough luck!" (Peter W., ABC/Ger)

The greater good

Trust in the ability and basic goodness of the individual also influences American attitudes toward the greater good. It leads to the idea that if each individual freely pursues his own happiness, the greater good will be a natural result. Unlike the German view, which holds that freedom, security and social justice are inseparable and need to be insured by the society at large, Americans look to their government as a guarantor of freedom rather than as a provider of security. Indeed, a large sector of American society harbors a deep sense of distrust toward the government and does not want the collective to impinge on their lives.

"I was taught in second grade not to trust the government." (Holly R., ABC/Ger)

"We Americans have more faith in the common sense of our fellow citizens than Germans have. We think that people will naturally abide by the commonly held principles of right and wrong." (Phil B., US/Ger/PRC)

"We have to find a balance. If we go too far on the collective impulse and tax people to the point of leveling out differences, then you remove the incentive. Germans and other Europeans are much more comfortable with a collective impulse, a concern for the common good. American concern for the underdog comes in the form of individual generosity and charity." (Alan K., US/Tw/Ger)

Indeed, due to the generosity and love for action of individuals, American society benefits from a vibrant nonprofit and charity sector, one which the economist Peter Drucker called the third pillar of the American economy. Americans readily pitch in in times of need, assist when a disaster strikes, help an underdog, or possibly leave an extra large tip for a hard-working waitress. Americans are also actively involved as volunteers, whether this be in the church group, the local Friends of the Library, the community soup kitchen, or the volunteer force that serves as docents at a museum. Though membership in these groups tends to be temporary—leaving the group after a certain time may be necessary in a mobile society—these voluntary commitments are often strong. And since doing should also be enjoyable, Americans love to combine their volunteer activities with having fun. Organizers of a blood drive, for example, might get volunteer musicians to entertain their donors.

"I like the spontaneity of giving to others. If I have more than I need, I will put some money into the hands of that man in the street. Will he buy some booze with it? That's fine. Let him do it." (Richard M., US/Ger)

"In American society someone can move up the social ladder quickly. But at least in my Midwestern town, once people have made it to the top, they are expected to think of those at the bottom and they do." (Pamela Y., US/Europe)

However, as the social gap between the rich and the poor widened over recent decades, a deep political divide has arisen between conservatives and liberals as to how much government is desirable and how much of a safety net the government should provide. Whereas conservatives hold that the government cannot be trusted and contributions to the collective well-being should be voluntary, not written into laws and funded by taxpayers, a more liberal sector of society, more in tune with European views, maintains that the society as a whole must take more responsibility for the social and economic security of all. Perhaps not surprisingly, many of my American conversation partners who lived or had lived in Germany belonged to the latter group.

"I think the view of the common good has deteriorated in the US. It's very hard to get Americans to agree on social security or health insurance. The Michael Moore movies showed the country to be very divided. Forty to fifty percent of the people were not willing to spend more tax money on such programs. It goes back to the fabric of America: If you are not rich it's your own fault. You are not living your life right. If you do your own thing, you'll be secure and the greater good will take care of itself." (Jonathan L., US/Ger/PRC)

⇒ *"In America we don't have a sense of having things in common with others, or of having to contribute to a common purpose within our society. Americans are very short sighted and self-centered. Europeans see a bigger picture." (Angelina H., US/Eur)*

⇒ *"Europe is much more community minded than we are. We have this thing about space and freedom. It's much less about community." (Richard F., US/Ger/Asia)*

⇒ *"In Germany people have more of a sense of social obligation. In the US the percentage is not high. We demonstrate social responsibility because it is a nice thing to do. For Germans it is an obligation. Our kind of social responsibility benefits primarily the individual. I miss the German job security and its social net." (Marianne L., US/Ger)*

⇒ *"I regularly donate blood. I did so when I lived in the US, and I do so now here in Germany. I noticed that in Germany blood donors come from a wide cross section of society, from all walks of life. In the US, it's a much narrower spectrum. Here people are more socially aware, more engaged. In the US if you do something good, you do it locally and personally, not for the wider common good. It probably would be good to have a combination of both kinds of philanthropy." (Peter W., ABC/Ger)*

Although American reactions to the German idea of the greater good suggest a notable difference between the two cultures' approaches toward fulfilling their society's social responsibilities, American and German reactions vis-à-vis the greater good in Chinese societies were very similar. Like Germans, Americans bemoaned the Chinese lack of social consciousness and responsibility toward the public. As one of my American conversation partners stated it, "Compared to Europe the US is very conservative, but compared to Asia America is very liberal."

⇨ *"For the Chinese there is no greater good. For all practical purposes, the other guy, the one you don't know, does not exist." (Jonathan L. US/Ger/PRC)*

⇨ *"The Chinese don't identify with society, only with the family. They have no trust in laws or government, which is why evading taxes is an avocation, to say the least. People don't see any benefit coming to them from the government —so why contribute to something you can't control. Neither do the Chinese trust nonprofit organizations. The fear is that people in the organization will abscond with the money. Volunteering for some public benefit is also still at an infant stage. More often it's seen as foolish, unless it's for status." (Harry M., US/Asia)*

⇨ *"The Chinese distrust the government, the bureaucracy, the police, the IRS, any kind of public institution. In the US we are much more trusting of institutions." (Anthony M. US/Asia)*

⇨ *"In China you have this warm and tight family safety net which takes care of you. But it comes with obligations. And when this small personal web is broken, life is brutal. Everybody is on his own." (Diane P., US/PRC)*

⇨ *"I missed a basic order in Chinese society, people showing some consideration in public places and cars stopping for red lights." (Andrew M., US/Asia)*

⇨ *"As for social issues in Taiwan, it's almost as if they were not there. It's a lack of awareness, people not seeing—or not wanting to see—certain situations. In the past talk about being gay or gays was hush, hush. When it was AIDS people said, we don't have AIDS in Taiwan. Or domestic violence, or prostitution. There are now organizations, private and church related, that help prostitutes and others, but for the most part there is still a denial that there are social problems." (Julie L., US/Tw)*

* * *

Notes

[1] Lin Yutang, *The Importance of Living* (New York: John Day), 402.

[2] Cathy Bao Bean, *The Chopsticks-Fork Principle: A Memoir and Manual* (New Jersey: We Press, 2001), 56.

[3] Lin Yutang, 12.

V. Discovering Your Shade of Gray

The advantage of living abroad is that you see manners and customs from the outside and you see that they do not have the necessity which those who practice them believe. You cannot fail to discover that the beliefs which to you are self-evident to the foreigner are absurd.

—W. Somerset Maugham, *Of Human Bondage*

Though our reasons for going, the length of our stay, and the degree to which we partake in the host society color how much we gain from the experience, living in another country opens up new perspectives and broadens personal horizons. Regardless of whether we are a good or a bad fit in the foreign culture, we will never be able to forget that there is another way. Several of my respondents were surprised to find that during their stay overseas they learned more about themselves than about the host country.

"Once you leave your country, all of a sudden you see yourself and your country in a new light. You realize what some of your own values are, because you miss them, or perhaps you are glad to find out that there are better ways than those at home." (Beatrice A., US/Asia)

"I was born and raised in Germany, but I learned more about my own country after I left than during all those years before." (Anne B., Ger/Tw/PRC)

"When I left Taiwan for Germany I was prepared to see and learn about Germany. What I was not prepared for was that by leaving Taiwan I learned a lot about my country and myself. I had taken what I knew about life and living for granted and was like a frog in a well." (Chung C. Y, f, Tw/Ger)

The role of language

A new language is a new life, says a Persian proverb. Indeed language plays an important role in our self discovery. Languages are windows to the world. Our native language offers a clear view but it also frames and limits our sights. Things and concepts that are outside this field of vision simply do not exist. Being proficient in a second language means looking out through two windows, which opens up a wider vista. Thirty-six year old Richard Simcott, a British polyglot who studied more than thirty languages, described the importance of language learning: "Each language has its own way of expressing thoughts and ideas; so you get a real insight into diverse thinking. Language carries the culture of the country that uses it and when you internalize it, it becomes a part of you too." Simcott's fellow polyglot Alex Rawlings expressed it in a similar way: "Each new language gives me an entirely different perspective on the world. And exposure to different cultures allows me to see things in different ways, and to develop a whole new understanding of the way things work." [1]

Because language determines not only *how* something is said, but also *what* is said, each language nudges the speaker into a certain frame of mind. Not surprisingly, multilinguals often describe themselves as a collection of selves. For their 2003 study, linguists Jean-Marc Dewaele and Aneta Pavlenko asked over a thousand bilinguals whether they felt like a different person when they spoke different languages—nearly two-thirds said they did. [2] When I asked one of my Chinese conversation partners whether she felt like a different person and if so, which of her two language personalities she liked best, she said, "Yes, I do feel like a different person and for several years I liked my English self the best. But now I like to be my Chinese self. In Chinese we are less direct and that is closer to my character."

Those who speak a second language realize that language and culture are inseparable and that language is more than a tool to transmit information. In many cases becoming fluent in another language generates a sense of personal growth and confidence.

"Before I left the US I had everything I wanted and was very content. But as a history major I had to take two years of language and something happened when I took German: I developed a certain hunger for the world I had just learned about." (Jim S., US/Ger)

"Only after I gained fluency in German did I begin to recognize the underlying cultural issues." (Mark R., US/Ger)

"It's not only that the Chinese language is difficult for Americans, but it's the different way of thinking that's hard for us to understand." (Jenny A., US/Tw)

"When we spent a year in China my eleven-year-old daughter said one day, "Mom, I used to think that people are the same everywhere, that they only speak different languages. But that is not so. People are not the same; they are different!"' (Hope S., ABC/PRC)

"To me language is more than a tool. A feel of life goes along with it. It's more like music or a painting." (Meghan F., US/Ger)

Lack of recognition of the importance of culture and its connection to language may contribute to the relatively low American interest in acquiring foreign language skills. While Americans generally consider knowledge of a foreign language to be a bonus when traveling or doing business, many are unaware that language is a prime vehicle for valuable insights into understanding themselves and others.

Study abroad programs at American universities, which are a good way to give people an opportunity to live in another culture, have multiplied over recent decades. However, a Harvard student, who spent a year in Europe, explained the situation from the student's point of view, "The American academic highway has no easy off ramp to study abroad. It's linear. You build on each semester toward that successful professional track." [3]

In Germany, and more generally throughout Europe, the acquisition of foreign language skills is highly valued. Though Americans often assume that this is due to geography, perhaps the importance that Germans and other Europeans attach to foreign language skills is due less to geography and more to their awareness of the importance of culture and their understanding that culture is embedded in language.

American personal change

Only a few weeks after a young friend of mine left Hawaii for a study program in Europe, I received a postcard from him. "Being here for a week has already changed my view of the world!" he wrote. The statement seemed a bit premature, but given some time living abroad many Americans, like the Germans and Chinese, are likely to see themselves and the world in a new light. For many the overseas experience serves as an eye opener.

> *"When I first went to China I was shocked the most by my own ignorance about who we are." (Peter D., US/PRC)*

> *"When I spent two weeks with a friend in her home in Germany, her father was appalled to find that I had little knowledge and no particular interest in the Chinese part of my heritage. He firmly sat me down in the library of his house and presented me with some books on Chinese culture and civilization. What shocked me more than anything was to see how shocked he was over my disinterest and lack of knowledge." (Holly R., ABC/Ger)*

A new self-perception

Andrew J. Bacevich, Sr., an American historian specializing in international relations, said this about the American self-perception, "I have come to believe that perhaps the greatest failure to which American political leaders are prone and perhaps to which we as a people are prone, is an inability to see ourselves as we really are." [4]

While Americans tend to feel strongly about individual differences at home, when living in another country, their own cultural commonalities became more apparent. Several of my respondents reported having become aware overseas that there was something that made them feel American and that as Americans they too had their share of cultural commonalities. As a result they changed from having little appreciation for "cultural baggage" to discovering that they had their own.

> "As Americans we have been taught that we are individuals, so diverse that nothing will describe us. But I discovered that when Americans go abroad they act very similarly, no matter whether they are from the South, West or East." (Harry M., US/Asia)

> "I thought my grandparents were just individuals. That's how they were. But then I discovered that they were really Scandinavian in a lot of ways." (Jonathan L., US/Ger/PRC)

> "When I lived in Europe it was much more obvious to me how American we are." (Angelina H., US/Europe)

> "I think there is a unique layer to each country, a kind of cultural DNA which nourishes and conditions its people. To me it is clear that it is a layer, though I think most people think it is their character. As an individual we can reject a particular piece of the layer, though we grow up in a certain surrounding and much of our interpretation of the world reflects that. I guess that's why there is such a thing as a 'mainstream society.' Now, after having lived overseas for many years I am wondering how much of me is really me and how much of me has been programmed into me by being American." (Helen V., US/Asia)

Besides seeing their own cultural commonalities more clearly, Americans living overseas also became more aware of the cultural diversity in their host societies.

> "Overseas I discovered that there are many different ways to live and my world became more differentiated. Before I was thinking in terms of 'us' and 'them,' with 'them' meaning all the other countries, all non-differentiated. Now my world is larger and encompasses more differences." (Meghan F., US/Europe)

> "Growing up in New Jersey I thought I knew Europe, but when I got there I found I did not know it at all. It is much more diverse than I thought." (Jonathan L., US/Ger/PRC)

"Americans don't seem to realize just how culturally, ethnically and racially diverse Germany is. We wrongly assume that we are more diverse than Europe." (Jenna H., US/Ger)

"The longer I live here in Germany the more I realize that there are cultural differences, and that talking about them with my friends, even if we disagree, enriches us." (Larry R., US/Ger)

Having broadened their own view of the world by living overseas, my American conversation partners were quite critical of their fellow Americans in terms of their limited interest in and knowledge about the rest of the world.

"If you are not interacting with the people of your host country, you are living in a bubble. Yet somehow many American expats don't see the bubble." (Paul R., US/Asia)

"My 'ugly American' was a fellow outside Taichung [a city in central Taiwan]. He was an air force sergeant, who was married to a Chinese woman and had retired in Taiwan. When I met with him in a restaurant, it started to rain and he remembered that he had left his house with the windows open. Afraid that things were going to get wet inside, he became more and more agitated. He could not get on the phone and call the house boy, because, as he said, 'the stupid boy did not speak any English.' I was thinking to myself: You have been living here for twenty years and you can't say how to close the window in Chinese?!" (Jim M., US/Tw)

"I get tired of all the complaining by Americans overseas. I was especially surprised to find American diplomats to be such a complaining lot, very condescending. My own father would never have understood if I told him that Germany or France have a better health care system than the US. For him, we are the best. Period." (Jonathan L., US/Ger/PRC)

"Americans often ask me how I adapt to the 'lower' standard of living in Germany. So I tell them that I think the quality of life in Europe is actually higher than in the US. I feel safer in the streets here and I like the fact that friends have more time for each other and that restaurants and cafes do not rush us out the door by handing us the check the minute we take the last bite. These kinds of things make me feel good here." (Jenna H., US/Ger)

"I enjoy the quality of life in Germany. Here there is more to life than working. There is time to enjoy simple pleasures such as having leisurely conversations with friends in a café." (Cara B., US/Ger)

"Americans think there is only one way, and if somebody else's way is different from theirs, it's got to be wrong. The Peace Corps was so valuable not because of what it did for the other countries, but because of what it did for young Americans." (Larry S., US/Asia)

Changing within

Not only did my American interviewees begin to recognize themselves as Americans and come to see a more differentiated world, they also realized that living overseas changed them within, sometimes in unanticipated ways. Those who lived in Chinese and other Asian societies tended to become more sensitive and more attentive to nonverbal communication. They also learned to slow down and go more easily with the flow.

"I learned in Asia that it is possible to convey volumes about one's feelings in a mere glance, a breath, or with a single word. When I go back to America and interact with people there, I often feel completely out of sorts and exasperated, because nobody seems to be paying attention to the verbal and non-verbal cues that in Japan I have grown so accustomed and attuned to. I find that I must beat Americans over the head with my meaning before they catch on, while in Japan the slightest ripple in interpersonal relations gives pause and leads to self-reflection." (Jason N., US/PRC/Asia)

"I now have a new concept of time. After coming back from Asia I no longer have the tendency that I see among many young Americans who complain that things are boring or are slow. I now have many more interests than before. For example, I like to look at regional and country histories to find out more about those places. Even while traveling I loved to go to bookstores. Before I did not have those interests. Like many other young men in Hawaii, I loved to go surfing. But now I don't find that satisfying any more." (Paul R., US/Asia)

"My experience with the Chinese bureaucracy made me more patient. I came to understand that business gets done behind the scenes and that you have to

look for clues about the meaning of any direct communication. This is useful for living here in Hawaii where the society is more Asian than on the US main-land and where the people expect Americans from the mainland to learn 'the local way.'" (Arnie E., US/PRC)

Americans who lived in German society adjusted to a different way of relat-ing to others. Geoff, a member and contributor to Germanway, a web-based group of Americans living in Germany, described his own change. "Some-thing happens to you when you move to a new culture. You change in ways that are unpredictable. In my case, I changed from a typical American who was friendly, but not intimately so, with my neighbors to a fully immersed vil-lage resident. Here everyone knows me and knows what I do. Here I cannot escape the glaring public eye of the village. But something else changed in me. . . . I liked it! Most Americans tend to be averse to such things. I have to say that I feel a real connection to my community here, something I never felt in the States." [5]

"When I came to Germany, I knew nothing about Germany and did not speak any German. Without language I read their body language, which made me think that Germans were pretty closed, not alive and friendly. But later I liked the people and the culture, and I also liked their distinction between the formal and informal 'you.'" (Joanne E., US/Ger)

"One of the reasons I choose to stay in Germany is that I have come to like the Ger-man directness and their slower way of getting to know each other. Making friends does take a long time but in the end you have a really close relation-ship." (Jenna H., US/Ger)

"I have never had to work so hard to make friends than when I lived in Germany, but in the process I became more serious, more open. Now, when I don't like something or can't do something, I will just say so. I did not do that before." (Jim S., US/Ger)

"I know the year in Europe changed me. For example, before I went I would be friendly with the person sitting next to me on an airplane or train. But when I traveled alone in Europe, people never initiated a conversation with me, and when I did, I could feel that they seemed a bit shocked, as if I were intruding

into their lives. Later I myself found it rude to do so. When on my flight back to the US the man sitting next to me started to comment on the movie I was watching on my laptop, it bothered me. Now I just don't want to deal with a stranger and find it annoying. Before I went to Europe I did not feel that way." (Angelina H., US/Europe)

"In America you have to appear fearless, even if you are scared, because that is a form of self-protection. I hated to feel unsafe and being constantly afraid in the neighborhoods where I lived in New York and Baltimore. Now living in Berlin my life is different. I am 'Berlinicized.' I feel very safe and I like it, but it also means I have lost a lot of my wariness." (Jenna H., US/Ger)

In a Wall Street Journal article Jessica Scott-Reid, a Canadian freelance writer, describes her own adaptation to Europe. "As I adapted to life abroad, becoming more cultured and open-minded, I became less social and outspoken. Expatriation turned this once over-the-top extrovert into a quiet and more mindful introvert. And for that I am grateful." [6] Becoming more introverted, or as Scott-Reid describes it, shifting "from being more out-there to more in-here" appears to be a rather common change Americans undergo in Europe.

German personal change

If Americans in Germany tended to adjust by becoming quieter and more inner directed, Germans in America were likely to change in the opposite direction, becoming more social and more outgoing in dealing with strangers and people they did not know well. Those living in Chinese societies tended to become less direct and pay more attention to social forms of politeness. However, along with giving up some of their directness, Germans also seemed to lose some openness and trust.

Relating more casually

In the US my German conversation partners were apt to become less reserved, more sociable.

"I used to share the German discomfort with strangers but I learned in the US that it's something that can be unlearned. Soon after I came back to Germany I had to go to register with the residents' registration office. While there, I heard a couple of people speak English to each other. So I immediately asked them where they were from, which is something you cannot really ask in German. The words <u>Wo kommen Sie her?</u> ('Where do you come from?') already sound intrusive. With that sort of reserve, you don't get to know a lot of new people. So I am glad I learned another way." (Olga K., Ger/US)

"I used to be much more inhibited and think that if people at a party or some other group event stand or sit there a bit forlorn by themselves it's okay. I might even have thought that it was their own fault since they came without knowing anybody. But after having lived in the US I have become more sensitive. I now more easily approach people I don't know." (Marie W., Ger/US)

"In the US I became much more comfortable interacting with people I didn't know well, which means that now I am having a hard time living in Germany again. When I start talking to strangers in the store they look at me as if I were an alien." (Susanne C., Ger/US)

Toning down directness

The assumption of separation between content and audience allows Germans to leave personal feelings out of the equation and be direct and objective. Because neither the Chinese nor many Americans share that assumption, Germans learned to tone down their directness and be more careful about how they said things.

"I have fully adjusted to the American way of politeness and soft indirectness. Now I like it that way, so much so that when I go back to Germany I am sometimes shocked at people's directness." (Katharina N., Ger/US)

"I now work very hard at not saying things so directly. So when I have to reject something, instead of saying 'no' right away, I now try to come up another suggestion to soften the impact." (Ulrike B., Ger/US)

"I used to think that it was stupid to pay attention to the Chinese forms of politeness. And they have many. But now after six years of togetherness, my Chinese wife has 'Taiwanesed' me. I am now more ready to adjust to social form." (Hans B., Ger/Tw)

"After spending a year in Hawaii, where the social mores are quite Asian, I became more careful about how I say things. In Hawaii people are more responsive to the feelings of others than what I was used to. There, being sensitive is seen as a good thing. But here in Germany, this trait is not recognized as something valuable. It comes out in a lot of silly little ways. For example, once when my friend Peter and I were preparing a fruit salad, Peter cut the apples into pieces that were too big for me. Not wanting to hurt his feelings, I asked, 'Would you mind if I cut them into smaller pieces?' 'Why do you ask me for permission?' he shot back. In my mind I had not asked for permission. I just didn't want to hurt his feelings. Since this kind of sensitivity was of no concern to him, he could not think of anything other than that it was a matter of permission. There are many other occasions where I now find people in Germany to be insensitive or inconsiderate. I am sure that has something to do with my having lived abroad because before I went, those things were not an issue. They never came up." (Olga K., Ger/US)

Less negativity, more acceptance

Along with becoming more sensitive in their communications with others, Germans also became less critical and negative. Instead of indulging in the German habit of M&J (complaining and whining), they became more accepting.

"I have undergone a personal transformation in how I think of things. I used to complain a lot about all of the things that weren't perfect in this world. But now I am much better at going with the flow and about accepting things I cannot change." (Regine F., Ger/US)

"I learned overseas that I could tolerate a lot more than I thought. When I studied in Japan, I had very little money. So I lived in a room which had no heat, even during the winter when it was very cold. But it felt good to know that I still

could manage. Nowadays, if there is a cockroach in my hotel or things don't go so well, it's okay. I can deal with it. I no longer want to or need to complain. I've got a thick skin now." (Sabine D., Ger/Asia)

"After marrying into a Chinese family I began to accept and adjust. Overall I have become hardier, better able to adapt to new circumstances. " (Elena M., Ger/ Tw)

"We Germans have a tendency to see things as well as ourselves in a negative light. In Taiwan I found that people are more neutral or they make things sound beautiful even when they aren't. I had to live overseas to realize that some German ways are really good. I think at least for my postwar genera- tion our negativism is an aftereffect of World War II. Because of those years, in the eyes of others and in our own eyes, nothing about Germany could be good." (Marie G., Ger/Tw)

Loss of trust and closeness

While gaining in sensitivity and losing some negativity generally felt like a pos- itive change, certain adjustments to the different social environments overseas ran counter to deeply held values. In Chinese society, for example, some of my German conversation partners felt it necessary to give up not only their habitual directness, but also their openness and trust in order to protect themselves.

"I used to trust people to be honest, but in China I have had to learn to look out for my advantage. If you tell the truth people will use it against you, which means that I now have become very distrustful. I don't want to be used by others or be deceived yet another time. But having to be constantly suspicious and on the alert is not my nature and it stresses me out." (Friederike G., Ger/PRC)

"When I came to Taiwan, I was naïve and trusted people to be honest. By now I am much more suspicious, aware that I need to protect myself." (Karin S., Ger /Tw)

In the US my German conversation partners did not sense the same need for distrust and self-protection. However, adapting to the American casual and tangential style of relationships felt like a loss of sincerity and closeness.

"Over the years I've come to the conclusion that 'knowing someone well' is different for an American and a European. So I've had to adjust my expectations with regard to relationships to avoid being disappointed. I now get along fine with people, though I miss our sincerity and closeness." (Regine F., Ger/US)

"When a close German friend came to visit me in the US, he sensed a new distance between us. And it was true. I didn't reveal my innermost feelings the way I used to in Germany. Americans just don't do that. I am glad though that since returning to Germany I have changed back to being open again." (Olga K., Ger/US)

"After living in the US, I needed to readjust to Germany: sing fewer praises and be more sincere." (Marie W., Ger/US)

Chinese personal change

Because Chinese family and societal expectations of the individual to follow cultural norms are strong, personal change seems to be somewhat more difficult than for Americans and Germans. Even over a distance, family roles and loyalties must be maintained, which means that personal change may cause feelings of guilt over disappointing the family. In addition, the Chinese preference to stay within their respective groups tends to hinder a full immersion overseas, making a deeper personal change less likely. Nonetheless, change does occur, though it may be less openly displayed.

"We are used to the social pressure of everybody needing to be the same. It takes a lot of courage to be different." (Pai T. Y., f, Tw/US)

"We are trained to adjust. So when we go back home after living overseas we need to readjust and fit in or else family and society would disapprove and we'd feel excluded. This is especially true for women." (Tsou P.Y., f, Tw/US)

"Now that I am back in Taiwan, I am proud to say that nobody can tell that I spent ten years living in Germany." (Hsieh S. H., m, Tw/Ger)

Becoming a stronger individual and less relational self

In spite of the social pressures to stay within the Chinese tradition of the relational self, several of my Chinese respondents reported having gained a stronger sense of individuality overseas.

> "For the Taiwanese, life is fate. So people are okay with doing what is expected of them and they don't look for other options. But I have seen something else. So here I am in my thirties and am already in a mid-life crisis." (Yeh H. S., m, Tw/US)

> "We Chinese think we are responsible for the feelings of others. I must not make others sad or have them worry. I used to like to be part of a group and I'd want to make others laugh. Not any more. Now I don't like to be in groups and trying to make others happy stresses me out. Before I lived in Germany, if I saw that someone in our group was not happy, I'd be sure to send someone over to cheer him up. Now I think, maybe that person wants to be alone. I accept that and trust the other." (Pian Y. F., f, Tw/US)

> "I learned in the US to talk to strangers. Most Chinese are afraid of being used by others, but since I lived in the US I don't have that feeling any more." (Hu T. H., m, Tw/US)

> "I liked the freedom people in Germany have to live their lives the way they want to and I learned from my German teachers that I can look for my own happiness. 'You are over thirty years old,' they told me. 'Don't look to others for happiness. Find your own.' I don't want to have regrets, but pursuing your own way is considered selfish here. It takes courage in Chinese society." (He Y. Y., f, Tw/Ger)

> "Before living in Germany I cared more what other people thought of me, because in Taiwan people worry a great deal about how others view them. But I now have more of a sense of self and when others may not have such a good opinion of me, it doesn't affect me as much as before. It's not that I am proud of myself for not wanting to be like them, but if I am happy with myself that is fine. I have many new friends now, and my relationships with them are different from those with my original friends." (Ku H. J., f, Tw/Ger)

"Going to Germany changed me. In fact, it changed my entire life. In Taiwan people think they are happy, but their happiness depends on how others view them. Even before I left Taiwan, I felt I was a bit different from my Chinese classmates, but in Germany people encouraged me to find my own way and not be guided by what others think of me. I have come back to Taiwan, but I now have a new outlook on life. I want to develop myself, learn more and do things well. But that means giving importance to the capital 'I', and to do that takes courage in Taiwan." (Sun W. T., f, Tw/Ger)

Perhaps Fan Y. (m, PRC/US) summed it up best when he said, "In America I learned to be concerned about becoming the kind of person I want to be."

Money is not the most important thing

Though money continues to be at the center of their lives for many Chinese, several of my Chinese interviewees began to feel differently, to a degree that if they returned home their changed priorities would likely invite conflict with their families.

"I no longer see my life driven by money and wealth, which means I would not be able to move back to live with my family in Hong Kong." (Liang J. C., f, Hong Kong/US)

"I worked for many years and have saved enough money to take care of myself. So at this point money and material things are not the most important thing for me. Living in America now, I'd rather follow a simple life style, and have time for family and friends." (Sung M. K., f, Tw/PRC/US)

"Now I want to be happy and the job and money are no longer everything. But we Taiwanese don't think about life in this way. We men want to make money and buy a house. Before I was that way too. I was just looking toward getting that PhD in order to get a well-paying job. But now it's enough if I am happy with what I am doing. If I marry a girl without money or without a good job, that is okay. Or if I don't marry at all, that is okay too. But I know I could not convince my parents of this." (Tu C. L., m, Tw/US)

A changed view of child raising

Along with a greater emphasis on the individual and a lesser concern with money, several of my Chinese respondents began to see the Chinese way of child raising in a more critical light.

> "My family lives in Singapore and my parents sent me to Canada at the age of eight because they did not want me to go through the Singaporan authoritarian education. In Canada I somehow ended up living with a German family where I learned first-hand what a real family is or can be. What is this Chinese family value if you can send your eight-year old alone to Canada? I would never ever do it to my own son." (Chung S. H., m, Singapore/Tw/US)

> "If parents send their children to the US to avoid military service or for education, they do it—at least in their own minds—for the good of the child and the family. Once in America though, the children may no longer see it as sacrifice but rather as irresponsible." (Pai T. Y., f, Tw/US)

> "Some years back many Taiwanese who lived in the United States sent their young children back to Taiwan to be taken care of by grandparents or relatives. Nowadays quite a few don't have children to begin with and those who do have children are beginning to take more responsibility for them." (Tu C. L., m, Tw/US)

Gains and losses: Discovering your shade of gray

A mind that is stretched by a new experience can never go back to its old dimensions.

—Oliver Wendell Holmes Jr.,
former associate justice of the Supreme Court

Feeling more confident and alive

Repeatedly my conversation partners remarked that living overseas had made them more confident in their ability to navigate the world. They came to feel more comfortable in their own skin and less likely to stress out over inconveniences and unfamiliar ways. Overall it meant feeling enriched and more intensely alive.

> "After having seen life elsewhere, I realize that there are totally different ways of living, of looking at things. The experience opened my horizons and enriched me. If you live your life sitting on a chair facing the same direction, you don't know what is behind you and beside you. If you turn around you see more. It may be something bad, but you learn something and you change within. It also makes you feel more alive." (Nikki Z., Ger/Europe)

> "Recently I went back to Germany for our fortieth high school class reunion. All but three of our original classmates attended, four of us having travelled from overseas to be there. It did not take long for the four of us to gravitate toward each other, because we felt different—younger than the others. When the others talked about their lives, they spoke mostly about their pensions and children. Sometimes there was also a negative tone to what they said, as if they were disappointed with life. Those of us who lived abroad had much more to talk about. We also seemed to have more energy to spare." (Ursula L., Ger/Tw)

> "After working in the US for a year I brought back a new clarity of what I want to do with my life." (Anna K., Ger/US)

> "In the US our individualistic upbringing teaches us to be self-confident, but before I went overseas this sense was more a hypothetical feeling. As my small geographic world expanded with age and mobility, this feeling became more real. Now, after having lived overseas I know I can handle situations as they come up. I have the confidence that I can go and make my way." (Andrew M., US/Asia)

> "When I was in Germany I had so much energy every day. It was a new world, so much to experience, such a happy feeling. I also developed more self-confidence. Before I went to Germany I had a certain fear, not knowing what to do

with my life. Now I have a direction, something I did not have before. I now know that what I want is reachable, which means I am no longer afraid of the future." (Jim S., US/Ger)

Among the people who return home after living overseas, the newly found confidence and vitality often lead them to soon leave home again for another international adventure. But even those who were not a good fit in their host culture tend to treasure the experience and be happy with the person they have become.

You can't go home again

When long-term sojourners overseas return to their home country they often feel like strangers in their own land. Usually the realization that they can never feel completely at home again is an unexpected and intensely painful discovery, until they realize that it comes with having enriched their lives in other ways. For many the overseas experience represents a loss and a gain at the same time.

"As a teenager, I felt that I was really a changed person when I returned to Los Angeles after having lived for a year as a high school exchange student in Mexico City. This same feeling really hit me squarely in the face when I took my mandatory home leave after one year of working for a community development organization in Vietnam in the late sixties. One of my workmates who was from Ohio and I left Vietnam together but then split up as I flew to see my parents in Los Angeles and he flew on to Ohio. We were expected to stay for a month, but after only one week in Los Angeles, I decided that I no longer belonged. I had changed but my friends had not. I remember that one day my dad, who was a very observant person, asked me to meet him at his office for lunch. Over the meal he told me that he sensed that I was probably getting ready to return to Vietnam early. I told him that he was a mind reader as that very morning I had called my workmate in Ohio and since he too was feeling that it was a mistake to have come home, we both agreed to head back to Asia. We changed our return flights and spent the rest of our 'home leave' in Hong Kong before heading back to Vietnam. Now, decades later, I have discovered that for me 'home' is more a set of relationships than a physical place.

I have lived most of my adult life in Hawaii but I don't know that I really call Honolulu home. As long as I can maintain meaningful relationships with immediate family and stimulating links with key friends and colleagues I can be happy no matter where I live." (Harry M., US/Asia)

"I like the fact that the people here in Germany take ample time to get close to one another. I think it would be difficult for me to go back to the US and feel at home again. In the US people are always on the go and they take little time to sit and enjoy each other's company." (Jenna H., US/Ger)

"After many years in the US I have taken on a more bubbly personality and become more casual and freer with strangers. I probably was a bit like that even before I left Germany, which made me a good fit in the US. However when I returned to Germany, I found it difficult to retrain myself to be more reserved." (Heike V., Ger/US)

"When I was away from home I saw the lights of my country. After I came back home I became more aware of the shadows." (Alex J., Ger/US)

Keeping the "most precious"

In spite of the various changes and adjustments my conversation partners made when living overseas, they tended to hold on to what they considered the most precious aspects of their home culture. For Americans this was the customary lightness in relationships, one that allows easy contact with others while at the same time retaining individual freedom.

"The thing I came most to appreciate about America when living in Asia is its 'tangentialness.' It means to me that everyone is free to go their own way, and is expected and encouraged to take full advantage of this freedom." (Jason N. US/PRC/Asia)

"I think the best part of American culture, is our informality. It allows us to break through more quickly if you want to meet the other." (Tony K., US/Ger)

Germans pointed to the value of truthfulness and sincerity, and their feelings for nature and the environment as the best parts of their culture.

"In China I discovered that to me truthfulness ranks higher than politeness, which often feels like a lack of sincerity or reliability. I think of honesty as the best part of German culture and as the single most important difference via á vis China and the United States. This applies to honesty, both in terms of directness in communication and of a relative absence of dishonesty in daily life. In Germany friends, family and the public are more likely to detect and sanction dishonesty." (Oliver K., Ger/PRC/US)

"To me the best part of German culture is our value of honesty along with a concern for the quality of life. One day, soon after I returned from the US and spent a day canoeing down the Spree river with a couple of friends, relaxed and enjoying the pine tree scent and the floating water plants, it occurred to me that there are certain values we and many other Germans share: Environmental consciousness, a distaste for artificialness—in food, as well as in manners—and the value of self-reflection." (Olga K., Ger/US)

For my Chinese respondents, including individuals who had grown up in the US, family commitment and the Chinese way of maintaining human relationships continued to be at the heart of their cultural self, something they were unlikely to give up.

"To me the best part of Chinese culture is our commitment to the family and our politeness." (Tang P. H., f, Tw/US)

"I grew up in the US, so I feel comfortable there. Yet in the big things, such as family and marriage, I am Chinese." (Matthew C., ABC/Tw)

"I have changed in many ways, but with respect to human relations I am Chinese." (Peter W., ABC/Ger)

> *We shall not cease from exploration,*
> *And the end of all our exploring*
> *Will be to arrive where we started*
> *And know the place for the first time.*

T.S. Eliot – "Little Gidding" (the last of his Four Quartets)

* * *

Notes

[1] Martin Williams, "Natural born linguists: what drives multi-language speakers?" The Guardian (US edition, 5 September 2013). www.theguardian.com/education/2013/sep/05/multilingual-speakers-language-learning

[2] Alice Robb, "Multilinguals have multiple personalities," *New Republic* (April 23, 2014). www.newrepublic.com/article/117485/multi-linguals-have-multiple-personalities.

[3] Nathan Heller, "An American in Paris," *Harvard Magazine* (July/Aug 2005). harvardmagazine.com/2005/07/an-american-in-paris-html

[4] Chris Berdik, "First a soldier: CAS Prof. Andrew Bacevich. Part two: A straight talker rethinks war," *Bostonia, Alumni Magazine of Boston University* (spring 2007).

[5] Geoff Galiz, "Where a house is a home," (August 10, 2009). (www.german-way.com/where-a-house-is-a-home)

[6] Jessica Scott-Reid, Wall Street Journal (Aug 19, 2015). blogs.wsj.com/expat/2015/08/19/expat-introverts-when-living-abroad-changes-your-personality/

Epilogue

I confess that it has taken me a very long time to complete this book—over ten years! Probably long enough for many of my respondents to have forgotten about our conversations long ago. However, I thoroughly enjoyed the process. I learned a great deal from living in different places of the world, but exchanging experiences with my conversation partners taught me just as much. I will always cherish having had opportunities to meet so many kindred spirits.

The divergent views expressed in this book do not let us forget that the world is populated with people who think, feel, believe and act differently. Cultural differences and barriers due to culture and language are real. But meeting the world gives us an opportunity to open our minds, and hopefully our hearts, realizing that there are drawbacks and advantages to each culture.

Understanding another culture and our own also prepares us to be flexible in our adjustment, helping us recognize which of our attitudes and habits we can and may want to change and which ones we want to keep in order to stay true to ourselves. When I was in charge of student exchange programs at the university, I often alerted our outgoing students before their departure that their year abroad would change them, that they would come back as a different person, but that most likely they would be happy with the person they had become. If I saw these students after their return they invariably confirmed that prediction.

As for me, someone who has spent many more years living abroad than in the country of her birth, I have changed in many ways. However, even though I can never "go home again," after writing this book I realize more clearly than ever before that I have not shed all characteristics of my German home culture:

To this day I prefer openness and honesty over politeness. So I am sorry to say that by American standards I may still be "blunt!" Though to be honest, maybe I am not really sorry!

Acknowledgments

My heartfelt thanks go to the nearly one hundred individuals—American, German, Taiwanese and Chinese—all of whom generously spent many hours with me sharing their experiences and insights gained while they lived abroad. We met in homes, coffee shops, offices and libraries, in Hawaii, California, Taiwan and Germany. Since they provided the content, there would be no book without them.

Many of these conversations partners also contributed by introducing me to others with relevant experiences, thereby expanding the scope of information available to me. Similarly, during my six-month stay in Delmenhorst, Germany, Helmuth Riewe, a reporter for the local newspaper, the *Delmenhorster Kreisblatt*, published an article on my book project in which he invited interested readers to get in touch with me by calling the newspaper. As a result, numerous people contacted me. Thank you Helmuth Riewe and thanks to your newspaper.

Later, when trying to mold information I had gathered into a cohesive whole, I admit to often unabashedly steering conversations with family, friends, acquaintances and coworkers toward my topic enlisting them to help me overcome whatever difficulties I happened to encounter in my writing at that moment. Thank you Debbie Dunn, Judy Van Zile, Phyllis Young, Ursula Magaard, and Rosemarie McElhany for hearing me out and sharing your ideas, always with patience and unwavering support. Then when I hit a road block and considered abandoning the project altogether, Jane Maeda came to my rescue. For an entire year Jane faithfully appeared every Wednesday afternoon at my house, ready to read and discuss what I produced during the previous week. Her suggestions and detailed feedback on the various drafts kept me on track. From the bottom of my heart, thank you Jane.

My gratitude also goes out to those who read and commented on the final draft or parts thereof: Bonnie Abiko, Kim Simpson, Yuan-Hui Li, Olivia Key, Garry Mitchelmore and Lynn Pullen. Each one of them contributed by eliminating mistakes, identifying inconsistencies or improving wording or organization. I am indebted to May Izumi for editing the manuscript, to Heide R. Li, Royalene Doyle and Rosemarie Greenman for their assistance during the prepublication phase, to Michelle Li Bothe for the cover design.

Lastly, I beg for forgiveness of all those who have been with me over the years and whose names I have failed to mention.

ABOUT THE AUTHOR

Born in 1942 in an eleven home village Dr. Gertraude Roth Li grew up in post war Germany. After her father was killed on the Russian front during the war, her mother faced the challenging task of raising four children during difficult economic times. That experience, however, did not dampen Gertraude's passion for learning and her curiosity about people in other parts of the world. At nineteen she left Germany to improve her high school English by working for a year in the United States before returning to Germany to study Chinese. Initially hired by a retired professor and his wife in Cambridge, Massachusetts, to help their daughter with an infant for one summer, Gertraude ended up staying with the couple for nearly ten years, during which time she studied at Boston University and Harvard. Along the way she not only improved her English, but also learned Spanish, French, Chinese, Japanese and Manchu—the latter for academic research as part of a Ph.D. in History and Asian Languages. Over the years that followed, Dr. Li lived in Switzerland, Taiwan and Japan, worked professionally in refugee resettlement and university international programs, and together with her husband Yuan-Hui Li raised two trilingual daughters. After calling Hawaii home for thirty-four years, the Li's now reside in Highlands Ranch, Colorado.

Other publications by Gertraude Roth Li

Numerous ethnic guides to help American sponsors become familiar with the cultural backgrounds and likely challenges faced by refugees from Southeast Asia, Africa, Afghanistan and Poland. Written for World Relief Refugee Services (1981-84).

"Trends in Japanese Higher Education," in *International Education Forum* (Spring 1993).

"Higher Education in Hong Kong: International or Local?" in *International Education Forum* (Fall 1995).

"The Manchu-Chinese Relationship, 1618-1636." Chapter in *From Ming to Ch'ing* (1979).

Stille Gedanken (Still Thoughts), by Dharma Master Cheng Yen, 2 vols. (2000). Translated from Chinese into German for the Tzu Chi Foundation.

"Manchus and State Building before 1644." Chapter in the *Cambridge History of China*, Vol. 9 (2002).

Manchu: A Textbook for Reading Documents (2010).

Made in the USA
Monee, IL
27 March 2021